The Charrette
HANDBOOK

The Charrette HANDBOOK

The Essential Guide for Accelerated, Collaborative Community Planning

By The National Charrette Institute

Principal Authors **Bill Lennertz** and **Aarin Lutzenhiser**

Editor and Contributing Author **Breesa Culver**

Foreword by **Andres Duany, AICP**

Cosponsored by **The National Association of Realtors**
The Knight Program in Community Building at the University of Miami

American Planning Association
Chicago, Illinois
Washington, D.C.

This handbook is based on the NCI Dynamic Planning curriculum originally created by Bill Lennertz, Steve Coyle, and Aarin Lutzenhiser.

Cover and book design by Lubosh Cech

ISBN (paperback):
1-932364-21-8 and 978-1-932364-21-9
Library of Congress Control
Number: 2006923523

Printed in the United States of America

CONTRIBUTING AUTHORS

David Brain
Ben Brown
Dan Burden
Marcela Camblor
Anthony J. Costello
Steve Coyle
Andres Duany, AICP
Mark Farrar
Andrew Georgiadis
Raymond L. Gindroz
Peter Katz
Douglas Kelbaugh
James Kennedy
Oliver Kuehne
David C. Leland
Gianni Longo
Peter Musty
Kristen Paulsen Pickus
Elizabeth Plater-Zyberk
Bruce Race, AICP
Harrison B. Rue
Ken Snyder
Galina Tahchieva

ACKNOWLEDGEMENTS

For their generous financial support of the creation of this handbook, we would like to thank:
The National Association of Realtors®,
The Knight Program in Community Building at the University of Miami,
McLarland Vasquez Emsiek & Partners, and Mark Farrar of Millennium Partners.

NCI would like to thank Andres Duany and Elizabeth Plater-Zyberk for their inspiration, support, and technical advice. We are grateful to our peer reviewers: Joseph Molinaro, AICP; Rick Bernhart, FAICP; Steve Coyle; and Victor Dover, AICP. In addition, we would like to thank NCI's students and clients who have helped refine and improve the original NCI Dynamic Planning curriculum. Thanks are due to the American Planning Association for publishing this book and thereby making its content widely available. Thank you also to Lubosh Cech of Oko Design Studio for his inspired layout and graphic design work.

cha•rrette \shuh-RET\ *n.*

1. a multiple-day collaborative design and planning workshop held on-site and inclusive of all affected stakeholders.

[From French charrette (cart), from Old French. Anecdotally, professors at the École des Beaux Arts in Paris during the 19th century collected architecture students' final drawings in a cart for jury critiques while students frantically put finishing touches on their work.]

Contents

Foreword

Andres Duany, AICP

It is only recently that citizens have begun to participate in the planning of their own communities. Involving the public in planning decisions used to be a rare thing and one not considered necessary. Elected officials and their planning departments would retain expert consultants and simply get on with it.

Looking back at the built evidence, this method worked rather well up to about 1940, after which cities began to look and to function rather more poorly. It took the next three decades of recurring disappointment to gather anger enough to organize an alternative. It has been a long campaign of protest and reform. Today, urban planning routinely includes the advice and consent of those to be affected by its outcome.

The early decades of the past century, when planners were implicitly trusted, also saw the fruition of great reform movements. Their planners were trusted because the evidence was everywhere that the life of citizens improved under their advice. From these planners came the great neighborhoods and main streets, the parks and civic buildings that are cherished wherever they survive. The sections of our cities that we still value most were produced in those years.

And then things changed. Without here listing the reasons why, many municipalities ceased to initiate their own planning, which had so evidently been for the common good. With some exceptions, developers became dominant and the municipal planning departments became reactive—the processors of developers' plans. With the pressure to deliver housing quickly immediately following World War II, developers became careless and diagrammatic in their proposals, and the minimum became the maximum. And something else: The automobile was still beyond reproach, so it became the determinant of codes and standards. Whatever the car wanted it got. The old delicate urban fabric was torn apart by big roads and parking lots and hideous new building types. The human walking was inadvertently forgotten as the measure of community. When the big developer and the big car called the shots the result was sprawl. Across America, fine, old, beloved places were eviscerated, and equally beloved open space was lost.

Democracies, it has been said, do not avoid mistakes but they do eventually correct them. With the problems of sprawl becoming evident, the people took it upon themselves to gradually take charge of the planning process. The people have in fact become so powerful that public participation has itself become the planning process. Visionary planners and developers have responded with smart growth. Has it made things better? Yes.

Has it been all for the best? . . . Not always.

The public process can lead to negative outcomes as randomly as projects exclusively in the hands of developers. The process can too easily be undermined: by the possible ignorance of the participants (the act of showing up to a meeting does not necessarily qualify a person as an informed contributor); by lack of representation (well-organized minorities can be tyrannical with an absent majority's best interests); and then large numbers of people "just showing up" can be swayed, becoming indistinguishable from the mob rule that our American founders were so careful to manage in their conception of republican government. Questionable outcomes have been so persistent that it is now obvious that the process of public participation must be as well crafted as the process of any properly constituted deliberative body. That process, over time, has been refined in the charrette.

The charrette process is here described, analyzed, and made useful by a group of very experienced practitioners. Over the past 15 years, in the National Charrette Institute founders' practices and through the observation of others, the NCI dynamic planning process has become a refined instrument. It is an instrument inclusive not just of the citizens and neighbors of a projected plan, but of everyone who matters. The charrette is about dynamic balances. It is about principles balanced by process, about the interests of the few balanced by those of the many, about experts being balanced by those who know nothing except how things really should be, about public benefit and private gain.

A proper charrette brings into being a collective intelligence . . . and it does this with stunning efficiency. No one should waste his time. No one should feel stymied. The negotiations should take place—not during the adversarial circumstances of the municipal hearing when the plan is already fixed—but during the ongoing creation of the plan, when most plan components are at the maximum pitch of flexibility.

When it comes to development decisions, the people have the power. It is now up to the people to wield it responsibly. If they do not—there is no one to suffer the consequences but themselves. Be careful. Look about you. Become responsible. In a democracy, people get the cities they deserve.

Preface

Nearly every community in this country is feeling the dual pressures of growth and development. Change underlies community growth, and change generally proves difficult for people. Even when a planning initiative is based on a shared community vision, local codes and developments may not support it, builders may be slow to accept it, banks may not easily finance it, and public works and safety officials may not approve it. Additionally, many people are on guard regarding community development because of negative experiences with poor quality development in their area.

Many individuals have found that when they do engage in a public process it is less than satisfying because of insufficient methods for involving the public. For example, people are frustrated when they are given only three minutes in a public meeting in which to voice their opinions. Even when they are engaged, community members can feel alienated or apathetic if their input has no visible impact. Compounding this problem in many communities is an atmosphere of distrust surrounding the planning and development process. The result is that people are skeptical, anticipating a plan that will make things worse rather than better.

This book's authors and contributors have dedicated their careers to helping people make positive, transformative changes in their communities through the creation and implementation of community plans and development projects. The majority of their work can be categorized as smart growth based, and they share holistic approaches to their design and planning practices. These approaches often challenge development conventions such as zoning codes, transportation standards, and finance mechanisms. They can also challenge people's perceptions regarding growth strategies such as mixed-use, neighborhood commercial, and narrow streets. Early in their careers, these practitioners recognized that overcoming such challenges required that everyone affected by a planning effort be included from the beginning. Since the early 1980s, they have developed their own particular collaborative planning processes out of necessity to get smart growth projects planned, approved, and built.

In 2002, a group of these pioneering practitioners recognized the need to standardize and teach the effective methods for collaborative planning that they had been practicing and refining during hundreds of charrettes over two decades. To fulfill that need, the National Charrette Institute (NCI) was established as a nonprofit research and educational organization. There are many collaborative planning methods in use today, but NCI is interested specifically in holistic planning processes capable of facilitating lasting, transformative change. One example of this type of change is the adoption of a set of form-based codes, which prescribe the entire neighborhood form from street to block to building. This is in contrast to processes that accomplish only temporary or piecemeal changes, such as an overlay zone that allows a unique project to be built while the surrounding community remains the same.

NCI's first years were devoted to the creation of a curriculum for teaching holistic, collaborative planning methodologies to professionals and community members involved in community planning. The result was NCI dynamic planning: a three-phase, collaborative planning process centered around a charrette—a multiple-day, collaborative planning workshop. Dynamic planning offers much more than just a quick fix. After a charrette, people have been heard to say: "I have been a transportation engineer for 20 years and until today I never knew why the fire department needs 20 feet of street clearance," or "Now I understand why alleys are so important," or "This is the most creative experience I have had since college," and "I may not agree with the entire proposal, but my concerns were listened to and considered; I like how I was treated."

The dynamic planning curriculum has been taught by NCI for the past several years to federal and local planning agencies, private architecture and planning firms, and individual planners, architects, community activists, and developers through publicly offered trainings. *The Charrette Handbook* is based largely on the NCI Charrette Planner® certification training. This curriculum has been extensively tested and refined and has proved effective as a practical guide for improving the performance of even the most seasoned professionals who utilize public involvement processes.

Today, it is not enough to have a great project; you must also have a great process. Even the best, most creative, smart growth projects must have a good process. *The Charrette Handbook* was written to provide the tools and techniques necessary for creating and achieving a shared vision of a community to everyone involved in community planning and development. This book brings the basics of the NCI dynamic planning curriculum to the practitioner as a desktop reference for use in planning projects.

We recommend that you read this book in complete sections in order to best understand the context. Out of a need for clarity, the curriculum is presented in a linear, step-by-step fashion by phase, sub-phase, and each sub-phase's associated tools and techniques. However, dynamic planning is not necessarily a linear process. Some of the tools and techniques may need to be repeated cyclically throughout the life of a project. The tools and techniques are intended to provide the practitioner with a menu of all of the facets that should be considered when planning a project. All of these techniques may not apply to each project; however, it is recommended that each one be considered before it is discarded.

It is worth noting that collaborative, open meeting facilitation processes are referred to throughout the tools and techniques section and that such facilitation skills are imperative for dynamic planning project managers and charrette managers. This book itself is not a facilitation guide. There are numerous excellent books and trainings available on facilitation, some of which are listed in further reading in Section Five.

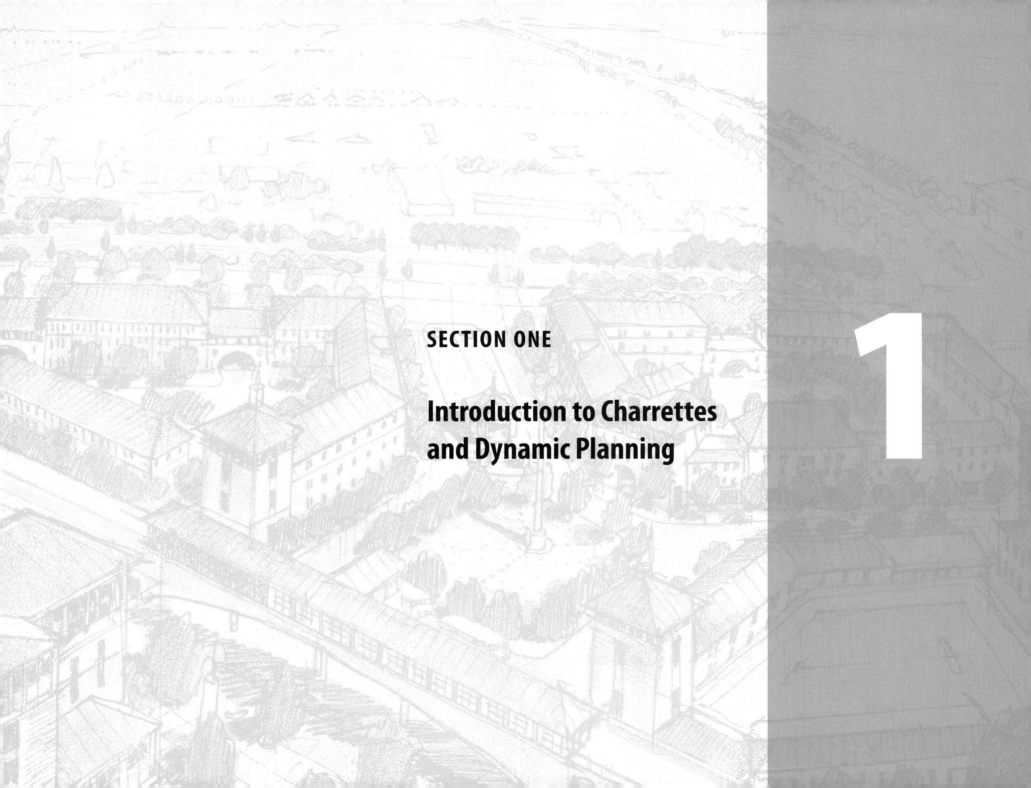

SECTION ONE

Introduction to Charrettes and Dynamic Planning

1

WHAT IS AN NCI CHARRETTE?

The term "charrette" means various things to various people. To some it simply connotes a meeting in which people brainstorm and perhaps sketch ideas; to others the charrette process is synonymous with public involvement. The charrettes on which this book is based are more than just brainstorming or public visioning sessions. They are distinguished from other workshops by their intense, collaborative nature and by their holistic approach, focused on a feasible solution. The NCI charrette is a collaborative design and planning workshop that occurs over four to seven consecutive days. It is held on-site and includes all affected stakeholders at critical decision-making points.

NCI charrettes are not typical planning processes. They are highly creative, energetic, and interactive community events: a combination of a barn raising and a New England town meeting. Community planning charrettes have a solid track record of attracting large numbers of people, including many who normally do not participate in land planning events. Charrettes are both educational and inspirational. Some incorporate picnics, tours, and interactive exercises; however, the creative atmosphere of the charrette studio itself is the underlying attraction.

Charrettes don't deal with single development issues in isolation. They move all design and development issues along the same track to allow each issue to inform the decision making for related issues. For instance, transit issues are considered in light of economic and market feasibility issues along with zoning plans and building codes. The charrette is also a democratic process in which all voices and viewpoints are aired and considered. It involves all disciplines from the start in an orchestrated series of "feedback loops" that chronicle decisions and opinions made along the way and provide a constant track record.

It is important to note that there are other models, in addition to the four- to seven-day charrette, for conducting an effective process that adheres to the dynamic planning values. These processes most commonly use a series of two- or three-day workshops to accomplish the three feedback loops required, essentially dividing the multiple-day charrette into segments (see charrette scheduling variations in Section Five for more information). The four- to seven-day charrettes have a unique capacity to quickly achieve a feasible solution with broad support.

An NCI charrette is:

- Usually more, but no less than four consecutive days
- An open process that includes all interested parties
- A collaborative process involving all disciplines in a series of short feedback loops
- A process that produces a feasible plan
- A generalist, holistic approach
- Phase two of the three-phase dynamic planning process

An NCI charrette is not:

- A one-day workshop
- A multi-day marathon meeting involving everyone all the time
- A plan authored by a select few that will affect many
- A "brainstorming session" that produces a plan but stops short of feasibility testing

A successful charrette cannot be a stand-alone process. It is one phase of the dynamic planning process, which requires extensive preparation and follow-through for plan approval and implementation. The dynamic planning process as a whole will be discussed in detail throughout this text.

WHEN ARE CHARRETTES USED?

The charrette is a sophisticated process that best serves the most controversial and complicated urban design and planning problems. Its capacity to bring all of the decision makers together for a discrete amount of time to create a win/win solution makes it one of the most powerful techniques in the planner's toolkit. The charrette is not always appropriate, but it is indispensable for contentious situations, such as:

- High stakes projects involving substantial public and private investment
- Volatile yet workable political environments—situations that are "hot" but manageable, as long as all the parties agree to participate in good faith
- Complex design problems such as mixed-use and mixed-income projects or challenging transportation problems
- Real projects that include imminent development

Charrettes can be used for virtually any type of planning project, including:

- Main street revitalization and infill
- Regional plans
- Comprehensive plans
- Transportation systems plans
- Environmental planning
- Rewriting development codes
- New community master planning
- Specific planning
- Redevelopment projects
- Affordable housing designs
- LEED building design

WHO SPONSORS A CHARRETTE, AND HOW IS IT FUNDED?

A private developer, a public agency (such as a city or regional planning department), or a non-governmental agency (such as a citizen planning advocacy group) usually sponsors a charrette. It can be funded by a single entity or by a group of funders such as in a public/private partnership. Charrette funding can come from various sources, such as public planning budgets, grants from smart growth grant-making bodies, or a combination of private developers and public planning agencies. When budgeting for a charrette, it is important to remember that the charrette event cannot be separated from the dynamic planning preparation and implementation phases. Therefore, it is not possible to budget for a charrette in isolation. The cost is completely dependent on project scale and complexity, how much preparation work has to be done, available resources, data collection, studies to be completed, and stakeholder outreach and engagement. The price for dynamic planning projects with a charrette, including preparation and implementation, ranges from $75,000 to $500,000, depending on the study area size, required technical specialties, and the final products. It is possible to reduce project costs through the use of professional volunteers, local agencies, and university architecture and planning departments. (See the text box in Section 1.5.2 for more on this topic.)

WHO RUNS A CHARRETTE?

A professional charrette manager generally runs a charrette. This person can be public planning staff or a private consultant, but it is key that he or she be highly trained to facilitate a variety of in-house and public meetings. Several planning firms across the country specialize in charrette facilitation, each with its own particular specialty.

WHAT IS DYNAMIC PLANNING?

Dynamic planning is a three-phase, holistic, collaborative planning process during which a multiple-day charrette is held as the central transformative event. Dynamic planning is designed to assure project success through careful charrette preparation and follow-up.

When a charrette project fails, it is most often due to a lack of preparation or follow-up rather than a poorly run charrette. Without proper preparation, which includes collection of base data and stakeholder outreach, the infrastructure may not be in place to support the outcome of the charrette. This can result in such problems as the emergence of an opposition group or the discovery late in the process of engineering data that challenge project feasibility. Without continued stakeholder communication, support for a project can wane over time.

The Three Phases of Dynamic Planning

Phase One: Research, Education, Charrette Preparation

Phase one of dynamic planning establishes the information and people infrastructure for the project. Establishing the information infrastructure includes the identification, creation, and collection of all base data necessary to perform the project planning and design during the charrette. Creating the people infrastructure includes identifying and engaging all those whose involvement is necessary to produce a feasible outcome that will be supported by the community. This requires early and ongoing collaboration between the project sponsor, project management team and those immediately affected by the project (including community members), all relevant decision makers, potential supporters and blockers. Furthermore, in order to gain their long-term support, these stakeholders must be treated with respect and assured that their input will have an impact on the outcome. This phase is about becoming "charrette ready," that point at which all of the information and the people are in place. Depending on the project, this preparation process can take anywhere from a minimum of six

weeks to nine months. By the end of phase one, the information, people, and physical logistics required to start the charrette must be in place.

Phase Two: The Charrette

The charrette is the catalytic event of the dynamic planning process. It is a collaborative event that lasts four to seven days. The goal of the charrette is to produce a feasible plan that benefits from the support of all stakeholders through its implementation. A multidisciplinary charrette team, consisting of consultants and sponsor staff, produces this plan. It takes place in a charrette studio situated on or near the project site. During the charrette, the charrette team first conducts an open public meeting to solicit the values, vision, and needs of the stakeholders. The team then breaks off to create alternative plans, testing and refining them with the goal of producing a preferred plan. The charrette is organized as a series of feedback loops through which stakeholders are engaged at critical decision-making points. These decision-making points occur in primary stakeholder meetings, several public meetings, and possibly during an open house throughout the course of the charrette. These feedback loops provide the charrette team with the information necessary to create a feasible plan. Just as importantly, they allow the stakeholders to become co-authors of the plan so that they are more likely to support and implement it.

The charrette needs to last at least four days for the simplest of projects, and six to seven days for a standard project, in order to accommodate the required feedback loops. Processes that last less than four days usually do not allow enough time to perform feasibility testing and to deal with major stakeholder issues. Some firms have developed processes lasting less than four consecutive days, which is usually done by breaking the longer charrette into several three-day events about a month apart. (Alternative charrette schedules are addressed in Section Five.)

The Value of the Pleasant Hill BART Transit Village Charrette

Mark Farrar
Principal, Millennium Partners

The charrette process proved invaluable in our entitlement effort for the Pleasant Hill BART Transit Village. Prior to utilizing the charrette, we had spent more than five years and a significant financial investment using traditional entitlement efforts without success. We were introduced to the concept of a charrette by Contra Costa County in 2000 and began the process later that year. Over an intense several months, we were able to bring all of the stakeholders together in the same room for a rational discussion of the issues. As a result of the charrette process, all of the disparate viewpoints were successfully melded into a viable project for both the community and the developer. The charrette results were then packaged into a development application and submitted to Contra Costa County for discretionary project approval. As a result of the charrette, the project had already been reviewed and accepted by the

>>

Phase Three: Implementation

Two major processes follow the charrette. The first is product refinement, during which the charrette team tests and refines the final charrette plan to assure its feasibility. The second is based on a relationship strategy in which the project sponsor continues to work with the stakeholders to maintain their support of the plan. The dynamic planning process concludes with a post-charrette public meeting, usually no more than four to six weeks after the charrette, during which the revised plans are presented for final public review and input.

DYNAMIC PLANNING BENEFITS AND FEATURES

Meaningful Involvement

Conventional planning workshops can be initially engaging for the public. However, a single workshop, or even a string of workshops held over weeks or months, can lose its impact if the design process disappears behind the scenes. In dynamic planning, people see the results of their input immediately reflected in plans in the next day's progress update. They know that their opinions were heard and feel their individual contributions were appreciated. It is this process of participation, review, and validation that encourages people to remain enthusiastically engaged. In conventional planning, it is much more difficult to acknowledge and validate all voices as efficiently and effectively.

Trust in Government

Charrettes are a positive way to channel public interest that can otherwise manifest as uninformed opposition and protest. Participation in the planning and design of a community-based project gives people the opportunity to influence decisions that affect their daily lives. When done correctly, the charrette promotes trust among community members, developers, and government through meaningful public in-

volvement and education. It fosters a shared community vision and often turns opposition into support.

Feasible Plans with Minimal Rework

The charrette makes economic sense. Because all parties are collaborating from the start, no viewpoint is overlooked, which allows projects to avoid costly rework. Also, the charrette allows for fewer and more highly productive work sessions, making it less time consuming than traditional processes. Everyone suffers when a project in which many people have invested time, energy, and money has to go back to the drawing board. Community members suffer because their precious time has been wasted on a plan that sits on the shelf. Elected officials suffer because their constituents have one more reason to distrust government. The developer suffers because of the money wasted in planning costs and in interest paid. Dynamic planning continuously strives for the creation of a feasible plan through inclusion and collaboration, increasing the likelihood of a project being built.

Exceptional Design

Dynamic planning promotes creative problem solving. During the charrette, a group of specialists (the charrette team) and single-interest parties (the stakeholders) collaborate, employing a generalist approach in the pursuit of the best ideas. This results in a holistic solution. The preferred plan produced during the charrette reflects the most creative solutions that meet the test of feasibility.

AN EXAMPLE DYNAMIC PLANNING PROCESS: THE PLEASANT HILL BART STATION AREA PLAN

In 2001, an exciting change began to take place in the community surrounding the Pleasant Hill BART station in Contra Costa County, California. The Contra Costa County Board of Supervisors, Redevelopment Agency, BART, local residents, business leaders, activist groups, and area employees, along with the developer, Millennium Partners, and consultants, convened to decide the fate of the BART transit hub. They created a shared vision and developed detailed plans and codes to implement it. With a 25-year history of failed planning attempts and contentious debates, more than 500 people collaborated and finally came to an agreement about how to develop the Pleasant Hill BART Station Area.

Over the course of a collaborative, holistic six-day charrette in spring of 2001, dozens of possible ideas were discussed and synthesized into a development plan that addressed participants' concerns. Following the charrette, the consultant team prepared a set of form-based codes to ensure that the designs created during the charrette would actually be implemented. In late 2002, the board of supervisors unanimously adopted the plan. Community support has continued through the project's lengthy implementation phase, and ground breaking was held in May 2006.

One example of the magnitude of the change that took place in this community during the charrette was the transformation of a community opposition leader. Because of the charrette, he became a plan supporter and is the chair of the advisory council that oversees project implementation. The advisory board assures that the built development will follow the final charrette plan. Because the community supported the final charrette plan and its members stayed involved through the implementation phase, the final development will match the vision created during the charrette.

The Pleasant Hill BART project is covered in detail as a case study in Section Four of this book and is referred to as an example in many descriptions of specific tools and techniques throughout Section Three. Following is an overview to provide the reader with an initial understanding of the dynamic planning process in practice.

Phase One: Research, Education, Charrette Preparation

The inspiration to use a charrette came from Contra Costa County Supervisor Donna Gerber upon the advice of consultant Peter Katz. In 1999, Gerber had witnessed the most recent failed attempt to plan the property. By all accounts that process was handled very poorly and left the neighborhood and surrounding jurisdictions negative and upset about any development on the project site. Gerber believed that the charrette process, combined with new urbanist planning principles, could provide a solution to the impasse. The fact that the surrounding neighborhoods and jurisdictions were distrustful of the project sponsors did not deter her from proposing a charrette. On the contrary, Gerber felt that this tense atmosphere would catalyze residents and engage them in a constructive workshop format. She also believed that for the project to be successful, many more people would need to be involved. She understood that the unique, magnetic quality of the charrette was the key to attracting the interest of those who historically did not participate in public planning projects.

Start with collaboration

In a dynamic planning process, each individual's unique contribution is valued for its potential to help the project become better. The Pleasant Hill BART project sponsors made collaboration the core strategy for reestablishing the trust of participants. True collaboration requires that participants are asked for their input *before* the design work begins to let them know that their contributions will have an impact on the outcome. When people are involved early in the design and creation of a plan they will support the results.

The first step toward collaboration was to place community representatives on the committee responsible for choosing planning consultants. Another important decision was to hold an initial public meeting four weeks before the start of the charrette to inform the public about the charrette process and to solicit their ideas for the project site.

>>

public and was unanimously approved by the County Planning Commission. The ability to combine the charrette process with the actual entitlement effort saved significant time and money in our development process. The return on investment was excellent given that the result of our charrette was an entitled project, and the development is currently under construction. For the developer, the charrette process should be viewed as part of the overall entitlement effort and supported as such. ∎

Focus on feasibility

In addition to addressing the community's vision, the project sponsors needed to ensure that the project would be feasible in financial and engineering terms. This required the collection and analysis of base data necessary to provide the charrette team with the information required for feasibility testing. The base data included transportation and economic existing conditions as well as analyses of the site and its subsurface conditions. A marketing study determined the demand for housing, retail, and other uses on the site. The dynamic planning process ensures that a project is feasible from financial, engineering, and marketing standpoints at each step in the process.

Phase Two: The Charrette

Designing in short feedback loops

After the charrette team set up the studio, held a debriefing meeting, and toured the area, a public kick-off meeting was held on the first evening of the charrette to introduce the players and issues and solicit public input. The highlight of the meeting was a "hands-on" workshop in which participants worked in small groups, each with a design leader, to describe and draw their visions for the project. A community representative from each team presented each group's top ideas to the whole assembly.

The next day, the charrette team started to create alternative concepts based on input from the meeting and existing project data and goals. As the concepts were developed, they were reviewed during daytime meetings with stakeholders such as neighbors, a technical advisory committee, bicycle and pedestrian advocacy groups, and BART representatives. These early reviews checked for any fatal flaws in the concepts prior to their public review.

The charrette did not deal with single development issues in isolation. The team moved all design and development issues along the same track to allow each issue to inform the decision making for related issues. For instance, the development economic specialist came prepared with a project financial model that she used to test the concepts. As soon as the planners developed a scheme, they provided her with the numbers and types of housing units, retail square footage, and number of streets and parks. Within a very short time, feedback was available about the economic feasibility of the developing concepts, allowing the team to make adjustments along the way. This quick reality check kept the team from wasting time on unsupportable options.

On the third night, the charrette team presented the tested alternative concepts at a public meeting. All stakeholders were engaged in a discussion about how the concepts were developed; how they performed against community values, policies, and feasibility standards; and what the trade-offs were. These feedback loops are the primary shared learning opportunities of the charrette. Through this process, stakeholders recognize that their input has an impact and, therefore, their participation is worthwhile.

Equipped with the input from the mid-course public meeting, the team then moved forward to develop a preferred plan. The plan was then refined through additional stakeholder reviews and detailed studies performed by the team. The team then prepared a complete presentation in preparation for the final charrette public meeting.

During this meeting, the team delivered a presentation to inform and inspire the stakeholders. All elements of the project were covered, including the master plan, building designs, economic and transportation impacts and strategy, and the form-based codes. Everything needed to move the project forward into implementation was addressed at a sufficient level of detail. At this meeting, yet another round of public input was gathered.

The charrette was indeed as much an educational event as a planning exercise. Everyone—from developer to community member—became aware of the complexities of development and design issues, and everyone worked together to try to accommodate these issues. In the end, the charrette yielded a comprehensive and detailed plan that met the basic requirements of all parties, ending the 25-year deadlock.

Phase Three: Plan Implementation

Testing and refinement
Creating a feasible plan is one of the most important strategies of dynamic planning. The plan created during a charrette has been reviewed in draft form by all specialists but requires further testing and refinement before it can be finalized. After the charrette, each specialist performs an analysis and proposed revisions. These final refinements help reduce the amount of rework required as the project proceeds through engineering and construction documentation. Due in part to this testing and refinement, the Pleasant Hill BART final development plan adhered closely to the charrette plan created five years earlier.

Maintaining support
Because the project management team valued collaboration and short feedback loops, a follow-up public meeting was held one month after the charrette. During this meeting, refinements to the charrette plan were presented and further community input was gathered and incorporated into the final charrette plan.

The BART project sponsors needed to maintain their effort to keep the project on track during the ensuing five-year period before construction would begin. An important part of this effort was the creation of a town architect position to administer the charrette plan and its associated form-based codes. The position was filled by a local architect and member of the charrette team. Another important step was the creation of the Pleasant Hill BART Station Area Municipal Advisory Committee, charged with advising county supervisors on the development application's adherence to the final charrette plan. A person who began his involvement at the forefront of neighborhood opposition eventually became the chair of this committee, a considerable indication of the neighborhood's commitment to the charrette plan.

During the implementation phase, Contra Costa County continued to hold public meetings on the status of the project as it went through the engineering phase and the development application was prepared. Plan implementation depends on keeping stakeholders in the loop as the project moves forward. This diligence was rewarded when the board of county supervisors unanimously approved the development plan with no attendee speaking in opposition.

DYNAMIC PLANNING VALUES
The most successful dynamic planning projects occur when the people responsible for shepherding the project through planning and implementation share the values that guide the way the project is run and how stakeholders are treated. The Pleasant Hill BART station area plan was successful in part because the project leaders, Contra Costa County staff, BART, and the developer shared a set of values that were reflected in the way the project process was conducted. They were committed to the creation of a healthy community designed through a collaborative process, based on shared learning and timely communication. Because of this approach, the project was able to endure many setbacks during its five-year implementation phase.

The following are core values central to defining how people work together in a dynamic planning process.

Community Health
Holistic planning processes based on local values produce solutions that support healthy communities. Healthy com-

munities improve the social, economic, and physical well being of their people, places, and natural environments.

Collaboration

Each individual's unique contribution supports the best outcome. When project sponsors maintain this value, stakeholders are viewed as members of the larger team who have valuable input and are essential to implementation. Therefore, all relevant decision makers, immediately affected parties (including general community members), and potential supporters and blockers are involved before design begins and throughout the project design process.

Transparency

Clarity in rules, process, and roles is essential to collaboration. Stakeholders know whether or not a process is genuinely collaborative, and any lack of openness will quickly erode their trust in the process. All information relevant to decision making must be made available to the stakeholders.

Shared Learning

Shared learning requires the involvement of all relevant viewpoints in the decision-making process. Shared learning facilitates new understandings that can lead to a change in people's perceptions and positions. Shared learning also reduces costly rework by assuring that the project plan includes the information required to assure its feasibility.

Direct, Honest, and Timely Communication

Collaborative work, based on shared learning, requires frequent communication and feedback between the project sponsors and the stakeholders. These feedback loops provide all parties with the reasoning behind decisions and knowledge of how their input affected the outcome.

DYNAMIC PLANNING STRATEGIES

The following 10 strategies are used in the most successful charrettes and are based on the dynamic planning values. These strategies should be referred to every step of the way when designing the process for a project using dynamic planning. The strategies are also useful when writing a Request for Proposals that includes a charrette and later while evaluating the submissions. Given the diverse interpretations of what constitutes a charrette, it is very important to be clear about what is expected when specifying one. NCI believes these 10 strategies should be active in any charrette process.

Work Collaboratively

True collaboration is based on valuing each individual's unique contribution. Therefore, anyone who might build, use, sell, approve, or attempt to block the project is involved before the start of design and throughout the project. It is important to involve stakeholders only at the point in a project when it is possible to consider their input. Including a broad range of positions and interests in the design and planning of a community leads to better quality plans with a higher likelihood of community support throughout implementation.

Design Cross-functionally

Holistic solutions require holistic approaches to a problem. This means that all relevant disciplines are represented and working together to achieve the same goals. Multidisciplinary teams of architects, planners, engineers, economists, market experts, public agency staff, and others work concurrently to build a feasible solution to community development problems from the onset of the charrette. When an important area of expertise is excluded from the process, changes and rework are likely to emerge late in the process at high costs in time and money lost.

Compress Work Sessions

Time compression facilitates creative problem solving by accelerating decision making and reducing unconstructive negotiation tactics. Time-compressed design sessions in the NCI charrette are full of energy and creativity. Uninterrupted focus on a problem often results in unexpected solutions to difficult problems. This strategy can be particularly useful in the eleventh hour of a negotiation when it becomes obvious that a decision must be made quickly for progress to continue.

Communicate in Short Feedback Loops

Regular stakeholder reviews build trust in the process, foster true understanding and support of the project, and minimize rework. A feedback loop occurs when a design is proposed, reviewed, changed, and re-presented for further review. This is a key strategy for the charrette and the entire dynamic planning process. Stakeholders are continually educated about the project process and plan's progress. They are brought into the process early and at proper intervals throughout so that their input can have an impact on the outcome. In many conventional planning processes, people may attend a great first meeting but then a long period of time elapses before the consultant team returns for a second meeting to present a final plan. Since the participants received no information between the first and second meetings they may not understand the thinking and learning that occurred in developing the final plan. Perhaps from their viewpoint, their input has been discarded with no explanation. This can cause stakeholders to distrust the consultant team and project sponsor and eventually lead to outright opposition to the plan. In a charrette, the result may very well be identical but people understand it, take ownership of the plan, and are willing to support it. After a charrette, people should feel that they were listened to and responded to. They may say something like, "May-

be all my ideas were not used but they were considered, and I know why."

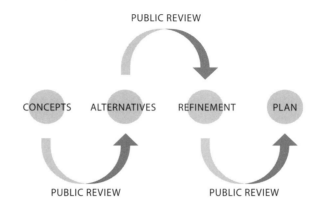

Figure 1 *Charrette Feedback Cycles*

Study the Details and the Whole

Designs at varying scales inform each other and reduce the likelihood that a fatal flaw will be overlooked that could result in costly rework. For example, in the Pleasant Hill BART project the location of the streets could not be verified without studying the layout of the parking garage. Looking at the details also supports shared learning by providing the information necessary for a well-rounded discussion about a proposal. To satisfy skeptics in the Pleasant Hill BART project, it was necessary for the charrette team to create detailed plans illustrating how multiple bus lines would be accommodated.

Confirm Progress Through Measuring Outcomes

By measuring progress through agreed-upon desired outcomes, the transparency of the decision-making process is assured, and people can see that the project is being implemented as planned. Early agreement among the primary stakeholders about measures of success allows the project team to illustrate how decisions are made. This is especially important when defending decisions to new stakeholders who may not have been involved in the charrette.

Produce a Feasible Plan

To create a feasible plan, every decision point must be fully informed, especially by the legal, financial, and engineering disciplines. The success of a community's work to plan and build together hinges on implementation. Plans that sit on the shelf contribute only to citizen apathy. From the beginning of a dynamic planning process, feasibility is a focus of the discussion, which brings a level of seriousness and rigor to the process for everyone involved. Plans that are built as drawn and agreed upon help build trust in government and collaborative planning processes in general.

Use Design to Achieve a Shared Vision and Create Holistic Solutions

Design is a powerful tool for inspiring a community to establish and achieve a shared vision. Drawings help illustrate the complexity of the problem and can be used to resolve conflict by proposing previously unexplored solutions that represent win/win outcomes.

A capable designer can change people's positions by altering their perception of the possible solutions. For example, if the only shared reference for neighborhood retail is a drive-thru convenience mart, a drawing of a friendly corner coffee shop can help change their minds.

Conduct a Multiple-day Charrette

The goal of a charrette is to take a project from a vision to alternative concepts, to a preferred plan, to a developed feasible plan, on to a final presentation. A minimum of three feedback loops is required to adequately involve the public in this undertaking. It takes between four and seven days to accomplish this work collaboratively. The first feedback loop is a warm-up, presenting many ideas that were generated based on stakeholder input. The second loop further engages people in the design and planning and shows them that the charrette team is listening and responding to them.

The third loop completes the cycle with a refined plan based on continuous input, feedback, and response. Without the full feedback cycle, the charrette team loses the opportunity to change perceptions and assure project support.

Hold the Charrette on or Near the Site

Working on-site fosters participant understanding of local values and traditions, and provides the necessary easy access to stakeholders and information. Charrette studios have been located in empty main street storefronts, community centers, high schools, and armories. From the viewpoint of the project manager, it is invaluable for a designer to be able to walk out, look at a site condition, and walk back to her drawing board to work on it. Working near a site is important in a charrette given the short time frame available. Working within a community gives the charrette team easy access to stakeholders and allows relationships to be built over a number of days. The open studio gives stakeholders access to the team and the plan throughout the day and into the evenings, making it possible for someone with a busy schedule to stop by even if she could not attend a scheduled meeting.

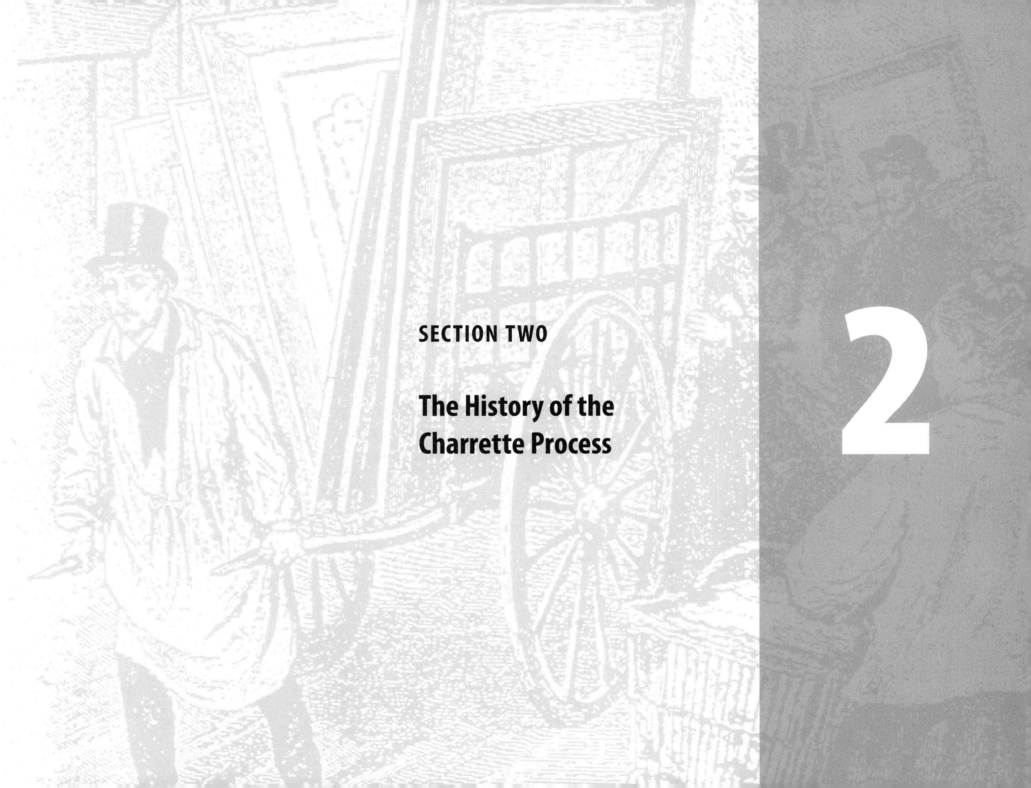

SECTION TWO

The History of the
Charrette Process

2

ORIGIN OF THE TERM

First, what does the word "charrette" mean? In French, "charrette" means "cart." It is often used to describe the final, intense work effort expended by art and architecture students to meet a project deadline. This use of the term is said to originate from the École des Beaux Arts in Paris during the 19th century. The process began with the assignment of a design problem, or "esquisse," and ended "en charrette" when proctors circulated a cart, or "charrette," to collect final drawings for jury critiques while students frantically put finishing touches on their work. Current community design and planning charrettes combine this creative, intense time compression, and peer critiques or "pin-ups" still common in art and architecture schools today, with stakeholder workshops and open houses.

THE EVOLUTION OF THE NCI CHARRETTE

The charrettes on which this book is based are more than just brainstorming or public visioning sessions. The NCI charrette is a collaborative design and planning workshop that occurs over four to seven consecutive days. It is held on-site and includes all affected stakeholders. Therefore, in researching the origins of this charrette process, we looked for trends and projects with these qualities.

The evolution of the collaborative, multiple-day, inclusive, on-site charrette is not a linear one. Its roots may be found in a variety of projects and processes, some related to land use and some not. Our challenge was to trace the origins of a process that has changed and evolved over time and has been used for various purposes. Some answers may be found in a discussion of general changes in trends and policies in the United States, particularly since the late 1950s; other answers are found by looking at some specific projects that were particularly innovative for their time.

Because we are discussing the origins of the NCI charrette, our research began with multiple day workshop-type processes. We looked for processes that were held on-site in the United States, and were stakeholder inclusive (collaborative), multidisciplinary, "groundbreaking," and helpful in advancing the field of public collaborative design processes for community planning.

Charrette Project Timeline

Until the 1960s, public planning agencies and private consultants made many land planning recommendations about the future without the input of the people who lived there. The Civil Rights movement of the 1950s and 1960s and other rights movements that followed, all based on making democracy work for everyone, had an effect on the way public planning decisions were made. "Processes for opening up the discussion of urban futures to the people directly affected by urban design recommendations began in a faltering and fragmented manner in the 1960s," wrote David Lewis, co-founder of Urban Design Associates. "Only in the late '60s and early '70s were efforts made to formalize procedures for receiving inputs from community members and to open up the discussion of alternative recommendations, so that community members would be able to respond to and buy into accountability."[1]

Advocacy planning and citizen participation began to take hold. Community design centers emerged to offer low-cost design services to disadvantaged and "grassroots" organizations. By the mid-1970s, radical sentiment had shifted to the environment and other rights movements such as feminism and gay rights. However, community involvement in architecture and planning has persisted and is on the rise today. Conversations about grassroots democracy and collaborative decision making can be heard across disciplines. It has become commonplace and often mandated to include some form of public participation in the planning process.

The following timeline of projects tracks the evolution of on-site collaborative design workshops with significant

Figure 2 *La Charrette, by Alexis Lemaistre at L'Ecole des Beaux-Arts c.1889*

Charrette Projects Timeline

1850
École des Beaux Arts, Paris, France
"Charrette" is used to describe the cart on
which completed student architectural
drawings are placed at the deadline for critique

1947
Urban Land Institute (ULI) Advisory Services
Panel in Louisville, Kentucky

1948
Caudill Rowlett Scott (CRS) Squatters in
Blackwell, Oklahoma

1960s–1970s
W.L. Riddick Community Problem Charrettes

1963
Carnegie Institute of Technology Master's
of Urban Design Program

1967
Urban Design Associates (UDA) Charrettes in
Pontiac, Michigan

1967
American Institute of Architects (AIA)
Regional/Urban Design Assistance Team
(R/UDAT) in Rapid City, South Dakota

1969
Community Based Projects (CBP) Program
of the College of Architecture and Planning
at Ball State University student charrette in
Indianapolis, Indiana   >>

stakeholder involvement. It is not all-inclusive but represents a series of significant moments. Doubtless and regrettably, relevant projects were missed because of the lack of remaining documentation. Each project/process is listed as it was termed at the time of the event. Most processes were called charrettes at the time, a few were simply called workshops or sessions, and in many cases such words were used interchangeably.

The following project processes took place in the United States between 1947 and 1987. All occurred on-site or within the communities on which they were focused. They were collaborative, meaning they included all relevant stakeholders throughout the process, and most were open to the public. The processes also included multiple-day workshops with professionals from multiple disciplines assisting a community to design and plan for its future building and development.

Processes were initiated for somewhat different reasons, but many of the project strategies were similar, as were the lessons learned. In most cases, firms and organizations ended up using similar processes in efforts to meet one or both of these goals: (1) complete projects quickly and efficiently, and (2) enfranchise community members and build community support for processes and products. Regardless of initial intent, all of the projects succeeded in accomplishing both goals. The most common intentions included a general interest in empowering community members; efficient use of time, money, and ideas; overcoming project opposition; serving local communities; and educating students through hands-on experiences.

In 1967 Urban Design Associates (UDA) set the goal of enfranchising citizens through urban design in the Pontiac project. Its focus was on involving the public and connecting them through the design and planning process. Similarly, W.L. Riddick was focused on involving and empowering citizens in underserved urban communities. The

AIA R/UDATs and Urban Land Institute (ULI) Advisory Panels recognized the value of bringing in outside experts to work with local stakeholders on the community's problems. Implementation strategies, carried out by local stakeholders, were also a focus of these early community assistance programs.

Caudill Rowlett Scott (CRS) initially traveled to a project site and "squatted" in an effort to recover lost time, money, and energy on an elementary school project. The firm was having communication problems working on a complex problem from a distance and discovered the value of involving users in the planning process. Many years later, Duany Plater-Zyberk & Company (DPZ) faced a similar problem and used a charrette to maximize efficiency of time and money on an out-of-state project. They also developed a process that allowed them to complete a project in one trip, minimizing rework.

Interaction, Inc. used a multiple-day collaborative process to work with and overcome adversarial attitudes from project opponents. Similarly, Centerbrook used a public involvement process after voters rejected a previous riverfront plaza plan. The firm needed a collaborative process to move the project forward, and the involvement of stakeholders in design and review feedback loops over many months helped build project support for implementation of the new plan.

The Community Based Projects (CBP) Program of the College of Architecture and Planning at Ball State University (BSU) also focused on public involvement and serving the communities in which they worked. The program's goals included giving community residents ownership in the process and products while educating students. The Muncie Urban Design Studio (MUDS) program was an extension of previous programs at BSU with the specific focus of serving the community in which they were located and providing a long-term resource for stakeholder involvement in community planning and design. The public involvement component of the Master's of Urban Design at Carnegie Mellon and the University of Washington student charrettes were founded on similar premises several decades apart. They served the communities in which they worked, advancing real, creative solutions for real users, while educating students through hands-on involvement in urban design.

The Solar Cities Design Charrette was a creative, multidisciplinary problem-solving colloquium in which experts gathered in California to work on prototypical case studies with broad applicability for real-world solutions.

Contemporary Charrettes

The emergence of the NCI dynamic planning process began with the 1987 Friday Mountain Charrette in Austin, Texas, conducted by Duany Plater-Zyberk & Company. It was the first of numerous charrettes conducted by DPZ, using a process that they continue to use and improve today. Bill Lennertz, NCI's executive director and co-founder, was the DPZ project manager for the Friday Mountain Charrette, beginning his 20-year journey to improve the process we now call dynamic planning. The Friday Mountain model became, and still is, the standard process for the work of DPZ and other firms that followed.

Since the mid-1980s, hundreds, if not thousands, of land planning and design charrettes have been conducted, mostly by private consulting firms, public agencies, and some citizen advocacy groups based on this weeklong, collaborative model within the framework of significant preparation and implementation phases. Other professional organizations and consultants have adopted similar but abbreviated versions of charrettes. Some examples are the American Planning Association's Community Planning Team Charrette in Greensboro, North Carolina, in 1995 and a number of short "environmental design charrettes" held by the American Institute of Architects's Committee on the Environment in 1995 and 1996. The AIA's R/UDAT program

continues, as do charrettes for green building and landscape architecture. University architecture and planning programs continue to offer student charrettes, most often within their own communities.

As this book was being written, NCI staff and board members were participating in a charrette of significant scale and importance for the revitalization of the Mississippi Gulf Coast following the devastation of Hurricane Katrina in the summer of 2005. When faced with the formidable challenge of producing plans for 11 coastal cities in six days, DPZ and the Congress for the New Urbanism turned to the charrette process. In a notable evolution of the process, 11 firms conducted their own "charrettes within a charrette," each focusing on one of the communities. It was also notable because of the scale. The overall charrette team was composed of more than 200 national and local professionals.

Charrette Project Timeline Details

Urban Land Institute (ULI) Advisory Services Panel in Louisville, Kentucky

In April of 1947, ULI convened the first of many Advisory Services Panels, in Louisville, Kentucky. ULI continues to offer Advisory Service Panels, providing objective analysis and advice on how to solve land use, development, and redevelopment problems across the United States today. Teams of ULI members provide technical expertise to cities, private developers, and other organizations, approaching a project from many perspectives, including market potential, land use and design, financing and development strategies, and implementation. The teams convene near the project site for five days, working with the sponsoring group, meeting with relevant stakeholders, touring the site, and conducting confidential interviews. The team's recommendations are made to the sponsor group in the form of a presentation on the final day and in a subsequent report.

>>

1970
Interaction, Inc.'s collaborative, multiple-day workshop in San Francisco

1976
Centerbrook Architects and Planners series of "design-a-thons" in Dayton, Ohio

1980
Solar Cities Design Workshop/Charrette at Westerbeke Ranch, Sonoma County, California

1980
Muncie Urban Design Studio's Muncie Urban Design Charrettes, Muncie, Indiana

1985
University of Washington Department of Architecture student charrette, Seattle

1987
Duany Plater-Zyberk & Company Friday Mountain Charrette in Austin, Texas

2005
Mississippi Renewal Forum, organized by the Congress for the New Urbanism and Duany Plater-Zyberk & Company in Biloxi, Mississippi

Ball State's Mobile Studio: Providing Technical Support for Small Town Charrettes

Anthony J. Costello
Professor Emeritus, Ball State University

In 1979, the development of a long-range plan for the community-based, service-learning component of Ball State University's College of Architecture & Planning (CAP) included among its goals a commitment to better serve the entire state of Indiana. As the director of the program at the time, I was challenged by the founding dean of the college, Charles M. Sappenfield, to devise both a strategic plan and methodology that would allow this to happen. At that time, Indiana had 495 incorporated towns and cities, 95 percent of which had populations of 5,000 or less. Spread across the entire state, and often a four-hour drive from Ball State's campus in Muncie, it was obvious that the charrette workshop was the optimum process to efficiently and successfully serve these far-flung and (mostly) rural communities. Therefore, my faculty colleagues Scott Truex,

>>

Caudill Rowlett Scott (CRS) Squatters in Blackwell, Oklahoma

In 1948, CRS held the first "squatters" in Blackwell, Oklahoma, on an elementary school project. The Austin, Texas, firm had a long commute to the project site that it found wasted a lot of time, money, energy, and creative ideas. The partners set up a temporary office and "squatted" at the school site until all of the design issues with the school board were resolved.

The process was effective enough that CRS incorporated the three- to 10-day squatters into their future projects for both programming and design to involve client and user groups in decision making. Stakeholders included clients, end users, and a multidisciplinary team of professionals that resulted in the client-user's approval of the current phase of the project.

"The squatters came about very accidentally," recalled Bill Caudill, co-founder of CRS, Architects, Engineers and Planners (originally Caudill Rowlett Scott). "We were trying to get the preliminary plans approved for these two schools in Blackwell. Wally and I were going back and forth trying to get their approval. We were running out of money, we were running out of time, and we were losing good ideas because we were having a real communication problem and we needed to solve it. How do you practice architecture five hundred and twenty-five miles from home? We were about to lose this job by default because we could not get it approved. I don't know if I thought of the idea or not; maybe it was Wally. But one of us said, 'By gosh, let's just get in the car, put our drafting boards in the car, and go to Blackwell. Let's set up office right in the board room and not come back to Texas until we get the damn project approved.' We drove one Sunday night to Blackwell and set up office early Monday morning; we just squatted, as we say, right in the boardroom. By Friday night we had complete approval on this project by the Board. In fact, it was

unanimous enthusiastic approval. While we were trying to solve a communication problem, we discovered something that we should have known all along—to involve the users in the planning process."[2]

Although CRS is no longer a firm, other firms continue to use the squatters approach.

W.L. Riddick Community Problem Charrettes

In the 1960s and 1970s, consultant W.L Riddick led a number of "community problem charrettes," which lasted seven to 10 days and were held in various urban areas in the United States. The community problem charrette is described by Riddick as "an activity that brings residents and people of expertise together, under the pressure of limited time, for the study of specific community problems."[3] Citizens took part in "working groups" to focus on specific problems. "Directly affected" citizens sat on a number of different committees including Finance, Publicity, Graphics, Building and Site, Citizens, and Hospitality. Also involved in the charrettes were professional experts, both from the community as well as consultants from outside of the community, city officials (as participants), and elected officials. The projects resulted in "results and recommendations of the working groups."[4]

Carnegie Institute of Technology Master's of Urban Design Program

In 1963, when David Lewis started the Master of Urban Design Program at Carnegie Mellon University (then the Carnegie Institute of Technology), he organized it to include citizen participation in the ongoing work of the design studios. It was one of the first educational programs in urban design in which students worked collaboratively within a community. Students worked hands-on with elected officials, agency representatives, and community members in communities in the Pittsburgh metropolitan region.

The program took the form of a series of working meetings with residents and community leaders from the neighborhood under study. The first group of meetings was part of the analysis of the area and included asking a lot of questions about conditions in the neighborhood and the community's aspirations for the future. The second set of meetings reviewed different design ideas. Then there was a final design presentation and discussion.

Urban Design Associates (UDA) Charrettes in Pontiac, Michigan

In 1967, UDA employed one of its first public participatory processes to enfranchise citizens through an urban design project for a human resources center in Pontiac, Michigan.[5] Initially funded by the Educational Facilities Laboratory of the Ford Foundation and then later by the local school board, the purpose of the project was to find a site for an educational facility that would combine primary education with day care and community college programs to serve a walk-in, racially integrated population.

The process included eight three-day charrettes over the course of 18 months. Stakeholder groups included the school board, Pontiac's political leadership, residents of the local neighborhoods, and a small contingent from the downtown business association. Project products included a master plan for the area and urban design for the building complex. UDA's early projects were focused on community involvement and community participation in urban design. The firm wrote in its *Urban Design Handbook*: "At the core of what we were doing was a sense of urban design as a language of democracy, a way of linking the individual and the family to the city—house, porch, and street, neighborhood, city."[6]

David Lewis writes, "R/UDATS and Charrettes have demonstrated that no one knows their urban communities more deeply and with greater concern than the people who live in them. Professionals and agency representatives who are on teams for the first time are amazed, not only by the knowledge of citizen participants, but at the quality and wisdom of their insights, and the determination of their aspiration."[7]

UDA has continued to develop and refine its charrette process for more than 30 years. See charrette scheduling variations in Section Five for details on the UDA charrette process.

American Institute of Architects (AIA) Regional/Urban Design Assistance Team in Rapid City, South Dakota

In 1967, the first Regional/Urban Design Assistance Team (R/UDAT) was held by AIA in Rapid City, South Dakota. James Bell, president of the Chamber of Commerce in Rapid City, South Dakota, met with a number of architects at AIA headquarters in Washington, D.C., including Andy Euston, then director of urban programs. Bell discussed the problems that Rapid City was facing, and the architects offered to gather a group of professionals to go to Rapid City as volunteers to work with local government officials and citizens. After some negotiations, "four team members, two architects and two planners were selected, and a packet of maps, aerial photos, statistics and other background information about Rapid City was sent to each."[8] The team met with local officials, architects, media, and citizens and made a presentation of their findings at the end of their visit. Shortly thereafter they mailed a brief written report. The results over time were powerful and had significant impacts on the community. "Back at the AIA, the architectural community was astonished and gratified," according to a history of the teams. "The value of the process was clear to the Urban Planning and Design Committee. It decided to offer the idea to other communities. And R/UDAT was born."[9]

R/UDATS are currently still conducted across the U.S. by AIA teams. The R/UDAT process addresses social, econom-

AICP, and Harry Eggink, and I developed the Small Town Assistance Program in 1980, relying on a charrette process that used interdisciplinary teams made up of faculty and students from the departments of architecture, landscape architecture, urban planning, and the program in historic preservation.

In 1980, there were logistical problems inherent in serving Indiana communities, where often the only copy machine was in the single town attorney's office and the nearest commercial slide-developing capability was often a 90-minute round-trip drive away. These issues had to be solved if the charrette process was to be instituted on a repetitive basis that efficiently allowed between two and four charrettes to be successfully completed each year.

Fortunately, a member of the Ball State board of trustees at the time was the president of Coachmen Industries, one of the largest recreational vehicle (RV) manufacturers in the nation. With a one-time, $60,000 grant and a five-year, $10,000 per year operational grant from the State of Indiana Department of Commerce, a 38-ft. Coachman RV was custom-outfitted to incorporate all of the technical capabilities that our quickly expanding experiences showed us were required.

The vehicle was self-sufficient with an electric generator and 50-gallon potable water supply and hot water heater. This allowed in-situ

>>

>>

land-reclamation studies in a state where strip coal mining had rendered many thousands of acres suitable for reclaiming as recreational and/or natural preservation areas. In addition, the vehicle contained a one-station darkroom (with capabilities for developing black and white film, making 8 x 10 prints, and processing E-6 slides), light tables, table and chair storage, a print machine, a copy machine, drafting boards, two computer stations (remember, this is prior to laptops!), and—most importantly—a large coffee maker, as well as a small microwave oven and refrigerator. On the exterior, a large roll-out awning provided a shelter for setting up the table and chair and conducting sidewalk interviews on the courthouse square or sheltering additional workspace.

The advent of laptop computers and graphic software, PowerPoint presentations, digital cameras, and other technology allowed most of the capabilities listed above to be carried to any site in two suitcase-sized containers. The CAP mobile studio, although used during approximately 25 charrettes, became an obsolete and not cost-effective resource. However, it did aid in allowing Ball State's CBP/Small Town Assistance Program to quickly gain a national reputation for serving the citizens of the Hoosier State's smaller communities in their attempts to revitalize their towns and/or nearby rural environs.

■

ic, political, and physical issues in a community. It combines local resources with the expertise of a multidisciplinary team of national professionals who volunteer their time to identify ways to encourage desirable change. The R/UDAT is four days in length with a team visit to the community prior to the event and a return visit by the team within one year during the implementation phase. Stakeholder groups include AIA and local leaders, and a steering committee representing a variety of residents, local government, businesses, institutions, and community groups. After listening to the concerns and ideas of residents, community leaders, and interested groups and viewing both the study area and the surrounding community, the team prepares and publishes a report, which includes a vision, action items, and timetable, and presents it in a public meeting on the last day of the event. Later, a report resulting from the follow-up visit analyzes the action plan, assesses progress to date, and makes recommendations that will aid implementation.

Interaction, Inc. Collaborative, Multiple-day Workshop/Charrette in San Francisco
In 1970, Interaction, Inc. (later Interaction Associates), conducted a five-day, multi-group, collaborative design and planning process—a "task oriented" charrette—for Far West Laboratories, a regional research laboratory of the department of education. Far West was moving its offices from Berkeley to the Mission District of San Francisco. The process included several break out groups and many plenary sessions, all of which used the Interaction Method of facilitation. Stakeholder groups included Far West Lab managers and staff, their architects, The Mission Coalition, local residents, local nonprofits who were interested in the space, and invited experts in the field of education, with 30 to 60 people involved much of the week.

Interaction, Inc. had been working previously with Far West Laboratories as its fiscal agent for a Carnegie grant called "Tools for Change" so it had access to management and an established relationship of trust. Members of Interaction, Inc. had been experimenting with the concept of a neutral facilitator as tool provider in a problem solving meeting and were influenced by Synectics and their ideas and courses in heuristic problem solving. The process also used the concepts of a recorder and documented group memory. David Straus of Interaction Associates writes, "The concept of an accordion, task-oriented conference also derived from our ideas about phases in problem solving and the design of collaborative processes."[10] He continues: "One key event involved the Mission Coalition trying to use classic organizer/adversarial techniques, which backfired on them as participants found that they were being heard and that process was truly collaborative. This was in the early days where all stakeholder groups were learning how to participate effectively in a collaborative process."[11]

Community Based Projects (CBP) Program of the College of Architecture and Planning at Ball State University Student Charrette in Indianapolis, Indiana
In 1969, the College of Architecture & Planning at Ball State University founded the Community-Based Projects Program (CBP), which sought to carry out the university's triple mission of teaching, research, and service. The program initially focused on Indianapolis, the state's capital and largest city, which was in the early stages of a major revitalization effort. The CBP program has always ensured that community participation is made a priority.

The first project the CBP undertook was a five-day design charrette for the Indianapolis Elementary School Community Center at 25th and Ralston Streets, Model Cities Neighborhood in Indianapolis. The project provided programming and conceptual design alternatives for a new elementary school that would also serve as a 24/7 community center. The main purpose was to engage the residents of the

African American neighborhood, whose children would be served by the new school, in a participatory process in order to give them ownership of both the process and product. In addition, teachers, administrators, and representatives of various community organizations participated.

The project was organized and sponsored by the following organizations: U.S. Office of Education (funding and planning); City of Indianapolis Model Cities Program (planning); Model Cities Neighborhood Citizens Advisory Committee (citizen input); Indianapolis Public Schools (planning and programming); and Ball State University College of Architecture and Planning (planning, design, graphic production, and public presentation of findings).

Project products included large graphic panels that covered three walls of the existing school's gymnasium for the public presentation of findings. These were condensed into a report given to the architect who was commissioned to design the school and had participated in the charrette.

Centerbrook Architects and Planners Series of Design-a-thons in Dayton, Ohio

In 1976, Centerbrook Architects and Planners held a series of televised interactive workshops, or design-a-thons, for Riverdesign Dayton in Dayton, Ohio. The project was a plan for a downtown riverfront plaza in Dayton. Voters had rejected a previous plan for the riverfront so the city hired Centerbrook to plan the plaza with public involvement.

First, Centerbrook established a centrally located, accessible project office in a downtown storefront. It was advertised in press releases and provided a walk-in office for community members to stop in and offer ideas. Centerbrook also established a steering committee, including public officials and community leaders and a citizen committee representing groups of stakeholders throughout the community. Six one-hour-long design-a-thons were broadcast approximately monthly over a six-month period on Thurs-

day nights on a local PBS affiliate.

The broadcasts were interactive; people could call in from home to make suggestions or have their questions answered by design professionals, city officials, engineers, and others. All the professionals involved (including architects, engineers, market researchers) had to simplify their jargon during the broadcasts to explain the project to a wide audience. Questionnaires were published in the local paper to help guide the design process. The main purposes of the entire process were first, to create a design that was easy to implement, and second, to gather public support for implementation. The final project products included a 130-page plan including 100 proposals plus an implementation strategy.

Solar Cities Design Workshop/Charrette at Westerbeke Ranch, Sonoma County, California

In 1980, a group of forward-thinking individuals gathered for a weeklong problem solving design process, which focused on three prototypical communities. Participants included a dozen architects, entrepreneurs, community organizers, transportation specialists, engineers, biologists, ecologists, agriculturalists, public officials, planners, and experts in public finance and design process. They developed case studies on three prototypical communities: an inner-city neighborhood in Philadelphia, a postwar suburb in Sunnyvale, California, and raw land within Golden, Colorado. Communities were revisioned into places "that, over the next 20 years, vastly reduced their dependence on fossil fuel, and increased community self-reliance and livability."[12] Conclusions included shared design principles with broad applications. The charrette resulted in a series of papers, which included plans, housing types, renderings, elevations, and energy use diagrams, all of which may be found in the publication *Sustainable Communities* by Sim Van der Ryn and Peter Calthorpe.

Student/Academic Charrettes at the Universities of Michigan and Washington

Douglas S. Kelbaugh
Dean and Professor of Architecture and Urban Planning, University of Michigan, A. Alfred Taubman College of Architecture and Urban Planning

U nlike a conventional charrette, academic charrettes produce competing proposals for the same problem from three or four teams. The shortest description of these multi-outcome workshops is "an illustrated brainstorm." It is a four- or five-day intensive workshop in which multidisciplinary teams of 10 to 15 graduate students led by three to four design professionals and faculty develop different design solutions for the same project and present them at a public meeting. Several thousand participants, including students, faculty, guest professionals, and community members have participated in more than 20 charrettes at the Universities of Washington and Michigan; and upwards of 7,500 people have attended the public presentations that end these events.

>>

Muncie Urban Design Studio's Muncie Urban Design Charrettes, Muncie, Indiana

In 1980, the Muncie Urban Design Studio (MUDS), a component of the Community Based Projects Program of the College of Architecture and Planning at Ball State University, was founded to serve Ball State's hometown of Muncie. The program is guided by the basic educational and public service goals of the college's Community Based Projects Program. One of the first MUDS charrettes, "Muncie Charrette '82," was held in April of 1982 and is still referred to as a critical benchmark in Muncie's downtown revitalization.[13] The project used an intensive three-and-a-half day charrette, organizing and conducting a major investigation of the White River corridor as it impacts and is impacted by downtown Muncie.

The MUDS program has operated out of four different "storefront studios" and has had a unique role in the city's redevelopment, particularly in "downtown revitalization, river corridor development, neighborhood revitalization initiatives, historic preservation efforts, and affordable housing programs in 'Middletown, U.S.A.'"[14] MUDS allows faculty members and students of Ball State University's College of Architecture and Planning to serve a wide range of public and nonprofit sector entities involved in community and neighborhood development, housing, social services, art, and culture.

The program continues to operate today. Its one- to five-day charrettes serve as catalysts for initiating long-term, community-based urban planning and design initiatives or projects. Examples of such projects include downtown revitalization, neighborhood redevelopment, and replanning and redevelopment of a federal public housing project. Stakeholders involved include local city government, community development agencies, planning commissions, housing authorities, newspapers, various community foundations, and community members.

University of Washington Department of Architecture Student Charrettes, Seattle

In 1985, Douglas Kelbaugh became the architecture chair at the University of Washington (UW) and organized a small academic event that grew into a large annual design charrette program. Early projects explored housing for the homeless. "They are meant to advance feasible but creative solutions to issues from real clients and users, as opposed to being a theoretical or pedagogic exercise for the sake of faculty or students," Kelbaugh explained.[15]

UW student charrettes focus mainly on the Seattle region, although two were held in Italy and one in India. "UW charrettes . . . always served a public agency, organization, or institution and resisted requests from private parties," Doug Kelbaugh writes. "Citizen participation is a practical matter of defusing obstructionism and developing strong ideas and shared ownership as much as a matter of common decency and democracy."[16]

UW charrettes last generally five days and involve major stakeholder groups including local officials, community members, charrette clients, local businesses, local institutions, local developers, and design professionals. Products include drawings and slides of four design solutions (one per team of 12 to 15 students led by faculty and distinguished local and out-of-town design professionals), a booklet delineating the project, publicity for the project (including a large final public meeting), and follow-up presentations to community groups.

(See also in this section "Student/Academic Charrettes at the Universities of Michigan and Washington.")

Duany Plater-Zyberk & Company (DPZ) Friday Mountain Charrette in Austin, Texas

In 1987, Duany Plater-Zyberk & Company held its first public charrette in Austin, Texas. The seven-day Friday Mountain Charrette resulted in a master plan and codes for a 500-acre new community. The charrette included opening and closing public meetings and two sets of meetings with primary stakeholders midway through the process. Major stakeholder groups involved included the developer, city officials, local architects, and local neighbors. Charrette products included a master plan, zoning codes, architectural guidelines, and renderings.

Friday Mountain was the largest project of its kind for DPZ at that time. The new demands associated with this project—given its physical size, the hilly site, the size of the development program, and its impact on the surrounding community—caused DPZ to search for new ways to do large land planning projects. The charrette was used for the efficiency of completing the project in one trip. It was also used for its ability to take the project to a high level of completion is a short period of time in order to minimize subsequent rework. DPZ's team wanted to create a process that could produce a plan for a complex project with a high level of efficiency and creativity and began their experimentation with and refinement of their charrette process with this project.

Mississippi Renewal Forum, Congress for the New Urbanism and Duany Plater-Zyberk & Company, Biloxi, Mississippi

In October of 2005, six weeks after Hurricane Katrina, the worst natural disaster in U.S. history, the Mississippi Governor's Commission on Recovery, Rebuilding and Renewal contacted architecture and town planning firm Duany Plater-Zyberk & Company (DPZ) to lead the planning effort to rebuild 11 Mississippi Gulf coast cities. Recognizing the enormity of the task, DPZ joined with the Congress for the New Urbanism (CNU) to tap a nationwide network of professionals.

The extreme urgency of the situation demanded an immediate response. The governor charged the design team with the task of completing an entire set of draft recommendations within five weeks and completing final reports two weeks thereafter. DPZ and the CNU turned to the charrette process to accomplish this formidable task. Four weeks after the initial contact, more than 130 planners, architects, engineers, economists, environmentalists, and sociologists from across the country and abroad joined over 100 local professionals for a six-day charrette to plan 11 coastal cities. In addition to the 11 teams formed, one for each city, there were also teams dedicated to regional environmental, social, financial, and transportation issues. Principals from national design firms led each team. Additionally, each team was seeded with local architects and planners responsible for taking the plans back to their communities. The teams also met with members of the general public during tours of the cities.

Products of the charrette included comprehensive presentations and reports for each of the cities and the region. Each report contained urban design, transportation, environmental, and economic recommendations for the short-, mid-, and long-term. Two days after the charrette began, the Governor's Commission and the local charrette team members organized a series of town hall meetings in each of the cities to present the charrette findings and solicit public input. The lead firms continued their work with several communities after the charrette.

>>

The charrettes have typically dealt with an urban design issue of social and civic importance. Three basic types have emerged: ones that tested new public policies or design ideas on real sites; ones that responded to requests for help from neighborhood groups or public agencies; and ones selected by the school that explored a particularly glaring problem or opportunity presented by a specific site. Most charrettes have been hybrids, for example, making proposals for an under-utilized site on behalf of a municipality. They have consistently advanced feasible but creative solutions on real sites for real clients and users, as opposed to being a theoretical or pedagogic exercise for the sake of the students. Their synergistic energy of friendly competition and collaboration typically resulted in ideas that conventional, linear consulting would not be likely to generate.

Each charrette has produced drawings, slides, a booklet of the teams' design proposals, and considerable local buzz and publicity for the project, including a final public presentation attended by hundreds of citizens, stakeholders, and officials. There have usually been follow-up presentations to other audiences, and the charrette outcomes have usually been widely published and aired by the local media. Sometimes they have precipitated the commissioning of consultant studies and/or built projects. Most charrettes have generated a shared vision for the public and provided a large gene pool of ideas for public discussion and dissemination, as well as adaptation by others and adoption by the community. ■

1   David Lewis. Unpublished writings.

2   Bill Caudill, interviewed by Larry Meyer for an Oral Business History Project, University of Texas, 1971. Sponsored by The Moody Foundation. Source: CRS Archives, CRS Center, Texas A&M University, College Station, Texas.

3   W.L. Riddick, II. 1971. *Charrette Processes: A Tool in Urban Planning*. York, Pa.: George Shumway. 1.

4   Riddick, *Charrette Processes*, 5.

5   UDA had previously employed a more limited public process in two projects in Pittsburgh in 1964, also funded by the Educational Facilities Laboratory of the Ford Foundation, when the Pittsburgh Board of Education fell under a Supreme Court order to integrate its secondary education.

6   Urban Design Associates. 2001. *The Urban Design Handbook: Techniques and Working Methods*. New York: W.W. Norton & Company.

7   Lewis, unpublished writings.

8   Peter Batchelor and David Lewis, eds. 1986. *Urban Design in Action: The History, Theory and Development of the American Institute of Architects' Regional/Urban Design Assistance Teams*. Raleigh: North Carolina State University Press.

9   *Ibid.*

10 David Straus. Unpublished writings.

11 *Ibid.*

12 Sim Van der Ryn and Peter Calthorpe, eds. 1986. *Sustainable Communities: A New Design Synthesis for Cities, Suburbs, and Towns*. San Francisco: Sierra Club Books. v.

13 Anthony Costello. 1995. "MUDS: A Focus for Urban Design Education in 'Middletown, USA.'" *Urban Design Studies* 1.

14 Costello, unpublished writings.

15 Douglas Kelbaugh. 1997. *Common Place: Toward Neighborhood and Regional Design*. Seattle: University of Washington Press. 14.

16 *Ibid.*

SECTION THREE

Dynamic Planning Tools and Techniques

3

Introduction

The tools and techniques section of this handbook provides the project manager and charrette manager with a practical guide for analyzing and organizing a project according to the dynamic planning process. It presents an organizational structure and a set of tools that can be adapted for each project. This handbook's authors and contributors, veterans of consulting practices, academia, and public agencies, recognize the value of a structured approach that offers relief from having to invent a different process for each new project. This tools and techniques section provides a template that the project manager can consult at the start of each project.

The tools and techniques are organized and presented according to the three dynamic planning phases and their sub-phases. Each phase and sub-phase begins with a diagram that locates the section within the dynamic planning process. In order to make the process easy to follow, each phase and sub-phase is presented as a linear set of events and tasks. However dynamic planning is an interactive process that often involves an iterative use of the tools. For instance, the stakeholder identification and preliminary analysis (task 1.1.3) that is first completed at the beginning of phase one is a living document that is updated continuously throughout the project. Every tool and technique might not be applicable to every project. However, we recommend that each one be considered carefully before it is dismissed.

RESEARCH, EDUCATION, AND CHARRETTE PREPARATION

1

1.1 Project Assessment and Organization

1.2 Stakeholder Research, Education, and Involvement

1.3 Base Data Research and Analysis

1.4 Project Feasibility Studies and Research

1.5 Charrette Logistics

THE CHARRETTE

2

2.1 Organization, Education, Vision

2.2 Alternative Concepts Development

2.3 Preferred Plan Synthesis

2.4 Plan Development

2.5 Production and Presentation

PLAN IMPLEMENTATION

3

3.1 Project Status Communications

3.2 Product Refinement

3.3 Presentation and Product Finalization

Figure 3 *Dynamic Planning Phases and Sub-phases*

Phase One: Research, Education, and Charrette Preparation

RESEARCH, EDUCATION, AND
CHARRETTE PREPARATION   THE CHARRETTE   PLAN IMPLEMENTATION

1.1 Project Assessment and Organization

1.2 Stakeholder Research, Education, and Involvement

1.3 Base Data Research and Analysis

1.4 Project Feasibility Studies and Research

1.5 Charrette Logistics

INTRODUCTION

As with many endeavors, the manner in which a project begins significantly influences the final outcome. In dynamic planning, a good start means beginning with collaboration. The value of collaboration and a cross-disciplinary approach dictates that everyone who has a guiding influence on the project must be involved from the beginning in an atmosphere of trust and respect. The foundation for broad project support is established when this value is reflected in the initial project communications and meetings. Therefore, the first organizational meeting (part of sub-phase 1.1) must include the core management team as well as anyone representing a specialty that will be involved in the project design. Far too often, disciplines such as finance and transportation are left out of the initial conversations. Significant rework can result when these specialties are brought into the process too late.

The tasks in phase one are designed to provide the support necessary for success and the preventions required to avoid possible difficulties in phase two, which is the charrette, and phase three, project implementation. A successful charrette (phase two) requires that the right people and information are present in an efficiently organized charrette studio. Effective project implementation (phase three) necessitates a shared understanding of the preferred plan by all of the stakeholders and their support of it.

Phase one consists of everything that must be done before the charrette begins. This includes organization, base data research and analysis, education, and logistical arrangements.

PROJECT ORGANIZATION

In a typical dynamic planning process, the sponsor, whether a public entity or a private development company, hires consultants to plan and run the process. More often than not, the lead consultant is a planning or architectural firm that contracts with a set of sub-consultants who provide expertise in such areas as economics, transportation, and the environment. The project manager for the lead firm works closely with the sponsor's manager. The level of involvement by the sponsor's manager varies from project to project but the consultant project manager is usually the person responsible for the planning, organization, and day-to-day project operations. The lead consultant may also have a charrette manager working under the project manager. In this case, the project manager is responsible for the overall operations of the project, including the relationships with the sponsor and primary stakeholders. The charrette manager is usually responsible for the setup and day-to-day management of the charrette.

BASE DATA RESEARCH AND ANALYSIS

Proper base data research and analysis is fundamental to the creation of a feasible plan. A cross-functional collaborative team process assures that no relevant piece of information is overlooked. The base information and its accompanying analysis necessary for the creation of a detailed plan should be readily available to the team during the charrette. Any shortcoming in this area can result in costly rework and a waste of valuable resources.

EDUCATION

The collaborative dynamic planning approach dictates that all who are closely involved have a shared understanding of the operating values and the project process. Each person must also be clear about his role and how the charrette will work. Within the planning and architectural professions, the word "charrette" is used to describe many different processes. This presents a challenge that requires constant attention throughout the project. The project manager should never assume that everyone is using the same definition of the word charrette. This understanding must begin with the project sponsor. It is not uncommon for a project manager to be so focused on community education that the education of the project sponsor and related agencies is overlooked. The project management team meeting that occurs at the beginning of sub-phase 1.1 is the first opportunity to create these important shared understandings.

CHARRETTE LOGISTICS

Charrette logistics include arrangements for the charrette team, studio, and schedule. The success of the charrette is heavily dependent on the chemistry and capability of the charrette team. The quality of the charrette studio and meeting locations can have a significant effect on the efficiency and overall success of a project. Logistics should not be left until the last minute. From early in the project, the charrette manager, in coordination with the project manager, works on the logistics required for an efficient charrette event.

Research, Education and Charrette Preparation Sub-phases

- 1.1 Project Assessment and Organization
- 1.2 Stakeholder Research, Education, and Involvement
- 1.3 Base Data Research and Analysis
- 1.4 Project Feasibility Studies and Research
- 1.5 Charrette Logistics

1.1.1 Objectives, Strategies, Measures Draft

1.1.2 Project Mission and Products

1.1.3 Stakeholder Identifiction and Preliminary Analysis

1.1.4 Complexity Analysis

1.1.5 Dynamic Planning Process Road Map

1.1.6 Charrette Ready Plan

1.1 Project Assessment and Organization

INTRODUCTION

The dynamic planning process begins with the assessment and organization phase. This commences when the project manager convenes a project management team meeting. The purpose of this meeting is to create a shared agreement between the project sponsor and team members on the project purpose and process. This shared agreement forms the basis of an efficient, well-orchestrated, team approach aimed at reducing rework.

The core team members and decision makers who will be guiding the project through to its completion all attend this meeting. In most projects, the project sponsor, the sponsor's staff, members of the lead consulting firm running the charrette, and possibly any political champions,

Sample Project Management Team Meeting Setup

Participants: Sponsor(s), lead consultants, public agency management, other promoters (elected officials, community representatives)

Meeting length: 3.5 hours

Agenda items:
- Introduction to project
- Project mission elements
- Charrette products list
- Objectives, strategies, measures draft
- Stakeholder identification and preliminary analysis
- Complexity analysis
- Process road map
- Charrette ready plan

for example a member of the city council who has a special interest in the project, attend this meeting.

Each of the project assessment and organization tasks results in a set of documents that will guide the team through the project. A draft of each one of these documents is created during this initial project management meeting. Two very important action items during the project management team meeting are (1) creating the overall project mission and (2) determining the specific products that need to be produced during the charrette. One of the most important products of this phase is the charrette ready plan. It lists all actions that must be accomplished, their timing, and the roles and responsibilities of each team member to prepare for the charrette.

1.1 Project Assessment and Organization Tools and Techniques
- 1.1.1 Objectives, Strategies, Measures Draft
- 1.1.2 Project Mission and Products
- 1.1.3 Stakeholder Identification and Preliminary Analysis
- 1.1.4 Complexity Analysis
- 1.1.5 Dynamic Planning Process Road Map
- 1.1.6 Charrette Ready Plan

1.1.1 Objectives, Strategies, Measures Draft

INTRODUCTION
The Objectives, Strategies, and Measures (OSM) document is a decision-making tool. This document represents a shared agreement on a prioritized set of clear, specific, measurable, and achievable objectives among primary stakeholders such as the developer, the principal government agency, and community groups. Establishing a set of measurable objectives and implementation strategies helps make the charrette process more objective and builds trust

between public and private parties. The OSM is an invaluable document for validating the charrette process and explaining it to those who enter the process at a later date. It is also an important guide for the charrette team's decision-making process as it works on synthesizing a preferred plan from alternative plan concepts during the charrette. Through the public input process, the objectives are defined as concise and achievable statements, each measurable by a set of criteria established early in the process and refined over time, to enable all participants to qualify and quantify the plan's performance. This is an essential step in securing broad-based support and trust throughout the life of the effort.

PROCESS
One method for developing the OSM is to create the first draft in the project management team meeting. The charrette manager leads the project team in an exercise for creating the OSM statement. The group creates a set of objectives by category, such as economic, environmental, circulation, social, aesthetic, legal/regulatory, and time goals and targets. The objectives can also address the degree of public input in key decision-making processes and measure degrees of success in providing participants with key information for meaningful involvement. The group lists the strategies for achieving each objective and then creates a set of measures for the performance of the strategies, such as fiscal impacts or financial contributions to local taxes. The OSM document that is created in the project management team meeting is then presented to other primary stakeholders such as the chamber of commerce and community groups for review, revision, and additions. At some point, the primary stakeholders may need to meet face-to-face to attempt to resolve any differences regarding the content of the OSM and achieve a set of objectives, strategies, and measures by consensus. Throughout the charrette, the OSM document

functions as a touchstone to help guide the community—public officials, staff, neighbors, organizations, businesses, residents, and other community members—in their decision making to create, test, refine, and implement the preferred plan.

1.1.2 Project Mission and Products

INTRODUCTION

Mission Statement
The project mission statement describes the overarching purpose of the project. It represents the higher-level purpose to which the project sponsor will devote financial and political resources to achieve. The mission will be used as a guide throughout the project for everyone involved. It will be used to describe the project to newcomers as well as to keep the planning effort on task. Without a mission, a team

is likely to engage in unproductive efforts that waste time and energy. This mission is initially drafted by the project management team in the project management team meeting and is usually amended by stakeholders, including the general stakeholders (public) as they become involved in the planning process.

PROCESS

Drafting the Mission Statement
Drafting a mission statement by committee can be a daunting task. To make it more manageable, the project manager may decide not to attempt to complete a written statement in the project management team meeting. Those present can simply agree on the elements of the mission. The elements should reference the objectives from the OSM. Once the elements are agreed upon, the project manager or another team member is assigned to write a mission statement that will then be circulated among team members for revisions. Dur-

TIP

Why and How OSM Works

Steve Coyle
Principal, HDR|LCA+Sargent Town Planning

In a small Southern California town, the charrette team for a large, private development began the charrette process by establishing a set of measurable objectives between the city and the developer. This effort to identify a list of goals (economic, civic, social, legal, educational, infrastructural, aesthetic) valued by the two entities helped make the charrette planning strategies more measurable and less subjective. The list of objectives for each also constituted many of the "deal points" for the future city/developer development agreement.

For example, one objective was to create a significant amount of parks and open space. The measures for the objective included the total acres used and the physical qualities of each type of open space. Since people tend to choose a plan they perceive to be "greener," whether or not their perceptions are correct, the use of accurate graphs and charts in addition to plans and renderings were recommended to more accurately compare the performance of two or more schemes.

By beginning the charrette with a set of measurable objectives, stakeholders can more fairly evaluate competing plans that employ standardized criteria as measuring tools. For instance, if the objectives

>>

Table 1 **Sample OSM Form**

Objective	Strategy	Measure
The project shall be economically feasible	Create a financial model and market study agreed upon by the city and developer	Financial and market analysis based on agreed upon models
The project shall promote convenient and safe walking and biking	A walkable, bike-supportive street system that is connected to the surrounding neighhoods	Street standards with design speeds and sidewalk designs based on current ITE street standards
The project shall provide basic services, employment opportunities, and housing	Mixed-use zoning ordinance	Financially and market supportable mix with a baseline agreed upon by the city and developers

>>

include reducing traffic impacts on the surrounding community, the projected traffic generated by a proposed plan might represent one essential criterion used to measure effects. In the charrette, each proposed concept might include the anticipated motor vehicle trips generated by homes, schools, and businesses within the boundaries of the site. One plan's clever design of mixed-use centers and transit to significantly reduce traffic should be evaluated against other schemes that employ a less walkable, more vehicle-dependant approach.

By employing the OSM tool, the charrette team can brainstorm, test, and refine the key design and planning strategies, in collaboration with stakeholders, that achieve the desired objectives. The OSM charrette plan will help build trust between public and private parties, lead to a fairer and more rigorous evaluation process, and provide the strategies required to achieve these goals within a measurable framework. ∎

ing the meeting, the team should make a list of elements under some basic category headings. Here is a good list of elements to begin with:

- Project products
- Politics
- Quality of life
- Economics
- Transportation
- Housing
- Design
- Environmental
- Cultural (minority issues, historic)
- Safety/security
- Process
- Timing

Project Mission Elements

First, list mission element categories, then fill in elements.

Sample Project Mission Statement

Here is an example of a mission statement created in a project management team meeting in an Alaskan city: "To create an economically feasible town center plan that describes an attractive, convenient, safe and walkable town center with a mix of uses and transportation choices to serve the surrounding neighborhoods and respond to the challenges of our northern climate. The project will be completed within a year's time using a collaborative process featuring a charrette."

INTRODUCTION

Charrette Products and Outcomes

The charrette products list describes specifically what needs to be produced at the charrette, at least in draft form, to assure project feasibility. This list is essential to the project manager. His or her job is to know what resources need to be assembled in terms of base data and people in order to produce this work during the charrette.

PROCESS

Creating the Charrette Products List

In a brainstorming session with the project management team during the project management team meeting, the charrette manager creates a list of drawings, studies, and documents that must be completed by the end of the char-

Table 2 **Example Project Mission Elements for Town Center Master Plan**

Element Category	Example
Project product	Town center master plan
Political	Serves the surrounding neighborhoods
Quality of life	Walkable, safe
Economics	Economically feasible
Transportation	Convenient transportation choices
Social	Mix of uses, affordable housing
Design	Responsive to the northern climate
Process	Collaborative charrette process
Timing	Completed within one year

Table 3 **Example Charrette Products**	
Product Category	**Product Example**
Transportation	▪ Transportation plan ▪ Traffic impact analysis ▪ Street sections
Environmental	▪ Environmental impact analysis and plan
Civil	▪ Stormwater management plan ▪ Conceptual grading plan
Landscape architecture	▪ Parks, open space, and trails plan ▪ Detailed park studies
Urban design	▪ Ground level and bird's eye renderings ▪ Building types ▪ Illustrative plan ▪ Detail site plan studies
Planning	▪ Regulating or zoning plan ▪ Housing impact analysis ▪ Form-based code elements ▪ Legislation language ▪ School impact analysis
Economics	▪ Fiscal impact analysis ▪ Economic and market feasibility study
Social	▪ Preliminary agreement indicating percentage of affordable housing

rette. A useful way to build this list is by category of work, such as transportation, civil engineering, landscape architecture, design, planning, and economics. This information is used to complete the complexity analysis and the charrette ready plan.

1.1.3 Stakeholder Identification and Preliminary Analysis

INTRODUCTION
During the project management team meeting, the project team creates an initial list of stakeholders who must be involved to assure project success. The team identifies the relevant stakeholders, the appropriate involvement for each, and a strategy for getting them to participate in the process. This stakeholder identification and analysis will be performed multiple times during the charrette preparation phase as information is obtained through interviews. This initial stakeholder analysis is therefore only the beginning of an ongoing process.

Understanding the "win"
Perhaps the most useful part of the stakeholder analysis is the identification of the "win" for each stakeholder viewpoint listed. Determining the win provides the information necessary to convince stakeholders that they should participate. Presenting the project as an opportunity for an individual to achieve his or her win is a way to create relevance and assure ongoing participation. A full understanding of a stakeholder's win is usually not attained until a discussion with the stakeholder has occurred. At the heart of any win is an underlying need. For instance, a stakeholder group might initially say that a win for them is to have nothing happen. But after further questioning, it becomes apparent

TIP

Engaging Community Members in Planning

David Brain
Professor, New College of Florida

The form and quality of public engagement in a charrette-based process is different from many practices commonly associated with participatory planning. For the most part, participation these days takes the form of collecting public "input." Whatever the effectiveness of such techniques, the public often appears only as a kind of reactionary force in the process, providing "data" that might or might not affect the outcome and reacting to the proposals that emerge—typically with anger and suspicion. Linkages between public discussion, the formulation of proposals, and final planning decisions often remain obscure and therefore suspect from the point of view of citizens.

Such participation mobilizes the public, raises expectations, and then routinely frustrates those involved when the plans finally put forth bear very little visible relationship to the public's experience of the process. So-called participatory planning processes routinely turn concerned and engaged community members into angry and distrustful NIMBYs.

In a charrette-based process, this common tendency can be reversed: NIMBYs can become involved community members with a sense of responsibility for

>>

>>

building consensus around community-based solutions and general faith in a legitimate democratic process can be restored. This is only partly a matter of making sure that the various stakeholders are adequately represented in the process. Research on democratic participation has shown that the form of the process matters as much as the extent of representation or the quality of the policy outcomes. In a charrette, community members are invited to engage in the substance (not just the fact) of proposals as they are being formulated, and they can see the substantive impact of their participation on a plan that they can realistically expect to see implemented. Community members come away with a sense of efficacy, having participated in meaningful decisions that are explicitly reflected in concrete outcomes. The charrette process provides community members with an opportunity to understand not only the consequences of particular planning and design decisions, but how their interests and concerns relate to others in the community when translated into built form.

A charrette can therefore boost the chances of successful implementation of a plan in two significant ways. First, the participants in a successful charrette end up with a sense of ownership of the vision and will therefore be prepared to defend it. They tend to have a deeper understanding of the issues and the trade-offs that accompany most planning decisions. Second, participants in the charrette will also recognize the opportunities that the plan creates for them to pursue their own interests in a way that contributes to the realization of a shared vision. This is, in fact, the very definition of civic engagement, the key to implementation in the context of market-based real estate development, and the secret to planning that is most likely to produce lively, beautiful, and resilient urbanism over time. ■

that the real win for the stakeholders is to maintain their privacy, security, and property values. Understanding these implicit needs is essential for the charrette team as it creates alternatives capable of delivering the win.

Stakeholder Levels

Stakeholders can be divided into "primary," "secondary," and "general" categories. General stakeholders, most commonly community members, are involved primarily at the public meetings. Secondary stakeholders are those with a keen economic or political interest in the project such as community art groups, schools, and churches. It is common to hold interviews with the secondary stakeholders before the charrette. The primary stakeholders are those with a strong influence over the project. These individuals hold political, jurisdictional, or economic positions, e.g., elected or appointed positions, or they own land nearby. The primary stakeholders must be involved at all key decision-making points. These are the people who are most frequently involved throughout the project. It is important to note that, regardless of their level, all stakeholders should be involved in major project reviews.

PROCESS

The purpose of the stakeholder analysis is to collect and verify crucial information. For the good of the project, and to ensure an inclusive and credible process, the charrette manager should never trust that the information provided by the client is the whole story. The following steps should occur during the project management team meeting:

1. Create a list of stakeholder viewpoints essential to a holistic process.
2. Identify the people who best represent each viewpoint.
3. List the people who must be involved because of their special relationship to the project.
4. Identify the issues that are important to each person and the viewpoint that they represent.

Table 4 **Stakeholder Levels of Involvement**

Stakeholder Level	Example Positions	Suggested Involvement
Primary	Elected and appointed officials (city council, planning commissioners, steering committee members), agency staff (departments of transportation, EPA, transit authorities), site property owners	Interviews before the charrette, meetings during the charrette, should attend all public events, may drop into the studio anytime
Secondary	Non-governmental organizations (historic and art groups, churches, synagogues), individuals with businesses or residences directly affected	Interviews before the charrette, possible meetings during the charrette, should attend all public events, may drop into the studio anytime
General	Community members	Should attend all public events, may drop into the studio anytime

Table 5 **Sample Stakeholder Analysis**

Viewpoint	Person / Affiliation	Issues	Win	Level	Outreach Strategy	Charrette Participation
Elected Official	Lucinda Wallis, Capital County	25 years of controversy, with nothing to show. Wallis is the project "champion."	A plan and codes agreed upon by the developer, and the neighborhood. A bulletproof public process. A national exemplar project.	Primary	E-mail, phone	Daily Team Meetings
Elected Official	Percival Moccasin, Capital County	Concerned about project costs. Interested in a non-controversial outcome.	A project that can be approved and supported by neighbors.	Primary	E-mail, phone	Public Meetings
Neighborhood Activists	Carrie Snodgras, Kris Tal, Terry Jensen, Medford District Improvement Association	Deep distrust of County Supervisors and staff. Traffic, visual impacts, property values, safety.	Minimal traffic impacts, maximum housing, low buildings across from neighborhood, pedestrian access, local retail only, no increase in transit parking. The county must keep its promise and build the regional trail.	Secondary	E-mails, letters	Separate Meeting
Neighboring Commercial Owners	Katrina Moskawitz, Hollywood Boosters	Workers have limited local services.	Compatible uses with existing business, amenities for office workers, traffic management.	Secondary	E-mails, letters	Separate Meeting
Developer	Tom Bates, Dick Bernard, Big Sky Development	Last development proposal failed.	Economic and market feasible plan.	Primary	E-mail, phone	Daily Team Meetings and Reviews

5. Establish what constitutes a win for each of these people.

6. Indicate each stakeholder's level of participation, especially for people who require separate charrette meetings in addition to the public meetings.

After filling out the chart in this manner, make sure that the following four categories of people are included:

1. Decision makers: If decisions are being made then decision makers need to be present.

2. Those directly affected by the outcome: Anyone whose property or business is affected should be there. Those living within the project area should also be represented.

3. Those who have the power to promote the project.

4. Those with the power to block the project: If there is any hope to gain the support of these people, it is better to bring them into the process earlier rather than later.

Charrette Steering Committees

Marcela Camblor
Urban Design Director,
Treasure Coast Regional Planning Council

True communication and genuine stakeholder input are goals of every charrette. Involving the public is key to a successful charrette but citizen participation doesn't just happen. The best, simplest, and most effective method is the "word of mouth" or "direct invitation" that comes from a resident or neighbor (not from the local government). People tend to listen to and trust their neighbors.

Establishing a Charrette Steering Committee is one very effective way to foster this community trust and encourage ownership of the charrette process. A group of 10 to 12 residents, property and business owners, and community leaders is established at least three months prior to the charrette. The design team educates this committee on the process, study area, design issues, and the importance of citizen participation. The committee meets often during the months prior to the charrette. With support from the local government and the design team, and using all available methods of advertisement, the committee assumes responsibility for publicity during the pre-charrette phase. The members of this committee become the link to the community and the press. The most dedicated Charrette Steering Committees usually remain involved for many months after the charrette. This long-term commitment ensures continuity of the concepts resulting from the charrette, but above all, guarantees that the stakeholders' vision is truly represented and respected over time. ∎

TIP

How to Assure a Proportional Demographic Representation

Gianni Longo
Principal, ACP – Visioning & Planning

Outreach is the most delicate phase in any public involvement process. Balanced and representative participation lends credibility to the effort, gains the attention of elected officials, and ensures that the resulting consensus is broadly shared. While publicity, through written and electronic media, creates general awareness of a process, outreach delivers participants.

An outreach plan should include a detailed set of strategies for how community members from all parts of a community can be approached and invited to participate in public meetings.

There are three types of concurrent sets of strategies that need to be implemented.

1. Geographic strategies are designed to ensure balanced participation from residents from all parts of an area, including rural, suburban, and city residents. For example, in the Birmingham, Alabama, 12-county region, 12 separate outreach committees were created and led by local leaders knowledgeable about how to reach out to local residents.

2. Demographic strategies are designed to ensure participation of those residents less likely to engage in a participatory process. These strategies typically

>>

1.1.4 Complexity Analysis

INTRODUCTION

The complexity analysis is a quick method for determining the overall difficulty of a project. When performed early in the planning process, it can help the project manager understand the magnitude of the task. The complexity analysis provides information to determine the research needed, the size of the team and its makeup, and the length of the charrette.

PROCESS

The project complexity analysis is an initial rating of the level of difficulty of a project by various categories of information. This analysis is key for deciding project work scope, team size and makeup, and project schedule. It can also illuminate areas that require additional resources or base

---

Table 6 **Sample Project Complexity Analysis Categories**

For each category, the team evaluates the degree of difficulty for each item and summarizes it in the analysis column.

Project Component	Analysis Summary
Politics	
Planning budget: Is it sufficient or will a tight budget limit necessary resources, adding stress to the project?	
Does the schedule allow for enough time to prepare for the charrette properly?	
What is required for project submittal for approvals? Is it very complicated?	
Number of jurisdictions affected: Are they all involved and informed? What are competing needs?	
Presence of opposition: What is their level of organization?	
Environmental	
Are there extraordinary site conditions such as topography, wetlands, or subsurface issues?	
Circulation	
Do plans for roads through the site challenge walkability?	
Perimeter streets: Do they pose any access or connectivity challenges?	
Economics	
Market feasibility: What is the quality of available market data? Is a new market study needed that will require resources?	
Developer: Are there willing and able development teams?	

data research. During the project management team meeting, the charrette manager leads the team through a set of questions according to different aspects of the project such as budget, time, approvals, site, politics, transportation, and economics. Each aspect is analyzed, its issues are explored, and the team determines the level of difficulty for each element. The team then stands back and makes an overall project complexity assessment and decides what additional work and resources, if any, are necessary.

1.1.5 Dynamic Planning Process Road Map

INTRODUCTION

The dynamic planning process road map plots the overall strategy for conducting the entire dynamic planning process. It is a guiding document for the project management team. The road map focuses on the major events and products of each dynamic planning process phase. Most importantly, it describes the public involvement strategy in terms of major events and meetings.

PROCESS

The dynamic planning process road map is completed in draft form during the project management team meeting. Having identified the mission, desired products, OSM, and stakeholders, and having completed the project complexity analysis, the project management team is well prepared to create the overall process strategy. This exercise is best done with a large wall chart or digital spreadsheet projected on the wall. The team lists the major phases, events, and products that influence the critical path of the project. This shows the phases, events, and products on a timeline and assigns roles and responsibilities for each task. The completion of this road map provides the answers to the frequently asked questions: "How long will the project take from beginning to end?" and "At which points will the public be involved and how?"

>>

target non-English speaking residents, minorities, and specific age groups such as seniors, youth, and the 20 to 39 age group. Each have different reasons why they might not choose to participate, and those reasons have to be addressed by outreach strategies.

3. Area-wide strategies are designed to engage community organizations such as clubs, professional associations, and church groups, to name a few. These organizations can use existing channels of communication, such as newsletters and electronic mailings, to inform their members about the goals of the process and the meeting schedules.

These three sets of strategies follow the principle that community members are more likely to participate when someone whom they know and trust invites them. ∎

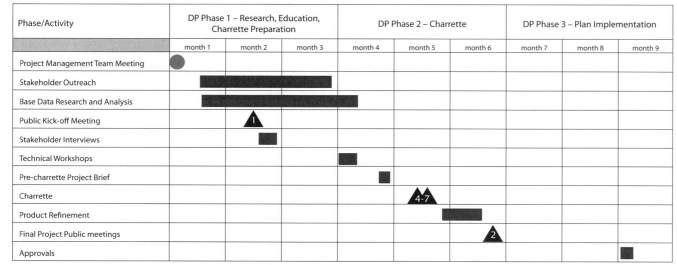

Phase/Activity	DP Phase 1 – Research, Education, Charrette Preparation			DP Phase 2 – Charrette			DP Phase 3 – Plan Implementation		
	month 1	month 2	month 3	month 4	month 5	month 6	month 7	month 8	month 9
Project Management Team Meeting	●								
Stakeholder Outreach		▮▮							
Base Data Research and Analysis		▮▮							
Public Kick-off Meeting		▲1							
Stakeholder Interviews		▮							
Technical Workshops			▮						
Pre-charrette Project Brief				▮					
Charrette					▲▲4-7				
Product Refinement					▮				
Final Project Public meetings					▲2				
Approvals									▮

● in-house meeting   ▮ ongoing task   ▲1 public meeting (one day)

Figure 4 Sample Dynamic Planning Process Road Map

Table 7 **Charrette Ready Planning Process Summary**

1. Make a running list of everything that needs to be done to complete the charrette products list using the following categories:

- Public and in-house meetings
- Outreach
- Site
- Buildings
- Economics
- Transportation
- Charrette logistics

2. Schedule deadlines for each

3. Determine responsibilities

4. Display in bar chart format

1.1.6 Charrette Ready Plan

INTRODUCTION

The charrette ready plan is a detailed investigation of phase one of the dynamic planning process road map. Completion of the charrette ready plan provides the necessary information to answer the commonly asked question, "When will we be ready to have a charrette?" This plan is essentially the project manager's work plan; it is a running list of all the tasks, their associated deadlines, and each team member's responsibilities. It must describe the tasks required to assure that the charrette team has the base data necessary for producing the charrette products. It must also list the tasks for assuring that the stakeholders are prepared and will participate in the charrette. The charrette ready plan can be created using a wall chart or project management software. The project team, generally at the end of the project management team meeting, creates the initial draft. This assures that everyone shares the same understanding of the process and, having created it themselves, they will be more likely to make it a priority and follow through on action items.

PROCESS

The charrette ready plan is developed during the project management team meeting. The most interactive method is to use a large wall chart and sticky notes. The project manager leads the team through an exercise of listing all major tasks with time frames under a set of categories. Each consultant contributes his list of the tasks required to have information on hand at the charrette to complete his part of the charrette products list. The tasks are written on the schedule chart under the specialty categories, and time frames are added. The entire team then reviews and revises the schedule until it reaches agreement on the dates for the charrette and other major milestones.

Conclusions for 1.1 Project Assessment and Organization

How a project begins affects the ease with which it proceeds. The project assessment and organization phase therefore forms the foundation for a project's success. During this phase, the project management team creates the tools to allow it to proceed efficiently. Especially important is the identification of stakeholders who will play a critical role in the process and to develop a strategy for their continuing engagement. The project management team meeting is the main event of this phase. Although it may seem more efficient for the project manager to complete this work in isolation, in the long term it is more beneficial to complete this work as a team. As its co-authors, the team members take ownership of the project assessment and organization. If there are any conflicting viewpoints about the project purpose, strategy, schedule, or budget, they should be dispelled by the end of the meeting. The exercises and research accomplished during this phase assure a unified team approach and a road map for success.

The dynamic planning strategies at play in the project assessment and organization phase are:

1. **Work collaboratively.** Collaboration between team members in the early stages of the project forms the foundation for a smooth project process.

2. **Design cross-functionally.** The formation of a multidisciplinary team assures limited rework and creative solutions.

3. **Produce a feasible plan.** The project management team's approach to project organization is strongly influenced by the end goal of creating a feasible plan. When working toward a feasible plan, the necessity of extensive charrette preparation is vital.

Phase/Activity	month 1	month 2	month 3	month 4	month 5
Public and In-house Meetings					
Project Management Team Meeting	●				
Public Kick-off Meeting		▲			
Conceptual Sketching and Testing		●			
Economics					
Market Research and Analysis	▬▬▬				
Economic Model			▬		
Transportation					
Transportation Existing Conditions	▬▬▬				
Transportation Model					
Site					
Site Analysis		▬			
Stakeholder Engagement					
Attend Neighborhood Meeting		▲	▲		
Bus Tour			▲		
Smart Growth Lecture			▲		
Stakeholder Interviews		▬			
Technical Workshops			▲ ▲ ▲		
Charrette Logistics					
Pre-charrette Project Brief				▬	
Charrette					▲

 in-house meeting   ongoing task    public meeting

The Value of Collaborative Project Analysis

Project sponsors often develop assumptions about a project's scope and budget without a proper assessment process. In one such project, a consultant was able to change the sponsor's preconceptions by holding a one-day project organizational meeting. With all of the sponsor's primary management staff in the room, the consultant led the sponsor through the same series of exercises outlined in this chapter. At the end of the day, the project sponsors were able to recognize that their previous assumptions about scope and budget were incorrect and that they needed more time to prepare for the charrette. They also realized that the charrette needed to be longer and that they required more funding in order to execute the project correctly. This meeting, in which the sponsor and project management team developed a shared understanding of the project purpose and goals and work necessary to achieve them, resulted in a successful project. ■

Figure 5 *Sample Charrette Ready Plan*

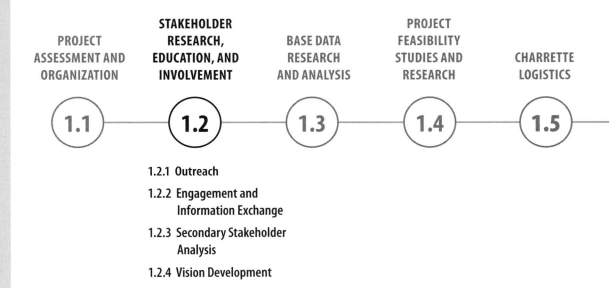

1.2 Stakeholder Research, Education, and Involvement

1.2.1 Outreach

1.2.2 Engagement and Information Exchange

1.2.3 Secondary Stakeholder Analysis

1.2.4 Vision Development

INTRODUCTION

A comprehensive stakeholder analysis and involvement program is perhaps the most effective tool for preventing post-charrette project failure. A proper stakeholder analysis will uncover a project's potential promoters and blockers and identify the issues that matter to each group as well as the outreach and engagement tools to use. A strategy can then be developed to illustrate how involvement in the charrette and throughout the project will directly benefit participants. Numerous examples exist of projects in which a small but well-organized group of opponents successfully undermined the charrette outcome. However, in projects in which potential blockers are identified and engaged early

Table 8 **Outreach and Engagement Tools**
Outreach Tools
▪ Phone calls
▪ Faxes, e-mails
▪ Web notices
▪ Flyers
▪ Mailings
▪ Signs/banners
▪ Door hangers
▪ Newsletter/newspaper announcements
▪ TV announcements
▪ Radio announcements
▪ Reverse 911 system calls (automated recording on the police emergency system that calls every home and business in the targeted area)
Engagement Tools
▪ One-on-one meetings
▪ Confidential interviews
▪ Neighborhood meetings
▪ Meetings at churches and local organizations
▪ "Living room coffees"

on, they often end up as promoters. Success depends on the charrette team's level of understanding of the opponents' interests and its ability to establish a mutually beneficial relationship.

1.2 Stakeholder Research, Education and Involvement Tools and Techniques

- ▪ 1.2.1 Outreach
- ▪ 1.2.2 Engagement and Information Exchange
- ▪ 1.2.3 Secondary Stakeholder Analysis
- ▪ 1.2.4 Vision Development

1.2.1 Outreach

PURPOSE

The purpose of the outreach phase is to establish contact with the individuals and organizations identified in the stakeholder analysis. The result of this initial contact—whether it is by phone, e-mail or printed advertising—should be an immediate, positive perception of the project. This first contact sets the tone and expectations and should therefore be orchestrated carefully with a well-crafted outreach strategy. The desired outcome of the outreach phase is for all those contacted to be excited about and interested in participating in the project.

PROCESS

The outreach process ideally occurs at three levels: the large public gathering, such as lectures and workshops; the group meeting, such as neighborhood organization steering committee or chamber of commerce meetings; and the individual or small group meeting, which consists of one to five people. The project management team, led by the public involvement specialist, develops a strategy for contact-

ing stakeholders. A successful outreach program is based on a clear set of main messages about the project purpose and process. These main messages should be used in all outreach communications including press releases, presentations, and individual conversations. An effective outreach program describes the project in terms of its relevancy to the targeted audience, the basis of which are the "wins" described in the stakeholder analysis. An example of a main message is: "The project will seek to provide a balanced solution to the housing shortage for people who work in Springfield."

It is worth noting the importance of a comprehensive e-mail and address list of project stakeholders. The project manager should use all available sources in the creation of the master list and should not rely on any one source alone. For example, government agency contact lists often include only those people who regularly attend public meetings. In order to solicit broader participation, it is critical to build a list that includes more than just the usual meeting goers. Additional lists may be obtained from such sources as community service groups, churches, and schools.

1.2.2 Engagement and Information Exchange

PURPOSE

Appointed and elected officials do not always fully represent their constituency, and sometimes the most influential people in a community are not visibly public figures. It is therefore critical to locate and engage influential individuals in the community—especially those not immediately apparent. The project management team must be diligent in its efforts to identify and reach these people.

For example, in one Memphis neighborhood, an 85-year-old community member was the institutional source

TIP

Community Strategy for Charrette Participation

Kristen Paulsen Pickus

Director of Planning Services, Davis Office, Moore Iacofano Goltsman, Inc. (MIG)

As Andres Duany has said, "The best plans are touched by many hands." To gain diverse participation, the charrette practitioner must be creative, persistent, responsive, and resourceful. The most successful community engagement campaigns have certain elements in common.

Authentic Involvement

The charrette team should ask for input only if it is prepared to listen carefully, respond to what it hears, and incorporate the ideas (or the intent behind them) into its plans whenever feasible. The goal should be to enable people to participate, with clear vehicles for giving input and a transparent process for responding to people's ideas and concerns. Community members have a depth of knowledge and understanding of the area, a fresh perspective, and a dedication and commitment to their community that improves and enriches even the best plans.

Organized Flexibility

A good stakeholder involvement plan must be an example of organized flexibility. It is important to have a systematic way of identifying (and then contacting) all of the major stakeholders in a community, utilizing appropriate vehicles of communication and creative methods of engagement. Equally important is flexibility, leaving holes in the plan to allow the process to take you where it may. Invariably as you move through the process of stakeholder interviews, you will gain new insights and information. The people you interview will lead you to other groups or individuals who can contribute to the process or even to new ways of communicating. A flexible plan leaves available time and resources that can be allocated as new opportunities are presented.

For example, during the Pleasant Hill BART charrette in California, a good working relationship with Bay Area Rapid Transit public rela-

tions staff meant that we were not only able to put ads in the BART newsletter, post fliers on the BART bulletin boards, and have announcements ("passenger pulls") available at the station exits (tasks that we anticipated), but also to work with BART to develop a new communication method that had not been used before: hanging a large banner at the station to advertise the charrette. For a project in Marina, California, which our research showed had a large Spanish-speaking population, stakeholder interviews provided the information that there was also a growing Korean population in the area. This knowledge allowed us to create trilingual posters, flyers, and meeting materials that successfully drew participants from the entire community.

Relationship Based

Successful stakeholder engagement is all about putting a face on a process and/or plan. It is about relationship building, which is more of an art than a science. It involves caring about people, treating people with respect, honoring their opinions, respecting differences, and being genuine, responsive, and worthy of their trust. This can be accomplished with openness, consistency, a positive attitude and clear, regular communications. A good charrette is a celebration of the community—past, present, and future. Charrette events should be friendly, engaging, and fun.

Resource Intensive

Finally, this process takes energy, resources, and time. For the Pleasant Hill BART charrette, we wanted to keep community members involved, excited, and up to date on the project as it evolved over the course of the week. Our team often worked late into the night, and I can remember sending midnight e-mails to update everyone on our list about new developments and modifications to the plan that had happened during the day.

Good stakeholder involvement is an investment—an investment that must be maintained throughout the charrette process from beginning to end. But it is an investment that can yield incredible rewards. The process builds the groundwork for future civic engagement and long-lasting community support that is a gift to the project—and the community—for many years to come.

STORY FROM THE FIELD

Personal Outreach Meetings

During the preparation for one charrette, the project manager of a very contentious transit-oriented development identified, from his early research, the key people leading the project's opposition. First, the project manager made personal phone calls to the opposition leaders and offered to make a special trip to their location for an introductory meeting. The result was a casual get-together in the living room of the opposition's organizer. This meeting set the genial tone that allowed the creation of a working relationship between the opposition leaders and the project management team. In this case, the opposition eventually lent its support to the final plan. Making personal contact with people and treating them with respect is fundamental to a successful project. ∎

Publicizing a Charrette

Raymond L. Gindroz
Chairman, Urban Design Associates

Without people a charrette would be pretty pointless—as if you were holding a party and nobody came. Even more damaging is an unbalanced representation of points of view. Special interest groups with a particular agenda are much more likely to organize and turn out a crowd than those without one, but it skews the process. Broad and balanced stakeholder representation is vital to a successful charrette. So, the most important challenge when designing the process within which a charrette takes place is to establish effective communication with potential participants. The techniques used to do this vary from project to project depending on the constituencies that need to be engaged.

The mainstream media should be involved in this program. Hold a press conference, issue press releases, use local TV access, and post information on appropriate websites. This should be done well in advance to announce that a charrette is coming, then immediately before the first part of the process as well as before, during, and immediately after the charrette. Ideally, there will be media coverage throughout the charrette. This often encourages people to participate by physically visiting the site or by viewing the charrette's interactive website.

However, it is best to rely on existing networks for

>>

of information for the neighborhood. She never attended a community meeting and she was never recognized formally. However, what she said could sway the whole neighborhood. For a successful project in this community, it was critical that someone on the project management team create a relationship with this woman. Failure to locate the real community influencers opens a project to a possible uprising by a non-represented group late in the game.

PROCESS

Engagement and information exchange is a two-way communication process. The project management team needs to transmit, with absolute clarity, the project purpose, process, and stakeholder involvement options. The team must also listen to stakeholders in order to identify their explicit as well as implicit needs. Knowledge of the implicit stakeholder needs is essential for problem solving. Reduction of cut-through traffic is an example of an explicit neighborhood need. An effective engagement process will identify the underlying implicit needs: neighborhood quality of life and individual safety. With this knowledge, the charrette team can create design solutions that address all of the community's needs.

Stakeholder engagement and information exchange requires the leadership of someone with an in-depth knowledge of local politics. Complicated projects are well served by public involvement specialists. The local public agency is sometimes capable of conducting this process; however, in many cases, its members are too close to the project and too politically charged to conduct a successful process effectively. In many cases, a third-party facilitator from the project management team is required.

Sometimes the stakeholder analysis calls for the involvement of individuals, such as business owners or out-of-town landowners, who are hard to reach or are uninterested in becoming involved in community planning projects. The

project management team must work creatively and diligently to reach these individuals. They must prove that the project is relevant enough to warrant their participation. Such people often require an individual one-on-one meeting, perhaps with a trusted friend, peer, or political ally, to convince them that their participation is critical.

Finally, the project management team must begin working to engage the press as early as possible. How this is accomplished varies from project to project and from place to place. Sometimes it is a chore to get the press interested, and other times they are eager to engage. If their eagerness comes from a sincere interest to help the project it may simply be a matter of providing them with information and access. If, on the other hand, they are bent on writing a story that requires conflict, the task may require a great deal of education. The key is to devise a strategy for working with the press early and throughout the project.

1.2.3 Secondary Stakeholder Analysis

PURPOSE

The stakeholder analysis should be updated continually as new information becomes available from conversations, interviews, and meetings. The secondary stakeholder analysis builds off of the initial stakeholder analysis completed in the project management team meeting. It is a revision that should be performed after initial interviews and at least a month before the charrette.

PROCESS

The project manager builds upon the initial stakeholder analysis by confirming stakeholders, their interests, and their wins. It can be developed after further information is gathered from field interviews with elected officials, community representatives, and other people with in-depth knowledge of the community. The project manager consults with the public involvement specialist as well as others in the community to create the secondary stakeholder analysis. The "others" are individuals identified by local members of the project management team. Often, these community helpers will look over the initial stakeholder analysis to ensure that no important group has been overlooked. Community advisory councils or steering committees are other important sources of information. Many jurisdictions appoint such groups to oversee a project. The most valuable role of these bodies is as community project champions in the recruiting of participants and in the community education process.

It is important to note that stakeholder analysis is an ongoing process that must be updated with information as it is received. It is a living document that is updated and referred to throughout phase one after the initial round of interviews and meetings with the stakeholders as identified in the initial stakeholder analysis.

1.2.4 Vision Development

PURPOSE
Charrettes that take place in communities with a shared vision of future growth have a distinct advantage. This shared vision may be the result of a recent community dialogue surrounding a comprehensive plan, zoning ordinances, or perhaps a well-publicized development project. The effects of growth are more easily discussed in communities where this framework is already present. In communities where no such dialogue or vision exists, the charrette takes on the added obligation of beginning this dialogue. Unless this is the stated purpose of a charrette, efforts should be made in the preparation phase to begin community discussions

about the vision of future growth. Without these discussions and some common ground prior to the charrette, it will likely be quite difficult to complete the planning work required during the short charrette time frame. Comprehensive and general plans often contain vision statements; however, they should never be taken at face value. It is important to assess the degree to which the community currently supports them. If the vision and values are indeed out of date, it may be necessary to engage the community to revisit and revise them as necessary.

PROCESS
The project management team has at its disposal a plethora of vision development tools, for example, workshops, tours, walks, lectures, and visual preference surveys. The following approaches are useful for easing a community into a charrette with a shared vision.

Public Kick-off Meeting
Virtually all projects can benefit from a public kick-off meeting that is held early in the dynamic planning process. This is especially true in volatile political situations where people are on their guard and apt to act defensively. They may assume that the project sponsors have already decided what they want to do. It is never too early to let the public know about the existence of the project. One purpose of a public meeting is to let people know about the project purpose, process, and their options for involvement. The other very important purpose of the meeting is to elicit information and vision elements from the public as a starting point for the project management team. A workshop in which small groups work together on well-orchestrated, hands-on exercises is an effective technique to use during this meeting. Such workshops allow community members to share their thoughts with each other and provide the charrette team with a basis for their early planning efforts. For more

>>

getting the word out. For example, in a city with a strong tradition of civic leagues (especially where their importance is recognized by the political leadership), it is possible to use whatever means of communication they currently use, such as newsletters, a Listserv, or word of mouth.

At the most basic level of communication, all participants at the public meetings should be asked to provide contact information so that follow-up minutes and letters may be sent. A newsletter or website that reports on each event can ensure that accurate and consistent information is being circulated. This will encourage participants to return for the next step in the process because they see that their input has been taken seriously. Publicizing the charrette is more than letting people know it is happening. It is about getting accurate, objective news of its results communicated as well. It is not only important to get people to the party, but also to be sure that the memory of it will be positive, even for those who only heard about it. ∎

TIP

Walking Audits

Dan Burden
Senior Urban Designer and Director of Walkable Communities, Glatting Jackson

Walking audits are one of the most powerful tools to enable people to discuss common issues of interest for the design of streets, parks, safety, trails, and other features of their neighborhood. In many cases, complex and challenging issues are solved right in the field. These 45- to 90-minute teaching events are fun, healthy, democratic, and inspirational. Local media outlets love to cover these events. Variations on walking audits include bicycling, bus, and wheelchair audits. The basics of walking audits are:

1. **Role playing.** Some walking audits include role playing. The police officer pretends to be eight years old, while the fire chief pretends to be 80 years old. At stops, role players explain what works or does not work for them.

2. **Stakeholders are the experts.** Although a key facilitator conducts the walk, stakeholders with specific insights on landscaping, conservation, and placemaking help teach one another about preservation or development opportunities.

3. **Experts discover new answers.** A specialist, such as a fire chief, may discover how a new tool, such as a curb extension, helps him gain access to roadways.

>>

on this type of public workshop, see Section 2.1.4: Charrette Public Meeting #1.

Bus Tours

Bus tours are a very effective way to develop a shared vocabulary of good and bad community design. An afternoon spent with stakeholders visiting local examples of good and bad development and discussing these as a group is an effective way to develop a shared set of experiences and examples that can be recalled during the charrette. For example, it can be very helpful during the design session of a charrette to be able to remind stakeholders of a particular local public park as an example of the open space design issues at hand.

Technical Workshops

Technical workshops are educational events that focus on specific topics such as transportation, housing, retail, or parks. They are best held a month or two before the charrette. This is an opportunity for the charrette team specialists to provide information to community members related to their area of expertise. The purpose of the workshops is to provide the community with a holistic picture of the topics so that they will be informed charrette participants. An example of a desired workshop result would be community members understanding the effects that on-street parking has on travel speed, pedestrian safety, and retail markets.

Neighborhood Walks

The neighborhood walk is a fun and educational exercise that allows the project management team and stakeholders to learn about the project area together. Walks are mapped and carefully organized by the project management team. Routes are planned that will take a group of eight no longer than two hours to walk. Groups are led by a member of the project management team with a note taker and a volunteer renderer—often an architecture student or local

designer. An unlimited number of groups can be accommodated, although each group should consist of no more than eight people. Each group walks the route stopping at pre-assigned locations to answer a standard set of questions, followed by an open discussion. The note taker records the conversations and the renderer sketches ideas created by the group. At the end of the walk the teams gather and share their experiences and sketches. Sketches, notes, and maps are then assembled into a booklet. These booklets are invaluable resources during the charrette. The charrette team can use them as community-initiated departure points for the project plan.

Lectures

Another way to initiate discussions about growth within a community is to sponsor lectures by noted experts on topics such as sustainable design, traffic calming, and form-based codes. These lectures do not have to be specific to the project. They can provide a more generic view of challenges and solutions to community growth. Lectures are particularly useful in communities in which there has been little dialogue previously about growth issues and more education may be required prior to collaborative discussions.

Conclusions for 1.2 Stakeholder Research, Education, and Involvement

The stakeholder research, education and involvement subphase is vital in preparing for the charrette. The best stakeholder involvement processes are conducted by a project management team that values the stakeholders' contributions because these contributions have the potential to improve the project. In other words, the charrette team should not just go through the motions of soliciting "public involvement" but should realize that its diligence in involving

TIP

Confidential Interviews

David C. Leland
Managing Director, Leland Consulting Group, Urban Strategists

In most stakeholder involvement processes, it is necessary to do more than just hold public meetings. Many people are reluctant to speak in public and may not feel comfortable doing so in a crowded public meeting. Also, there are some issues that people want to discuss, but absolutely will not do so in a public setting. Confidential interviews are one technique for "public involvement" in a format that does not replace a large public meeting but rather complements it.

Lessons learned from conducting extensive confidential interviews include:

- The purpose of the confidential interview is to identify both facts and trends.
- Invitations for the interview should come from a respected individual.
- Invitees must have confidence that the interview will be confidential.
- The interviewer must be skilled and knowledgeable about the subject.
- Interviews can be one-on-one or in small groups (of two to four persons).
- Notes may be taken, but no comments should be attributed to individuals.
- Interviews are best carried out by a consultant without the client present
- The setting should be comfortable—have necessary props (maps, photos, etc.).
- Don't control the conversation—let it flow where it goes.
- Occasionally bring the discussion back to the general topic.

When the interviews are over, thank the participants, summarize the pattern of results, trends, agreement, disagreement, significant problems discovered, barriers revealed, solutions suggested, and so on. Send the participants a summary of the overall findings and patterns. This information can be coupled with other research and other public opinion. The process always reveals matters of significance that will not be discussed in a large public forum, yet are fundamental to the success of the overall project. ∎

community members will have a positive impact on the final plan.

During this phase, it is essential that the initial contact between stakeholders and project representatives is positive. All potential stakeholders must be treated with respect. This is especially true when contacting those who normally do not participate in community planning projects. These are often the very people who you most need to engage. After the first contact, stakeholders should have a clear understanding of the project purpose and process and understand its relevance. They should feel compelled to get involved and know how to do so.

The dynamic planning strategies at play in the stakeholder research, education, and involvement phase are:

1. **Work collaboratively.** The project management team's approach to engagement is based on a value for collaboration as a necessary means to project success.

2. **Communicate in short feedback loops.** Communications should be frequent enough to keep stakeholders interested and informed.

>>

4. **Wheelchairs** are brought out on some walks so that all participants can learn the challenges of existing street conditions.

5. **Groups stop frequently** each time there are new teaching points on how to repair a corridor, create a crossing, or make some other improvement.

6. **Create solutions on the spot.** Workshop members may pause in quiet locations to design a curb extension, mini-circle, or other feature. ∎

1.3.1 Base Data Research and Gathering

1.3.2 Strengths, Weaknesses, Opportunities, Threats (SWOT) Analysis

1.3 Base Data Research and Analysis

INTRODUCTION

The charrette is a major undertaking requiring significant resources for its preparation and execution. Once the charrette begins, it is crucial that the necessary resources are readily available for the charrette team to take the project to the level of detail required to assure feasibility. There should never be a time when a team member says something like, "If we only knew exactly where the heritage trees were located then we could precisely plan the location of the main boulevard," or "If we only knew exactly where the street rights-of-way and property lines were we could determine if the sidewalk will be wide enough for outdoor dining."

Members of a charrette team should be experts on all base data concerning their areas of specialty. It is also the responsibility of the charrette team to make sure that all members of the community are given access to *all* of the base data. An effective method is to post all information

The Vision Process in Community and Regional Planning

Gianni Longo
Principal, ACP – Visioning & Planning

In the 20 years since Vision 2000 in Chattanooga Tennessee—the first and one of the more successful visions in the country—the vision process has undergone a profound transformation while remaining true to the basic principles of inclusiveness, transparency, careful design, and commitment to implementation. Visions have become indispensable tools in community and regional planning activities and have been catalysts in bringing together public, private, and civic interests to give form to a vision and successfully implement it.

A vision process brings together a diverse cross-section of residents to develop an agreed-upon preferred future and recommends how that future can be realized. A vision process may be applied to neighborhoods, cities, and regions. It may be designed as an open exercise to elicit ideas on all areas of interest to a community, or it may be focused on planning issues, thus creating a foundation of consensus for plans at all scales.

The implementation of a vision process follows three phases. The first is organizing the vision to determine who will lead the effort; tailor the process to the area; and promote broad-based participation through publicity, education, and outreach.

>>

and research on the project website. Pre-charrette educational sessions (task 1.2.4) are also a way to discuss base data. In a charrette, the public flow of information is paramount, and any action that can possibly be perceived as a "back room deal" can throw a charrette off course. Also, there can be no perception that the charrette team is missing vital information. When, for example, previous studies of the area are overlooked, an opponent of the project could bring it up in a public meeting. Such an occurrence will not only embarrass the charrette team and sponsor but could derail the entire process. At the very least, it will result in a general lack of trust. When this happens, an outside group may be able to take over the process. When previous studies are taken into account, participants feel that their past efforts are valued.

1.3 Base Data Research and Analysis Tools and Techniques

- 1.3.1 Base Data Research and Gathering
- 1.3.2 Strengths, Weaknesses, Opportunities, Threats (SWOT) Analysis

1.3.1 Base Data Research and Gathering

INTRODUCTION

The primary guide for base data research is the charrette ready plan (task 1.1.6). This document lists all of the information that needs to be gathered and prepared prior to the charrette. The project manager oversees the work done by each specialist in accordance with this plan, which usually includes at minimum an existing conditions report.

PROCESS

Initiating base data gathering is the responsibility of the project manager. The manager requests all existing reports, plans, and studies from the project sponsor, local planning agencies, local universities, and possibly community advocacy groups. After analyzing and cross-referencing this information with the charrette ready plan, the project management team can decide if new studies are necessary or if existing studies can be updated with fresh data. New studies are then commissioned as necessary. It is very important to determine the level of community investment in previous planning processes. A group or community may view these documents as virtual contracts with the planning authority. In this case the project manager must assure that the documents are used as the foundation or departure point for the project planning effort.

Geographic Information Systems (GIS) mapping is becoming an indispensable base data gathering and assessment tool. The maturation of interactive GIS software makes it a powerful tool throughout the dynamic planning process. In the base data phase, GIS software can be used to provide a comprehensive picture of a existing state of a community in terms of transportation, stormwater, wetlands, energy consumption, housing types, demographics, air quality, and other measures.

1.3.2 Strengths, Weaknesses, Opportunities, Threats (SWOT) Analysis

INTRODUCTION

The Strengths, Weaknesses, Opportunities, Threats (SWOT) analysis is a tool borrowed from the business world. Often, when launching a new business plan or product, a product team will conduct a SWOT analysis to refine its business strategy. The product team examines the product's qualities and conditions external to the company, such as competition and market forces. The same type of analysis can be very useful in preparing a strategy for and planning land planning and development projects.

Table 9 **Common Categories of Base Data**

Site	Existing conditions map, geotechnical study, base maps, aerial photographs
Transportation	Traffic counts, future projects planned, Transportation System Plan (TSP)
Market	Demographics, buyer profiles, demand analysis, housing types
Economics	Financial pro forma model
Politics	Decision-making process, relevant organizations and positions
Environment	Government regulations, analysis models/data for impact analyses
Planning	Previous plans, regulations and standards, policies (including previous attempts to develop the property)
History	Local built environment, culture
Project Program	Mix of uses: housing types, commercial types, public uses, open space

By this point in the dynamic planning process, enough base data and stakeholder research have been completed to perform a SWOT analysis for the project. This valuable analysis can be used to inform the planning documents created during the charrette and the overall project implementation strategy. Like the stakeholder analysis, the SWOT analysis is ongoing and must be revisited as new information becomes available.

PROCESS

The project manager, in consultation with the project management team, performs the SWOT analysis after all base data have been assembled and analyzed and after primary stakeholders have been interviewed. The project manager assigns each specialist from the team to perform his or her own analysis. The project manager compiles the results and each analysis can then be further developed and refined in a project team meeting. This analysis will identify the re-search gaps (indicated in the weaknesses). It will also show those areas where attention can be focused and leverage can be gained (indicated in the strengths).

In the SWOT analysis, the project is reviewed by categories such as economics, market, transportation, site, and politics. For each category the following questions are asked:

Strengths

What advantages does the project have that the team can leverage and focus on? For instance, advantages of the site may include views, open space, and easy topography.

Weaknesses

What liabilities are inherent to the project? Liabilities may include high groundwater, poor soils, or even toxic contamination.

>>

The second phase is the conducting of the vision process itself. This includes three types of meetings. Generative meetings gather ideas, using techniques ranging from brainstorming to visual surveys. Analytical meetings refine the material generated using techniques to draft goals, address critical questions, and identify implementation strategies. Finally, deliberative meetings lead to the selection of a preferred future or planning scenario and to community priorities.

The third phase is implementing the resulting vision while sustaining the interest and energy created by the process itself. Charrettes are commonly used to implement specific projects within the vision. Within the context of dynamic planning, it is therefore best to conduct a vision process in the research, education, and charrette preparation phase, prior to holding a charrette. ■

TIP

Educate and Inform the Public through Technical Workshops

Steve Coyle
Principal, HDR|LCA+Sargent Town Planning

In order for communities to make well-informed decisions, they need to be equipped with sufficient knowledge of both general and specific features of planning. Members of the public can learn about these features during technical workshops. These optional events are designed to educate and prepare the public and the agency staff on particularly important or complex technical, regulatory, or political elements of a project in advance of a charrette. These workshops, which precede the charrette by as little as one week but no more than six weeks, should ideally take between two to four hours on a Saturday afternoon. Each workshop offered should focus on a specific, critical component of the planning effort to be undertaken during the charrette.

For example, for an upcoming charrette to create a new municipal transportation plan, a series of workshops, featuring recognized experts, would include a discussion on topics such as speed limiting design, public art, safety, truck routes, transit, access management, right-of-way encroachment, and street design principles and techniques. The workshops would expose residents to current transportation options and concepts, provide answers to questions, and encourage a discourse on the feasibility and suitability of these options for their city. This information

>>

Table 10 **Sample Strengths, Weaknesses, Opportunities, Threats (SWOT) Analysis from the Pleasant Hill BART Station Project**

	Strength & Opportunities	**Weaknesses & Threats**
Site	The site is completely paved, with good utility access, so it has good physical redevelopment potential.	There is a conflict between the requirement to replace all BART parking on the site, and the need to maintain the BART functions during construction.
Transportation	Direct connection to the Iron Horse Trail. Regional access via BART.	Site is bordered on three sides by heavily trafficked roads, making pedestrian and bicycle travel difficult.
Economics/Market	BART station is a possible anchor for development and a people generator for a major public space.	Recent slowing of the economy may cause rents to stabilize or decline and vacancies to inch up.
Design	The view of Mt. Diablo from the station platform and from higher buildings.	The 7-story BART parking garage is a huge, utilitarian, imposing structure, adjacent to residential.
Political	The county will provide political leadership and management for the duration of the project.	BART Strategic Plan, to maximize regional transit access, convenience, and ease of use through effective coordination among transit providers, may present obstacles to design of an urban village.
Environmental	An existing oak grove greenway at the southeast corner of the site could be protected and enhanced.	Except for a grove of oak trees on the southeast corner of the site, and a few on the northeast corner, there are no natural features on the site.
Development	High quality, well-financed developer has been designated for the project.	The developer needs to proceed with construction within two years of commencement of planning.

The Importance of Base Maps

One of the most fundamental base data requirements for the charrette team is a correct base map that includes property lines, rights-of-way, existing buildings, trees, and topography. For example, the Pleasant Hill BART station project was well funded and well staffed. Even so, the team did not have an accurate base map to work from at the charrette. It was only 24 months later that the engineering team discovered this fact. The result, although it did not drastically alter the charrette plan, did cause considerable rework that could have been avoided if the correct base plan had been available during the charrette. ■

Opportunities

In light of the strengths, what opportunities present themselves to the project management team? For example: a forecasted market need for the project's housing component.

Threats

What are the potential "external" threats to project success and implementation? Examples: competing projects, political opposition, and changes in government policy toward brownfield mitigation requirements.

In this example, the strengths and opportunities are listed together as are the weaknesses and threats. This approach generally works well for planning projects.

Conclusions for 1.3 Base Data Research and Analysis

Base data gathering and research is essential when preparing for a charrette. It provides the information necessary for the charrette team to create a feasible plan. This information also helps the project management team develop its strategy for implementation. The quality of the work done during the base data gathering phase directly affects the quality of the charrette outcomes.

The dynamic planning strategies at play in the base data research and analysis phase are:

1. **Study the details and the whole.** The research completed during this phase provides the necessary information to study the project at the level of detail determined by the charrette products list.
2. **Produce a feasible plan.** A feasible plan begins with credible research and analysis.

would then be folded into the team's research and would provide the basis for the development of the objectives, strategies, and measures (OSM) used to evaluate transportation alternatives. Each workshop should be summarized and recorded to document facts, ideas, and recommendations for goals and objectives regarding the topical area.

The workshops may also be utilized to introduce controversial issues like increasing density and affordable housing, and to describe technical regulatory methods like form-based codes, environmental conditions, and the principles behind neighborhood planning. ■

TIP

Base Data Research Needs

The base data research and gathering sub-phase of a project should be carefully managed to avoid unnecessary costs. The project manager should be diligent in questioning the need for lengthy research reports. There are certainly times when these reports are necessary, usually when there is an absence of current data, such as demographic and market information. However, it may be acceptable for a specialist to complete an executive summary in place of a costly and lengthy report. For example, an economics consultant may complete an executive summary instead of an entire market report. The consultant then attends the charrette with the summary and, equipped with her knowledge of the local market and the brief studies that she has completed, will be able to provide valuable advice to the charrette team. ■

TIP

High Tech Tools and Dynamic Planning

Ken Snyder
Director of Planning, Tools and The Planning CoLaboratory, Orton Family Foundation

High tech tools, once intimidating for the average community member, have evolved rapidly to become a more user-friendly resource for enhancing the charrette process.

Web-based communication tools
Web-based communication tools offer opportunities to support each phase of the dynamic planning process. Content management, project management, and wiki white board tools can be used individually or in combination to provide important base information, community audits, and tours of resources that build stakeholder support and inform and engage members of the public about their community. Visualization tools such as photo galleries and web mapping can be used to gather feedback on visual preferences and as the groundwork for a common understanding of current conditions and possible futures.

Scenario planning and impact analysis tools
During the charrette, scenario planning and impact analysis tools offer real time solutions. These tools can demonstrate how indicators, such as proximity to stores and public services, are affected by alternative land use patterns.

Online decision support tools
The same online decision support tools available for the pre-charrette process also support the digital charrette by offering at-home community members opportunities to participate in public meetings in real time. Comments are entered into both home computers and computers located at meeting tables with results quickly available to everyone. Used in combination with keypad polling, these tools hasten feedback loops so that several iterations of discussions can take place in less time than in traditional meetings.

After the charrette, draft solutions that come from the public meetings, in addition to surveys and other information, may be posted online to provide a forum for community members to participate in the product refinement phase and watch how their ideas from the charrette manifest in real life over time. ■

1.4.1 Conceptual Sketching and Testing

1.4.2 Pre-charrette Project Brief

1.4 Project Feasibility Studies and Research

INTRODUCTION

It is essential that the charrette team begin the charrette with the knowledge and information necessary to work efficiently. For projects with a high level of physical design complexity, it is often necessary for the charrette team to conduct studies and research ahead of time. Examples of such projects are those in which the site conditions present a high level of difficulty, such as intense topography or a complex architectural component.

The tasks in this phase develop the team's capacity to work knowledgably on the project problem. This capacity is established by having access to the data and by exploring design and planning concepts as a means to become familiar with the problem. Work conducted in this phase is intended to minimize the charrette team's learning curve that otherwise could waste valuable time at the beginning of the charrette.

Building Sponsor Confidence with Conceptual Sketching and Testing

During one project, the developer/project sponsor was not convinced that the charrette was the right process for his project. A few weeks after the public kick-off meeting the charrette team conducted an in-house workshop in the developer's office. The workshop included members of the charrette team and the project sponsor's staff. Over the course of two days the group was able to investigate the project by sketching concepts that were simultaneously analyzed by the market and economics specialist from the developer's team. At the end of the two days the developer was convinced that the charrette would work. He felt less anxious about "designing in public." Additionally, the charrette team members were better prepared to do their work in the charrette. ■

1.4 Project Feasibility Studies and Research Tools and Techniques

- 1.4.1 Conceptual Sketching and Testing
- 1.4.2 Pre-charrette Project Brief

1.4.1 Conceptual Sketching and Testing

INTRODUCTION

The purposes of conceptual sketching and testing are to establish the charrette team's familiarity with the project constraints, to determine the range of feasibility, and to develop the sponsor's pre-charrette confidence in the process. The first two purposes relate directly to developing the team's capability to work with the planning problem. This process has been used by private developers to test proposed plans for "fatal flaws" and economic and market feasibility. Conceptual sketching can address a developer's concern about losing control of the project plan during the charrette by making him comfortable with the charrette team's understanding of his business and the project constraints. It is highly recommended that this sketching and testing be conducted only after a public kick-off meeting. The initial public kick-off meeting fulfills the promise to the community members that no design work has been undertaken without first soliciting their input. This tool is an option that is recommended for very complex projects and/or when the project sponsor is new to the charrette process. It is also essential that these sketches be considered only a learning exercise and that they are not brought into the charrette.

PROCESS

Depending on the level of project complexity, conceptual sketching can be conducted either as a half-day meeting with the project management team, or as a more intense one-to-two-day session that includes all of the project sponsor's advisors. The half-day meeting is used to create concepts that can then be tested for technical, financial, and market feasibility. These investigations are valuable for highlighting areas that require further research.

In the one- or two-day in-house workshop, the urban designers and planners, along with other members of the project management team, lead the process. The workshop requires intense involvement from the sponsor's staff. These are the people whom the sponsor turns to for advice regarding project design, market, and economic and engineering feasibility. The sponsor staff opens the meeting with a summary of the performance requirements for the project and how it fits into their business or policy strategy. The project management team then leads the workshop by brainstorming a variety of conceptual approaches to the project.

The team creates a series of conceptual approaches that are reviewed in a pin-up style meeting (see text box on pin-up process in section 2.2.2). The project management team considers the project mission, vision, objectives, strategies and measures, and all other previously agreed upon and given constraints for the project. The pin-up is an opportunity for all parties to be educated about alternative approaches to the plan.

Through these exercises, all members of the project management team learn the design, market, economic, and engineering impacts and realities of the project. The sponsor leaves the workshop assured that the project management team understands the organization's project goals. The project management team leaves with a greater understanding of the range of options and intricate project dynamics. Everyone is better prepared to enter the charrette with an understanding that will allow them to work efficiently and effectively.

CHECKLIST

1.4.2 Pre-charrette Project Brief

INTRODUCTION

The purpose of this brief is to provide a single resource that concisely summarizes the base data and research required for the charrette team to complete its work. It is a compilation of information from all previous phases of work including summaries on project assessment and organization, stakeholder research, education and involvement, base data research and analysis, and feasibility studies. This summary is an internal document for use by the charrette team and therefore need not be an expensive or highly finished document.

PROCESS

The pre-charrette project brief is a compilation of executive summaries created by each specialist that summarizes his/her pre-charrette research. The project manager assembles the base data with an executive summary from each specialist into a single document. This document becomes the guide for the charrette team on all available information and its location. The brief covers the results of the project management team meeting, the charrette ready plan, the project mission and products, the dynamic planning process road map, the stakeholder analysis, and the SWOT analysis. It may also include a community history section written by a local historian. The project manager assembles the report and distributes it to the project management and charrette teams at least three weeks before the charrette.

Table 11 **Pre-charrette Project Brief Checklist**

Document	Sub-phase Created
Project management team contact list	1.1 Project Assessment and Organization
Charrette team contact list	1.1 Project Assessment and Organization
Project mission	1.1.2 Project Mission and Products
Community history	1.3.1 Base Data Research and Gathering
Process road map	1.1.5 Dynamic Planning Process Road map
Stakeholder analysis and summary	1.1.3 Stakeholder Identification and Preliminary Analysis, 1.2.3 Secondary Stakeholder Analysis
Objectives, Strategies, Measures	1.1.1 Objectives, Strategies, Measures Draft
Base data summary by specialty (transportation, economics, etc.)	1.3.1 Base Data Research and Gathering
Strengths, Weaknesses, Opportunities, Threats analysis	1.3.2 SWOT Analysis
Conceptual testing summary	1.4.1 Conceptual Sketching and Testing

Conclusions for 1.4 Project Feasibility Studies and Research

The project feasibility studies and research sub-phase is a useful preparation step for projects with complex design issues. It can also be an effective means for verifying the project sponsor's mission, values, and goals. This phase involves a multidisciplinary team that conducts studies at various scales for the purpose of assuring project feasibility. This phase can also assure that the project management team, especially the project sponsor, shares a solid understanding of the process, and issues and dynamics that affect the plan before starting the charrette. The work completed in this phase plays an important role in reducing the learning curve, thereby increasing the productivity of the charrette team during the charrette.

The dynamic planning strategies at play in the project feasibility studies and research phase are:

1. **Create a feasible plan.** Developing an early understanding of the sponsor's programmatic and financial framework as well as the site constraints avoids time wasted pursuing fruitless studies.

2. **Work cross-functionally.** The degree of accuracy of the feasibility studies in part depends on having the right specialists involved.

3. **Study the details and the whole.** Feasibility studies must be detailed enough to address all issues related to project success.

1.5 Charrette Logistics

INTRODUCTION

The charrette is an intense, time compressed work session that depends on efficient and coordinated logistics planning. The last thing the charrette manager should be doing at a charrette is thinking about the lunch menu, who is going to pick up the next team member at the airport, or where to buy trash bags. The charrette manager is essentially setting up a fully functioning design office in a new location for seven days. Just like any design office, it needs to be supportive of creative work by a diverse team.

During the charrette logistics phase, the charrette manager must decide on the studio location and set-up. Decisions must also be made about the makeup of the charrette team. The schedule and agendas for meetings that take place during the charrette must be planned. Then, all of this information is summarized in a pre-charrette logistics summary report for distribution to the team prior to the charrette event.

1.5 Charrette Logistics Tools and Techniques

- 1.5.1 Studio Logistics and Set-up
- 1.5.2 Charrette Team Formation
- 1.5.3 Charrette Scheduling
- 1.5.4 Meeting Planning
- 1.5.5 Pre-charrette Logistics Summary

1.5.1 Studio Logistics and Set-up

INTRODUCTION

The charrette studio is a creative and dynamic environment that must accommodate many activities simultaneously. The primary function of the studio is as a place for the charrette team to work and meet, while accommodating the public. The combination of design studio, public reception, and meeting space is a significant challenge to the efficiency and workflow of the charrette. Adding to this challenge is the fact that the charrette team practically lives at the charrette studio. An average workday for the team lasts up to 12

Figure 6
Sample Charrette Studio Floor Plan

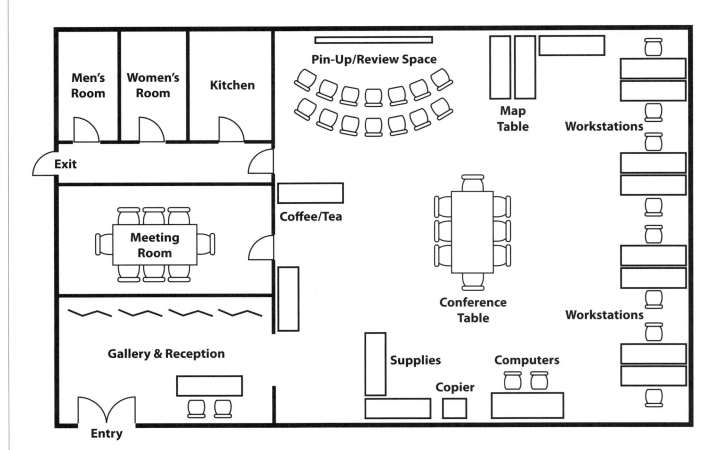

hours with occasional late-night work sessions. Therefore, meals are accommodated in the studio as well. Given these challenges, the charrette manager must think through and plan each day during the charrette in detail.

PROCESS

Choosing a Charrette Studio Location

Charrettes have been in main street storefronts, hotel conference areas, high schools, armories, historic mansions, barns, and even tents. The best charrette studios are in locations with local character, such as historic public meeting places. The difference between holding a charrette at an airport hotel versus a historic town meeting hall is vast. An uplifting and inspiring environment can have a strong positive effect on both the charrette team and the stakeholder participants. A key dynamic planning strategy is to hold the charrette on or near the project site. Every effort should be made to find a suitable studio location that makes visiting the site quick, easy, and convenient for stakeholders. It is highly recommended that the charrette manager visit the proposed studio location ahead of time to make a visual inspection. If a visit to the site is impossible then floor

plans and photographs should be provided by the charrette sponsor to assist the manager with planning and decision making.

Public Meeting Location

Public meetings might not be held in the charrette studio. It is often very difficult to find a large meeting space adjacent to the charrette studio. This is not a problem. Proximity of the charrette studio to the site and to the community should not be sacrificed in an effort to accommodate the larger public meetings. Public meetings can often be held in a high school auditorium, church, storefront, meeting hall, or other sizable public meeting space.

Studio Specifications

The minimum size for a charrette studio is approximately 1,500 square feet. When assessing the studio location, the charrette manager should consider basics, such as adequate windows (with shading devices to darken the room for projected presentations), good lighting, electrical outlets, and restrooms. A kitchen is desirable but not critical. The studio workspace itself can be accommodated in one large room. Within this room there must be an area for team workstations, dedicated locations for reference materials (such as maps and plans), a supply table, and an area for the computers and copier. There should also be adequate wall space for pinning up drawings and a central area with a large conference table for stakeholder meetings. A separate dining area is preferred, but a large conference table is sufficient. A separate room with a door for private meetings is also very useful.

Charrette Studio Gallery

Charrettes have failed due to an incoherent strategy for handling the public. Without a strategy for handling visitors during a charrette that buffers the charrette team from interruptions, little design and planning work will

Figure 7 *A charrette studio during the production phase*

Figure 8 *A studio gallery showing the use of foamcore boards*

be accomplished and the charrette team will be forced to work very late into the night.

Providing a buffer for the charrette team is the reason that the charrette studio gallery was invented. It is located in the studio reception area at the point of public entrance. The gallery showcases work in progress with some method for recording visitors' input. The gallery is staffed at all times by one or more greeters, usually a senior member of the charrette sponsor's staff who is knowledgeable about the project and the stakeholders. Visitors should be given a one-page summary of the project, process, and how they can stay involved. It is the greeter's responsibility to welcome the public in a gracious manner, find out who they are, and quickly assess how each person should be involved at that point in the charrette.

Primary stakeholders such as elected officials, landowners, and community representatives are usually escorted into the charrette studio to talk to the charrette manager and perhaps work with a member of the charrette team on an issue that is important to them. Most visitors to the charrette studio are happy just to view the ongoing work and engage in a discussion with the greeter. The greeter may ask

visitors to write their comments on flip charts, post-it notes, or questionnaires that are passed on to the charrette team. The gallery must be updated continually with copies of the ongoing planning documents throughout the week.

Charrette Equipment and Supplies

The charrette manager is responsible for ensuring that all supplies and equipment are available in the studio. Common 3' x 6' banquet tables are perfectly adequate for meeting and working. These tables can be transformed into drawing tables with the addition of cheap white illustration board taped to their tops. Padded chairs are important for each studio workstation. It is exhausting and demoralizing for a charrette team to sit on hard metal chairs for hours on end. A number of 4' x 8' foamcore sheets can be very useful to expand wall space for drawings (especially in rooms with a lot of doors and windows) as well as a means for transporting drawings to and from a remote public meeting location.

Desktops dedicated to the storage of supplies and reference materials plus plenty of garbage cans are essential in keeping the studio orderly and clean. The charrette manager is responsible for bringing all equipment including computers, printers, scanners, and networking devices. The charrette manager must also locate large-scale copy services, shipping services, and an office supply store. If these services are not within close proximity, volunteer runners can make things easier on the team. The studio must have telephone service and, ideally, high-speed Internet access. Consulting firms have been known to create their own charrette culture by bringing a small collection of planning history and architectural reference books often selected especially for the project. Some even bring their own espresso machines for late night sessions.

Charrette Food

Charrette food is often overlooked, yet it is central to a productive charrette experience. When charrette veterans reminisce about past charrettes, food is a frequent topic. When working intensely in the same place for up to 14 hours a day, food becomes a very important part of the experience. Food should not be left up to chance but should be planned well in advance. Some charrette practitioners actually include provisions for food in the charrette contract.

NCI recommends that a charrette team be fed interesting and healthy food. Be sure to check with each team member beforehand about any special dietary needs (such as vegetarian or kosher). The charrette manager should work with the sponsor and the caterer to suggest, review, and approve menus ahead of time. To prevent monotony, all meals should not come from the same caterer or restaurant.

It is a nearly universal standard for the charrette team to eat lunch on-site. Breakfast is usually eaten at the hotel or a local cafe. Most charrette teams eat dinner in the studio on those evenings when it is anticipated that intense production will be required, such as the night before a major presentation. Other dinners are eaten out, ideally at interesting local restaurants, researched by the charrette manager before the charrette begins. A fun way to get to know a community is to sample its regional cuisine.

1.5.2 Charrette Team Formation

INTRODUCTION

The charrette manager begins to compose the charrette team early in the dynamic planning process, once there is a clear picture of the problem at hand. The charrette team is the core group of planners, designers, engineers, economists, and others working virtually uninterrupted in the charrette studio, taking the project from a cold start to a preferred plan in a matter of days. Decisions about whom to include on the charrette team can mean the difference between success and failure of a charrette. These talented professionals must be chosen for their ability to solve the design problems and complete the required products and documents through an interactive team process in a public setting. The team is most often composed of consultants but may also include members of the sponsor's staff, such as public agency engineers and planners. While assembling the team, the charrette manager must consider each individual's professional skill set as well as how each person will function as part of the larger team. In short, there must be a balance between talent, personal skills, and ego. Strong ego is often associated with creative talent, but each charrette team member must, in the end, be able to let go and work along with the team for the benefit of the project.

Figure 9 *A studio work station showing the use of illustration boards as a drawing surface on a plywood table*

Table 12
Common Charrette Team Specialties
■ Planning and Urban Design
■ Economics and Market
■ Transportation Planning and Engineering
■ Architecture
■ Landscape Architecture
■ Public Involvement
■ Environmental and Civil Planning and Engineering
■ Local Specialists: Designers, Engineers, Historians
■ National Experts

CHECKLIST

Charrette Packing and Supply Tips

Oliver Kuehne, Senior Town Planner
HDR|LCA+Sargent Town Planning

TOP TEN TIPS FOR PACKING

1. **Create a supply checklist.** Specify what you need, and how many of each; take inventory a few days prior to leaving for the charrette as some items may need to be ordered.

2. Put **one** person in charge of inventory and packing. If everybody throws stuff in a suitcase you will likely forget something critical.

3. **Charrette suitcase.** Instead of trying to fit everything in one large suitcase, use multiple smaller ones and balance the weight, especially when traveling by plane. Use small containers or pouches to pack pens, markers, and other supplies, and keep everything consolidated and neatly separated.

4. **Pack valuable items,** such as digital cameras, in your carry-on bag (once it has passed security, checked luggage is no longer secure).

>>

PROCESS

To choose team members, the charrette manager considers information from the complexity analysis (task 1.1.4) and the charrette products list (task 1.1.2) as well as the project's scope of work. The complexity analysis indicates areas that will need extra work, and the product list informs what types of specialties are needed. For instance, a large greenfield development site may require several site planners to design several hundred acres in a matter of days. In addition to the usual group of specialties (see the table in this section), it is also helpful to have a local historian on the team. This person can provide valuable and inspirational information about the history of local planning in reference to the project site. Occasionally there is the need for a national expert to address key issues such as arterial design or retail mix. For instance, a transportation planner or engineer who specializes in pedestrian-friendly street standards may be brought in to discuss their benefits. This person is often required when working in jurisdictions with conventional street standards.

Charrette team members should share similar professional working values. One of the most important values is open, honest, and timely communication. There is no room for gossip or disingenuous attitudes during a charrette. A shared value for a holistic approach to community planning, commonly associated with smart growth movements, is invaluable. Team members must, however, remain open to input from stakeholders who share a wide range of views. Another value that should be shared by team members is a belief in true collaboration wherein all ideas are good ideas until proven otherwise, and the best ideas prevail. It is not uncommon for charrette teams to include a mix of people who are used to working together as well as those who are not. Consulting firms often have a group of professionals who regularly do charrettes and augment them with subcontractors. The addition of outside, and especially lo-

cal, professionals provides a fresh viewpoint on project that adds to the creative potential of the charrette.

Charrette Team Formation
The success of a charrette depends, to a great extent, on the ability of the charrette team to perform creatively while under the pressure of a compressed production schedule within a public workshop setting. The charrette manager should take into consideration the following when assembling a team:

Compatibility/chemistry
- Team players: A healthy ego must, in the end, bend to the team direction.
- Compatible design philosophy: Differences in design approach should not lead to an impasse.

Skills
- Multiple skills: People who are multi-talented can reduce the required number of team members, i.e., planners who can design a building, architects who understand retail and can produce renderings.
- Ability to work under pressure: Unexpected changes require people who are flexible. Also, charrette time constraints favor people who have the ability to manage their own time and produce under a deadline.
- Ability to work with the public: Designers must be able to work with people individually and in groups.

Local knowledge
- The team must include people who can provide an understanding of local history, politics, and unique local planning and building requirements.

Table 13 **Typical Team Composition for a Seven-day Charrette** (the number of each specialty varies per project)

Specialty	Final Product Responsibility
Planner	Master plan
Planner/Urban Designer	Detailed plan studies
Local Architect	Building types, assist with codes
Landscape Architect	Open space plan, park design
Environmentalist	Wetlands preservation plan, draft environmental impact statement
Renderer	Perspectives
Transportation Engineer and/or Planner	Street plan and sections, impact analysis

1.5.3 Charrette Scheduling

INTRODUCTION

The goal of a charrette is to take a project from a vision to alternative concepts to preferred plan to developed plan to final presentation. In order to guide a group of stakeholders through this process, at least three feedback loops are required. This takes a minimum of four days for simple projects and seven days for complex projects. One of the biggest differences between the NCI charrette and other processes is the extra time taken in the plan development phase to test and investigate design concepts in order to bring them to a level at which they can be approved, engineered, and built.

As previously discussed in section one, there are alternate models for conducting a process that adheres to the dynamic planning values. These models essentially divide the charrette into a series of shorter workshops. See the charrette scheduling variations in Section Five for examples of such processes.

Charrette Phases

- 2.1 Organization, Education, Vision
- 2.2 Alternative Concepts Development
- 2.3 Preferred Plan Synthesis
- 2.4 Plan Development
- 2.5 Production and Presentation

These phases are discussed in more detail in the charrette section of this book. However, it is important to consider the charrette phases prior to the charrette while creating the schedule. The charrette schedule must allow time to complete these five phases within a collaborative public process.

PROCESS

The Seven-day Charrette

The NCI charrette process has two major scheduling variations based on whether or not design alternatives have been created prior to the charrette. It is recommended that both

>>

5. Consider having a pre-packed charrette kit:

   Pros: You're less likely to forget something as it's always packed; saves time.

   Cons: Expensive at the front end; it's easy to forget to restock supplies.

6. **Prioritize.** Pack what's hard to find, leave behind what can easily be purchased at the charrette location.

7. **Label your supplies.** Art and drafting supplies are expensive and tend to get mixed with other firms' supplies.

8. **Pens and markers.** In advance of the charrette, establish a set of preferred line weights and marker colors for drawings and renderings; about three different line weights and 20 marker colors should do. Bring a set of pens for each team member, and pack at least two sets of markers, so more than one person can color at a time. Make sure to test all pens and markers before you pack them, so you don't end up with dried out ones.

9. **Dots and pins.** You don't always know what your display surface will be for maps and drawings. Pack plenty of draft dots, masking tape, and push pins. Bring foamcore boards and easels, or have them provided locally, if walls are sacrosanct.

10. **Unpacking.** Put someone in charge of unpacking the charrette suitcase(s). There's a tendency to just throw everything in a corner when you get back from a charrette, but taking the time to check everything and restock your supply is time well spent as it saves trouble when preparing for the next charrette.

>>

>>

TOP TEN MOST COMMONLY FORGOTTEN OR MOST MISSED ITEMS

1. Sign-in sheet for public events

2. Plenty of pens and markers for drawing and coloring

3. Flip charts for questions and comments at public events

4. Sticky notes

5. Professional-looking name tags for the charrette team

6. Basic set of tools for the studio set-up (hammers, screwdrivers, etc.)

7. White-out (for each team member)

8. Batteries for electric pencil sharpeners

9. Extension cords and power strips

10. Projection screen for PowerPoint presentations

TOP THREE MOST USEFUL ALL-PURPOSE ITEMS

1. Duct tape!

2. Duct tape!

3. Duct tape!

models be preceded by a public kick-off meeting (part of task 1.2.4). The first variation is the classic seven-day charrette model. This is the proven model for projects with complex design issues and/or political environments. In this model the charrette starts with a public vision from which alternative concepts are developed. The second variation, for conducting charrettes in less than seven days, is an adaptation of the primary seven-day model and will be discussed at the end of this section.

Different firms have variations on the seven-day schedule model. Some firms hold only two public meetings at the beginning and the end, and use open houses as a means to gather public input during the charrette. Some firms start the charrette with a public meeting on Friday night followed with a Saturday public workshop/picnic. These variations may be found in Section Five.

Overall Charrette Scheduling

The charrette schedule includes a number of different types of meetings and work sessions, tours, and meals. The charrette elements must be well planned and scheduled in advance, but include room for flexibility and inevitable changes. One thing that can be counted on in the charrette is that things will change and the unexpected will always happen. It is essential that the charrette manager build flexibility into the schedule to allow for impromptu meetings and changes of design direction. It is the nature of the charrette to change constantly—this is the nature of the creative process.

Table 14
Workflow for a Seven-day Charrette

DAY ONE
Organization, Education, Vision

■ The charrette team prepares the studio and holds a briefing meeting before departing on tours. The primary stakeholders are consulted, and a public vision is created or affirmed at an open public meeting.

DAYS TWO AND THREE
Alternative Concepts Development

■ Initial concepts based on project data and the public vision are created, tested by primary stakeholders, revised, and presented at an open public meeting.

■ Scheduled and unscheduled stakeholder meetings are held at the studio during the day.

DAY FOUR
Preferred Plan Synthesis

■ Alternative concepts are synthesized into a preferred plan based on analysis and stakeholder input.
■ Scheduled and unscheduled stakeholder meetings are held in the charrette studio during the day.

DAY FIVE
Plan Development

■ The preferred plan is detailed and tested for feasibility

DAYS SIX AND SEVEN
Production and Presentation

■ The charrette team prepares a complete set of drawings and data, then presents it to the public.

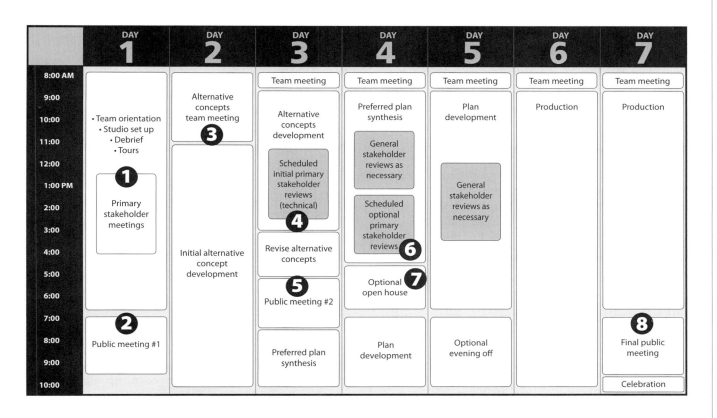

Figure 10 *Sample Overall Charrette Schedule by Phase*

1. **Informational meetings.** Check-in meetings with the most influential stakeholders before the first public meeting.

2. **Public Meeting #1.** Informational meeting and public workshop to create vision statements and drawings.

3. **Alternative Concepts Team Meeting.** Review work from public workshop exercise. Merge concepts into three or four sets. Assign teams to develop concepts.

4. **Initial Primary Stakeholder Reviews.** Reviews with approval agencies, vested landowners/developers, and community leaders, for testing validity of first set of concepts. Scheduled late enough after the public meeting to enable the creation of a set of alternatives, and early enough to revise them before the second public meeting.

5. **Public Meeting #2.** First public review of alternative concepts.

6. **Secondary Stakeholder Reviews.** Reviews with affected parties as necessary.

7. **Optional Open House.** Final check-in with the public on developed preferred plan.

8. **Final Public Meeting.** Presentation of complete plan drawings and supportive data, followed by public comment

Public Process—A Designer's View

Ray Gindroz
Chairman, Urban Design Associates

As urban designers, we find ourselves designing neighborhoods, towns, and cities—the most complex artifacts built by our civilization and the ones that have the most direct impact on people's daily lives.

As new urbanists, we come to these occasions prepared with a set of values based on the study of traditional patterns, a set of principles and tools for design, and images and ideas for beautiful urban places. But it is only through effective interaction with the place and the people of that place that we learn what to do with those sets of tools, principles, and ideas.

And so, we must enter each situation with a clean slate and explore the physical qualities of the place, study its history and culture, and listen to voices of those who have the most direct relationship to it and to its future. Then we know how to use our principles, tools, and patterns to serve it.

Urbanism is so complex and there are so many issues and directions to pursue that we could easily arrive at a dead end with a brilliant solution for the wrong problem. The charrette process, with its fixed schedule, brings clarity and focus to the situation. The short timetable makes it possible to build consensus and momentum on key issues. Without that focus, the process can wander aimlessly through the nearly

>>

>>

infinite issues that can emerge over a protracted time, with no tangible result.

It is in the public process that our design skills find a conscience to follow and through which we as designers are inspired to do our best. Design becomes the language of discovery. We view the early development of design alternatives as a means of learning more about the place and the aspirations of its people. Therefore, it is important to have sufficient self-confidence in our skills that we are not afraid to test ideas and let them be challenged. From the challenging, we are driven to reach beyond what we have done before and find new directions and solutions.

Urbanism in a democracy is a public art. The more the public is engaged, the better the art. ∎

Table 15 **Charrette Scheduling Checklist**

1. Decide on the days to begin and end the charrette.

2. Schedule opening and closing public meetings. Take local events into account, as well as national and religious holidays.

3. Schedule the daily team meetings.

4. Schedule informational stakeholder meetings on the first day. Refer to the stakeholder analysis.

5. Schedule alternative concepts development design time following the opening public meeting.

6. Schedule the initial set of stakeholder feedback meetings with those who have decision-making power over the project. These will include transportation, public works, fire, property owners, and community representatives.

7. Schedule any additional special meetings, i.e., special interests (those who have the power to block the project).

8. Schedule a mid-course public review (public meeting or open house), usually held at the end of day three or four.

9. Set the hours that the studio is open to the public. Limit the open hours during the final production phase.

10. Allow for extra stakeholder meetings to occur once the preferred plan is developed.

11. Schedule meals both in and out of the studio.

12. Allow time for production.

Common Charrette Scheduling Mistakes

Scheduling the first set of primary stakeholder meetings too early

The purpose of the first set of primary stakeholder meetings is to elicit the input of those who have a powerful influence and/or direct decision-making power over the project. These people normally include representatives from the department of transportation, public works, elected officials, developers, landowners, and neighborhood representatives. A common mistake is to schedule these meetings too early, i.e., before there are enough concepts developed to which they can respond. It normally takes at least a day if not a day and a half for the charrette team to review the results of the first public meeting, assess them, and develop a set of alternative concepts ready for the first round of reviews. Therefore, these meetings should not be scheduled until at least the end of the second day if not the late morning or early afternoon of the third day. The other factor determining when to schedule these meetings is the requirement of enough time (at least a few hours) to incorporate the solicited input into the design alternatives in time for the next public review.

Scheduling too many meetings

In an effort to be sure that all stakeholders are involved significantly in the charrette process, it is a common mistake to schedule too many meetings. Remember, meetings are held with all primary stakeholders prior to the charrette. The charrette manager must carefully study the stakeholder analysis to determine those people or groups who absolutely must be consulted during the first few days of the charrette. The obvious suspects are elected officials, any developers or landowners who plan to develop property in the near future, and anyone who has decision-making power over the project in any fashion. Some groups can be met with at the same time, such as schools, arts organizations, and parks

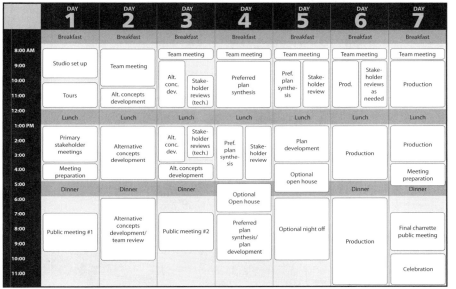

Charrette begins with input session, then design begins

4–6 weeks max.

Review & revise

Final review

Figure 11 *Sample Seven-day Charrette Schedule*

departments. The charrette manager needs to leave enough time in the schedule to accommodate any unanticipated meetings that may come up. One never knows when an important business owner or environmental group will appear at the charrette with a list of questions and concerns.

Not leaving enough time for production

One of the most common scheduling problems is not planning enough time to produce the final documents in an informative and attractive format for the final presentation. It is a disservice to the project sponsor and all involved not to be able to fully test the preferred plan and create the docu-

ments necessary to explain it. This final production phase usually takes at least a day if not a day and a half.

Scheduling the Public

To a great extent, the charrette's main function is as a public workshop. However, it is acceptable to limit public visiting hours to the studio to certain hours of the day and possibly to the first half of the charrette. The public should understand that the charrette has two phases: the creative phase and the production phase. The creative phase is the best time for the public to be involved—when the plan is being created and developed. This phase occurs in the first

TIP

The Pros and Cons of Enlisting Volunteers to Cut Costs

One way to mitigate charrette costs is to utilize volunteer design professionals, university professors, and students as part of the charrette team. Using volunteers can be very positive and cost-effective, but in order to be most useful, the volunteers need to be carefully recruited and managed. Often, volunteers can require a considerable amount of additional guidance.

There is very little room for philosophical impasses during a charrette; the task is challenging and time is short. At minimum, members of the charrette team should share basic values and philosophies toward community design. One way to prevent problems is to evaluate volunteers before the charrette by reviewing their professional work and/or by holding a team meeting where basic issues are aired and discussed. To be clear, debate among the charrette team members is encouraged and certainly can produce better results during the charrette; however, the debate should remain within manageable limits and should not threaten the team's ability to complete the assigned work. An example of an unmanageable type of debate is one in which some individuals endorse the use of traditional urban patterns and building forms and others do not. ∎

Why Four to Seven Days?

Often, first-time charrette sponsors resist holding a charrette for more than three days. When a sponsor has not been through a complete dynamic planning process, it is difficult for her to understand the benefits of holding a charrette over the course of four to seven days. Sponsors are often concerned about the resources necessary (both in terms of money and time) to complete a lengthy process. However, there are several risks associated with charrettes that are too short. Inevitably, unexpected political or engineering challenges requiring extra analysis or meetings will arise during the charrette (see the "Story from the Field" about an upset neighbor in section 2.3). If the charrette is too short to accommodate these analyses and meetings, the contentious issues may not be settled. An abbreviated process also will not allow enough time for the charrette team to solve the problem and to produce the final documents in an informative and attractive format for the final presentation. It is a disservice to the project sponsor and all involved not to be able to fully test the preferred plan and create the documents necessary to explain it. As a general rule, this final production phase usually takes at least a day, if not a day and a half. ∎

three or four days of a seven-day charrette. In the middle of the charrette, after the preferred plan has been chosen, it becomes more of a production event. The basic message to the community members is that if they expect their input to have any real impact on the outcome then they must get involved in the creative part of the charrette during the first few days. However, if a staff person is available in the reception/gallery area at all times, there is no reason to limit public hours except, of course, during meal times. During the last day of the charrette, the studio is basically off limits to the public since primary planning decisions have all been made and the team must focus on producing the final products. Particularly on this last day, the charrette manager must diligently protect the team from unnecessary or unproductive interactions with people, however well intended the suggestions may be.

Shorter Charrettes: The Five-day Variation

The second variation, for conducting charrettes in four to six days, is an adaptation of the primary seven-day model. In this model, the charrette begins with a presentation of design alternatives based on input received from a public kick-off meeting held four to six weeks prior to the charrette. During this kick-off meeting (see 1.2.4), the public is

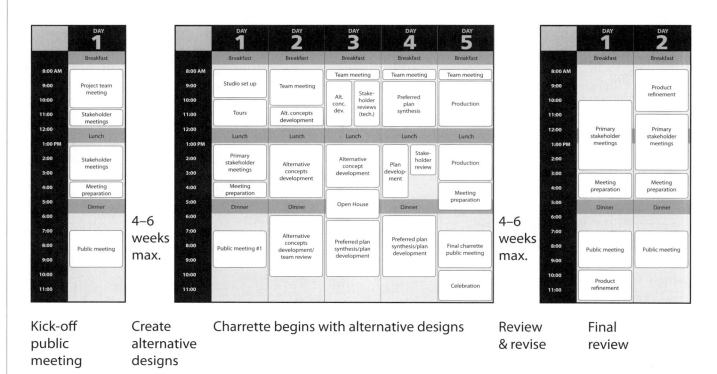

Kick-off public meeting

Create alternative designs

Charrette begins with alternative designs

Review & revise

Final review

Figure 12 *Sample Five-day Charrette Schedule*

asked to provide input regarding its vision for the project. This meeting authorizes the charrette team members to return to their offices and create design alternatives for presentation at the beginning of the charrette. This variation can be effective in saving costs, primarily in terms of space rentals and equipment and any additional staff costs for the charrette. However, it is a safe choice for only the simplest of planning projects and is definitely not recommended for volatile political environments. There is a danger in starting a charrette with design alternatives based on the results of the public kick-off meeting that some people may not have attended.

1.5.4 Meeting Planning

INTRODUCTION
Well-run meetings are the foundation of a successful charrette. One of the biggest challenges facing planners today is getting the right people to attend meetings and getting them to keep coming back. The project management team must devote substantial resources and political capital to get the right people to attend meetings. Many of these people may not be inclined to attend a public meeting in the first place. People have little patience for a poorly run meeting so the charrette manager must make it worth their time and energy to attend. This means that the meeting should start on time, adhere to the agenda, and achieve the desired outcomes. No one person or group should be allowed to dominate the discussion. The meeting space should be a safe environment for all ideas to be heard and where everyone is offered the opportunity to participate. Community members should leave the meeting excited that they are involved in the design of a plan for their community and knowing that their input has the potential to make an impact on the final plan.

There are at least six different meeting types that occur during the course of a typical charrette. They are the:

- Daily team meeting
- Pin-up
- Lecture
- Workshop
- Open house
- Forum

PROCESS

General Meeting Planning Process and Guidelines
A meeting is only as successful as the planning that precedes it. The charrette manager should take time to prepare carefully for each meeting by defining its purpose, desired outcomes, stakeholders, roles, decision-making process, agenda, and room arrangement.

Meeting Purpose and Desired Outcomes
The charrette manager should consult with the primary stakeholders to craft the meeting purpose statement. An example is: "To establish a shared understanding of the project purpose and process as well as the community's needs." Desired outcomes are related to the purpose statement but are more specific and results-oriented. Desired outcomes are the measurable results to be achieved during the meeting. Desired outcomes must be brief, specific, measurable, and conscious of participants' issues. Examples of clearly defined outcomes are: "Agreement on a start date for the new project" and "A list of community vision elements to be addressed in the project."

Stakeholders and Attendees
The charrette manager must also determine which stakeholders must be present for a successful meeting.

Charrette Scheduling Rules of Thumb

- Open and close with major public meetings
- Schedule at least three feedback loops
- Allow ideally two days, and a minimum of 24 hours, between feedback loops
- Meet with key stakeholders on day one: client, elected officials, head of opposition, etc.
- Meet with all stakeholders by end of day two: elected officials, agencies, developers, builders, community representatives, etc.
- Leave time for production

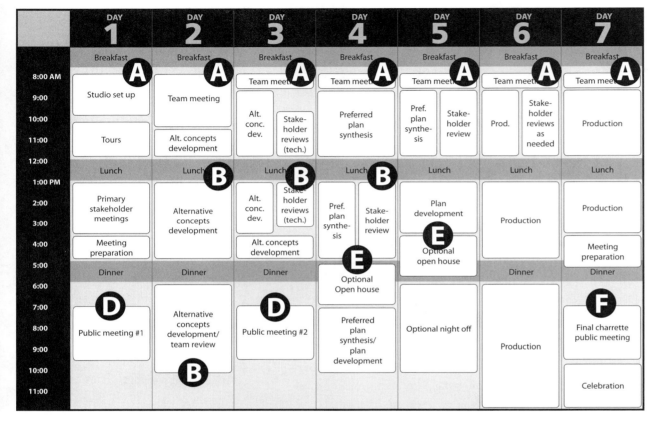

A = Team meetings   D = Workshop   F= Forum
B = Pin-up   E = Open house

Figure 13 *Charrette Meeting Types*

The stakeholder analysis exercise, which is performed early in phase one and revised throughout, is the source for determining attendance at the meeting. Remember that stakeholders generally fall into four categories:

1. Decision makers
2. Those directly affected by the outcome
3. Those who have the power to promote the project
4. Those with the power to block the project

Every effort should be made to contact these people to convince them that it is in their own interest to attend the meeting and that it will be worth their while.

Functions and Roles

The charrette manager must also decide on the appropriate roles that people will play in the meeting. It is recommended that all public meetings and some larger private meetings have a facilitator and a recorder. The classic role of the facilitator is to help the meeting participants achieve the desired outcomes. The facilitator helps the group focus its energies by staying on task, suggesting methods and processes, protecting all members of the group from attack, and making sure that everyone has an opportunity to participate. It is possible and not uncommon for the charrette manager or project manager to facilitate public meetings. It is recommended in this case that she maintain the role of facilitator at least 70 percent of the time, limiting content contributions to 30 percent or less. The recorder is a neutral, non-evaluating servant of the group. The recorder's responsibility is to create the "group memory" by writing down the basic ideas given on large sheets of paper in front of the participants. He needs to capture ideas well enough that they can be preserved and recalled at any time.

Decision Making

The charrette manager must make it clear to everybody at the beginning of the meeting how decisions will be made during and after the meeting. There are many different decision-making options available and a combination of options may be appropriate. The most common decision-making option for a charrette is consensus with a fallback option for the project sponsor to decide. Consensus requires legitimizing that the final decision may not be the first choice of some but everyone is willing to support and help implement it. Decisions that effect the direction of the plan should refer to any previously agreed upon objectives, strategies, and measures as well as values and policy statements. It is important that all primary, secondary, and general stakeholders are involved at these major decision-making moments.

Agenda

The final step in planning a meeting is creating an agenda that lets participants know what to expect from a meeting and acts as a road map to guide people through the meeting itself. The charrette manager creates the agenda to support the meeting purpose and deliver the desired outcomes. Each agenda item should correspond directly to a desired outcome. The agenda should list the agenda item and the time, process, and person or people responsible for each one. It is important to be realistic about the number of items/decisions that can be accomplished in the given period of time and include adequate time for start up and wrap up phases.

Room Arrangement

Every meeting has its own room arrangement. Even the best-planned meeting can fail if the meeting space is not arranged properly. A poorly arranged room can make it very difficult to create an atmosphere of collaboration. The charrette manager takes into consideration the types of activities that must occur while designing the room layout. Room arrangements for each dynamic planning meeting type are outlined in the next section.

Dynamic Planning Meeting Types

As mentioned previously, there are six basic types of meetings in the dynamic planning process.

Table 16 **Dynamic Planning Meetings**

PROCESS	APPLICATION	ROOM ARRANGEMENT
Daily Team Meeting Charrette team and project sponsor staff hold an organizational meeting to discuss the previous day's work and plan what they are going to accomplish. Usually takes place either during breakfast or afterward at the charrette studio.	Daily, first thing in the morning throughout the charrette	■ Square or u-shaped conference table situated in the middle of the charrette studio. ■ Flip chart for recording.
Pin-up An informal drawing review process in which members of the charrette team present/defend their work to their peers. All aspects of the design/plan alternatives are debated, weak ones are discarded, and good ones are merged into a stronger solution. This is a primary decision-making method used during the charrette. It is not uncommon for members of the community and stakeholder groups to participate. In doing so, everyone is made aware of the complexities of the problem and why decisions have been made so that they can continue to work toward a shared outcome.	Pin-ups are generally used only during the charrette and not in the other phases of dynamic planning.	■ The pin-up takes place in the charrette studio. ■ Drawings taped to large wall or panels. ■ "Jury" sits informally, close enough to see work.
Lecture In a typical lecture, a local official, historian, or important figure in the planning world presents important information about the project and/or planning philosophies. This information can help prepare people for the work to be done in the charrette. However, lectures are usually not used during the charrette itself since they are essentially a one-way conversation.	Used to inform and inspire participants about the project in preparation for a charrette. Occur most often in the early part of the dynamic planning process. This is commonly an educational presentation as part of the vision development phase (task 1.2.4) prior to the charrette.	■ Lecture-style rows of chairs, with a presentation up front. ■ Any relevant project information around the room.
Workshop Lecture format combined with an interactive exercise. A typical workshop begins with a concise informational presentation by the project team. This is followed by a presentation that equips the participants with the background necessary for the forthcoming exercise. The lecture should last no more than 45 minutes. The public is engaged in exercises led by facilitators at small group tables. Each group reports back briefly on their conclusions to the entire room full of participants. (See 2.1.4)	Initial visioning sessions, mid-course design reviews. Especially important for volatile circumstances. Commonly used in the initial engagement phase with the community and on the first night of the charrette. Excellent way to engage the public and provide a positive way to break down any suspicion or ill feelings that might be present.	■ Small tables, preferably round, eight people maximum at each plus the facilitator. ■ Flip charts at each table. ■ Reception area with take-aways. ■ Design in progress on the walls.
Open House The open house is an opportunity for members of the community to circulate through the charrette studio and review and give feedback on the design and planning work in progress. People circulate between the various stations (usually organized according to topics such as transportation, economics, the plan, codes) and talk to a charrette team member. People are given surveys to state their preferences and rate plans according to previously agreed upon criteria. Although there is no formal meeting agenda, presentations on major topics may be made once there is a critical mass of attendees. If there are contentious issues still to be resolved, people may become frustrated by the open house format.	Mid- or late-course progress reviews. Since this model does not support large group discussion, be cautious of using it early in the project before establishing the community's trust.	■ Exhibit stations are arranged around the perimeter of the charrette studio, often arranged by subject and staffed by charrette team members. ■ Greeting table with at least four staff people. ■ Tables for meeting in center of room. ■ Survey station near food. ■ Food table. ■ Literature describing the project and the charrette process should be provided.
Forum A forum is a lecture combined with an open house. The purpose of this meeting is to present a substantial amount of information and to solicit public input. As in the final charrette public meeting, the charrette team presents the final charrette products followed by an open house format wherein participants are allowed to talk directly to the charrette team members, view the exhibits and give feedback. (See 2.5.4 for more on the final charrette public meeting.)	This model is reserved for later project meetings with low volatility. Usually used only for the final charrette public meeting.	■ The room is arranged in lecture style with exhibit stations along the perimeter as for the open house. ■ Curved lecture style preferred. ■ Flip charts for recording. ■ Work in progress around the room. ■ Avoid long, narrow rooms that distance attendees from the presenters.

Sample Floor Plans by Meeting Type

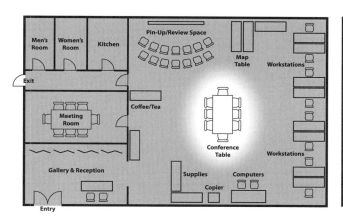

Figure 14 *Sample Daily Team Meeting Floor Plan*

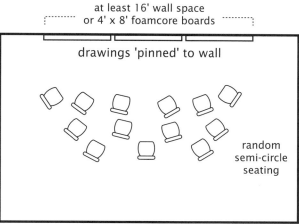

Figure 15 *Sample Pin-up Floor Plan*

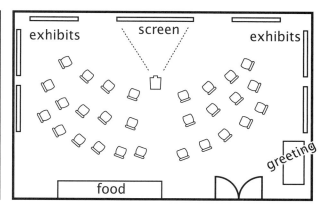

Figure 16 *Sample Lecture/Forum Floor Plan*

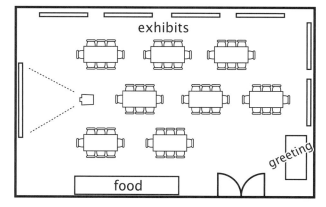

Figure 17 *Sample Workshop Floor Plan*

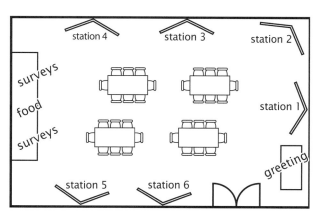

Figure 18 *Sample Open House Floor Plan*

Table 17 **Sample Agenda Worksheet**			
Title of meeting:			
Date, time, length:			
Location:			
Sponsor of meeting:			
Desired outcomes:			
Agenda:			
Topic (relates to desired outcome)	**Process** (how to reach desired outcome)	**Person** (who and how)	**Start Time**

1.5.5 Pre-charrette Logistics Summary

INTRODUCTION

It is the charrette manager's responsibility to ensure that the team members arrive at the charrette fully informed about the project and their roles. Failure to attend to this responsibility can result in precious time wasted during the charrette arranging for a team member's ride from the airport, or worse, trying to locate a team member lost in transit. Each team member should be apprised of the charrette schedule and all logistical details relevant to his or her role and responsibilities.

PROCESS

Team Logistics Summary Document

The charrette manager assembles a team informational packet complete with a description of the project, the charrette schedule, a contact list of the project sponsor team members, and a contact list of all charrette team members. The document should also include details regarding transportation, food, and lodging and should be distributed to the charrette team in advance of the charrette. This is one more way to save time during the charrette and one way that the charrette manager can ensure that his or her team arrives with a shared knowledge of the project.

Lodging

The charrette manager is responsible for reserving lodging for the charrette team. It is recommended that lodging be located within walking distance of the charrette studio, making it easy for charrette team members to get back and forth without a car and giving them some distance from the studio during their time off.

Team Scheduling

One way to maximize cost efficiency during the charrette is to stagger the arrival of the charrette team members. For instance, the code writer could arrive one or two days into the charrette once the basic plans had been decided upon. It is also possible to schedule renderers later in the charrette when it is clear what their assignments will be. It is important to apply this staggering concept carefully. On one hand, having people standing around waiting for something to do should be avoided; on the other hand, key consultants should not miss out on important conversations regarding the development of the plan. Finally, the charrette manager is responsible for arranging all transportation, including the rental of any necessary vans and cars.

Meal Planning

Meal planning should not be left to the last minute. The charrette manager should work with the project sponsor and caterers to review and approve the menus. This includes allowance for special diets, as there are always a few vegetarians to be accounted for. It is also very helpful to have a list of recommended restaurants set aside for those evenings when the team is dining out. (See 1.5.1 for more on charrette food.)

Conclusions for 1.5 Charrette Logistics

The charrette manager must take care of logistical tasks ahead of time so that he or she does not have to take time for them during charrette. Charrettes are highly creative events that are, of course, somewhat unpredictable. The charrette manager leaves room for the unexpected by planning and managing all that is controllable. This means that every effort must be made to promote ease and efficiency for the team.

One ill-conceived charrette took place in an airport motel in a northern Rust Belt city in the dead of winter. The charrette manager had failed to check out the studio before the start of the charrette. The team spent seven days in a windowless room with poor lighting, bad ventilation, and unpleasant hotel food. Needless to say, after only three days the charrette team was a grumpy group, and the charrette products reflected it.

The dynamic planning strategies at play in the charrette logistics phase are:

1. **Design cross functionally.** The project manager is responsible for assembling a team that will provide a cross functional approach.

2. **Compress work sessions.** The charrette schedule reflects a limited time frame that must be carefully orchestrated for an ambitious amount of work to be completed.

3. **Communicate in short feedback loops.** The charrette schedule must accommodate at least three major feedback loops punctuated by public reviews.

4. **Hold the charrette on or near the site.** The selection of the charrette studio, its physical attributes, and location are critical to a successful event.

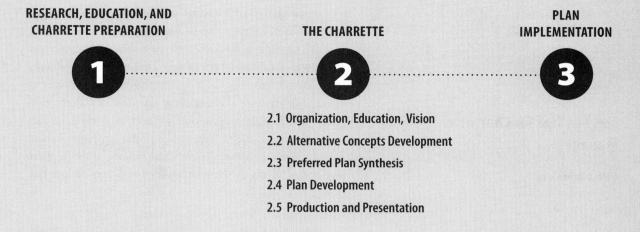

Phase Two:
The Charrette

INTRODUCTION

The completion of phase one signals that the people and the information are in place, assuring that the is project is "charrette ready." The charrette team and supplies needed arrive at the studio site and the charrette can begin. The focus of the charrette is the on-site studio. This studio is at once a fully operational design office and a public meeting place. The charrette team works nearly continuously in the studio to create and refine a plan incorporating stakeholder input along the way. One of the most common myths surrounding the charrette is that people must "quit their jobs" for a week in order to participate. This is not the case. The general public can participate in as few as three evening public meetings to make their contribution to the project's outcome. Although the charrette may last a week, the greatest number of people will review the most information during a few evening public meetings. However, if commu-

TIP

Top Ten Tips for Charrette Managers

Galina Tahchieva
Director of Town Planning,
Duany Plater-Zyberk & Company

1. **Assemble** a team of people with complementary abilities that fit the nature of the project. Most new urbanists are generalists capable of handling a broad range of tasks, but some have specialized talents—as illustrators, watercolorists, CAD experts, market analysts, and the like. The combination of characters and personalities also matters, as having a balanced variety of people makes a team efficient. The introspective thinker will complement the extrovert joker; the ambitious achiever will be balanced by the selfless helper. An indispensable team member is the charrette manager, who handles the logistics of the day-to-day charrette organization (travel, hotel, food). This frees the project manager to remain focused on the project, the team, and the client.

2. **Analyze** the project and formulate the task at hand. Then break the big task into smaller assignments that can be distributed among the team. Move people around if some of the tasks slow to a crawl. A fresh pair of eyes can bring a stagnant design to life.

3. **Start** work right away, not only to impress the client, but also to keep the energy level of the team high by seeing early results. This way, long hours

>>

nity members are unable to attend these meetings they may drop by the charrette studio almost any time.

The charrette is divided into two phases: the creative phase and the production phase. The creative phase generally lasts for the first half or two-thirds of the charrette, during which time the charrette team refines alternative plans into a preferred alternative, with the input of key stakeholders and the general public. Once a preferred alternative is decided upon, the charrette enters the production phase, during which the team studies and tests the plan in detail before preparing it for presentation at the final public meeting.

Charrette Sub-phases
- 2.1 Organization, Education, Vision
- 2.2 Alternative Concepts Development
- 2.3 Preferred Plan Synthesis
- 2.4 Plan Development
- 2.5 Production and Presentation

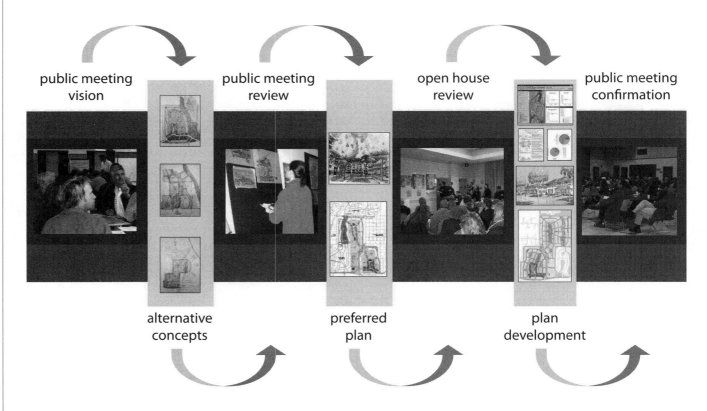

Figure 19 *Charrette Work Cycles*

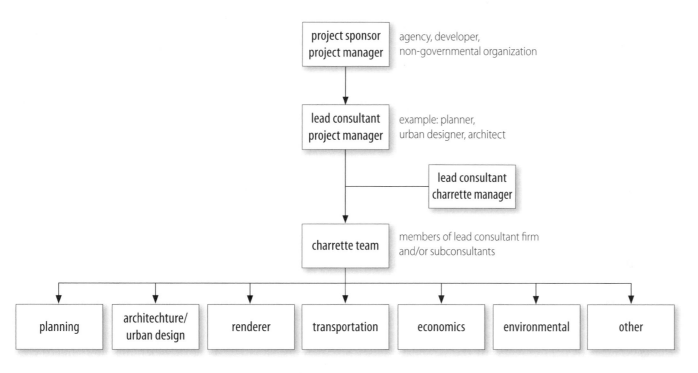

Figure 20 *Typical Project Management Organization*

CHARRETTE MANAGEMENT

There are two models for charrette leadership. In the first model there is one individual in charge of the entire project and process, acting as both the project manager and charrette manager. This individual is responsible for running meetings and maintaining relationships with the project sponsor and the primary stakeholders, and is also responsible for managing the charrette event. In the second model, which is appropriate for large and complex projects, one person acts as the project manager and another person acts as the charrette manager. In this model, the project manager maintains the primary relationships with the sponsor and the stakeholders and is responsible for leading the decision-making process and the public meetings. The char-

rette manager is responsible for logistical elements such as drawing production, transportation, catering, and organizing the charrette team. In this second model, the project manager and the charrette manager work very closely together.

The Charrette Team

The charrette team is a multidisciplinary team of specialists, usually composed of consultants. The primary role of the team is to plan the project in collaboration with stakeholders. Planners, urban designers, landscape architects, transportation planners, economists, and civil engineers are the most common specialties represented on a charrette team. An important aspect of charrette management

and all-nighters may not be needed.

4. **Encourage and motivate** the team at all times. Instill confidence by delegating responsibilities. All tasks are equally important; the details make the whole work.

5. **Think** about the bigger picture. Don't lose yourself in your own assignment. Monitor the studio, the meetings, and the team constantly. Try to predict crises.

6. **Communicate and coordinate** between the team, the client, and the charrette principal.

7. **Balance** the dialectic between collective and individual contribution. The charrette is both a democratic public process and also a democratic design process. Team contributions should be commended, while private ownership claims over design should be discouraged. The strength of the charrette is in its collective intellectual energy.

8. **Facilitate** fast decision making. Edit the information you communicate. Extract the essence from a situation or a meeting when you present it to the project manager and the team. Charrettes are short, and efficiency is crucial.

9. **Progress** from instinctive to deliberate thinking. The former happens at the beginning of the charrette; the latter is necessary for the final stages. Create a structure for spontaneity, improvisation, and creativity, but also welcome the initial chaos of the design process. It is the ideal medium for original ideas. Schedule the last two or three days for disciplined production.

10. **Keep** your sense of humor at all times, even when the PowerPoint doesn't work during a final presentation, or when someone in the audience is screaming, or even when there is a blackout in the studio. Good spirits produce good design. Remind the team constantly of its heroic efforts for the betterment of the world. ∎

TIP

The Media are Stakeholders

Ben Brown

If you're getting bad press—or no press—for a good project, you don't have a communication problem, you have a management problem. So engage the media the way you engage other key stakeholders.

Here's how:

- **Do your homework.** Know where locals get their news, and reach out to reporters and editors who specialize in topics featured in the charrette. Do it immediately, as part of pre-charrette research. And make the contact personal, one-on-one.

- **Sell the process.** Stress the charrette's inclusiveness and its bottom-line efficiency, both of which play to journalists' values.

- **Anticipate rough spots.** Assume reporters will be attracted to conflict and personality, the two big drivers of daily journalism. Defuse volatile issues with more information, not by secrecy.

- **Plan to explain and repeat.** Journalists arrive with varying degrees of knowledge and experience. Prepare fact sheets. Connect reporters with experts who can frame key issues and bring them up to speed.

- **Protect the spirit of openness.** Make clients and charrette team leaders defend any attempt to exclude reporters from any part of the process.

- **Tell the truth even when it hurts.** Admit problems. Allow no misleading information to stand—even if it temporarily benefits you. Honesty solidifies trust, which is the principal currency of communication. ∎

is knowing when to involve these different team members. The charrette manager must ensure that each team member is fully informed at key decision-making points, while not wasting the consultants' time by leaving them waiting for something to do. Most commonly there is a core design and planning team present throughout the charrette, with a number of specialists who may participate in key meetings.

Stakeholders at the Charrette

Charrette stakeholders can be divided into "primary," "secondary," and "general" categories. General stakeholders, most commonly community members, are involved in the evening public meetings held at the beginning, middle, and end of the charrette. General stakeholders may drop by the charrette studio any time. Secondary stakeholders are those with a keen economic or political interest in the project, such as members of community art groups, schools, and churches. Scheduled meetings with the secondary stakeholders are held during the first few days of the charrette. The primary stakeholders are those with a strong influence over the project. These individuals hold political, jurisdictional, or economic positions, either elected or appointed, or they own land nearby. The primary stakeholders must be involved at all key decision-making points for the charrette to be a success. These are the people who are most frequently involved throughout the charrette. (See 1.1.3 for more on stakeholder and analysis and stakeholder categories.)

Involving Youth

Whenever possible, it is helpful and important to involve young people in a charrette. Children often know more about the special places and paths in their neighborhoods than adults, and local schools are often willing to help involve their students in a charrette. Involvement techniques include workshops, art projects, and photo exercises. A pre-

sentation by a group of children can be one of the most profound moments of the charrette. (See text box p. 88.)

Public Communication

The charrette manager is responsible for communication with the public throughout the charrette via the project website and the local press. The website may provide instant notification about the proceedings of the charrette, and the charrette manager may post each day's work there. This is a safeguard against someone else controlling the message about the charrette proceedings. The adage, "If you don't control the message, somebody else will" is applicable to charrettes. This is especially true for the press. If the project manager has done her prep work, a good relationship with the press has been established well in advance of the charrette. The best situations are those in which the press is fully engaged with the project, attends all of the meetings, and reports extensively on the daily happenings of the charrette. The worst situation is one in which the press attends only one meeting and reports on the project inaccurately. This can be damaging to the charrette. One strategy is to convince the press to attend the first charrette public meeting. Once they see the uniqueness of the story they may be inclined to expand their coverage.

Charrette Team Communication

The charrette manager is responsible for ensuring that the team is fully informed about the project, the people, and the process. This is accomplished with the aid of the pre-charrette project brief (1.4.2), pre-charrette logistics summary (1.5.5), and the daily team meetings during the charrette. It is essential that everyone on a charrette team has a shared understanding of the main communication points because they will all be communicating with the public, including the press, and answering questions throughout the process.

2.1 Organization, Education, Vision

ORGANIZATION, EDUCATION, VISION — **2.1**
ALTERNATIVE CONCEPTS DEVELOPMENT — **2.2**
PREFERRED PLAN SYNTHESIS — **2.3**
PLAN DEVELOPMENT — **2.4**
PRODUCTION AND PRESENTATION — **2.5**

2.1.1 Start-Up Team Meeting

2.1.2 Charrette Team Tour

2.1.3 Primary Stakeholder Meetings

2.1.4 Charrette Public Meeting #1

INTRODUCTION

The organization, education, vision sub-phase occurs during the first full day of the charrette. Its purpose is to ensure that the members of the charrette team and the sponsor staff have a shared understanding of the project, the process, and their roles. At the conclusion of the first day of the charrette, all stakeholders should be completely clear about what is happening during the charrette and how they are going to be involved. Stakeholders will have participated in the first interactive session (charrette public meeting #1), during which they will have provided the charrette team with their knowledge of the study area and their vision of a successful project. Following this meeting, they should be convinced that their future involvement throughout the charrette will be well worth the effort.

TIP

A Youthful Perspective

Bruce Race, AICP
Founder, RACESTUDIO

In the United States, 25 percent of the population is under the age of 25. Besides being a large percentage of our population, young people will inherit the future we plan today. It is our responsibility to engage and empower young people in the community development process to involve them in making decisions about their futures.

Principles for engaging young people include:

1. Their Issues
Young people should define their own issues. Community development has to be important to them. It should reflect their perspectives.

2. Their Analysis
Young people should do their own analysis, learning about the environment and taking part in various observation and mapping methods.

3. Communication
Youth participants should develop their own communication strategies in which they identify stakeholders, audiences, and communication methods.

4. Advocacy
Young people should take the lead in advocating their positions. They understand the issues and have thought about how to communicate their preferred future.

Supporting young people has several important benefits. They learn about their community, and so do we, from them. Young people become empowered by owning a piece of the future, and communities gain a generation of informed and active citizens. ∎

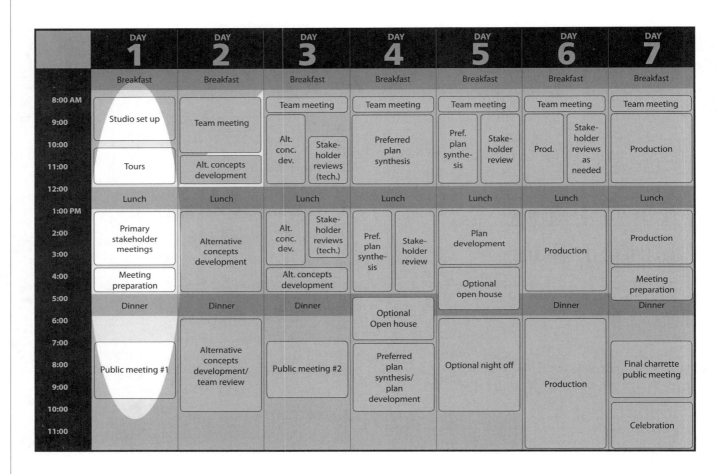

Figure 21 *2.1 Organization, Education, Vision Sample Schedule*

2.1 Organization, Education, Vision Tools and Techniques

2.1.1 Start-Up Team Meeting

INTRODUCTION

The charrette begins with a start-up team meeting, an organizational event for the charrette sponsors and all charrette team members. Some charrette team members have been working on the project from its inception, while others will arrive new to the project, only having read the pre-charrette project brief. Some members of the team will be making their first visit to the site. It is the charrette manager's responsibility to bring these people up to speed on the project as quickly as possible.

PROCESS

Attendees at the start-up team meeting most commonly include the project sponsor staff, the charrette team, and whenever possible, elected officials, and political champions who support the project. The meeting begins with an orientation and introduction of the project and the people involved. Each specialist delivers a brief summary of his work, which usually covers the project site's existing conditions. The charrette manager then orchestrates an open discussion to clarify all of this information. The meeting ends with a review of the schedule and task assignments.

2.1.2 Charrette Team Tour

INTRODUCTION

For the charrette team to truly serve the community, it must have a good working knowledge of the community's built history. Therefore, at the conclusion of the start-up team meeting, it is common for the charrette team and sponsor to tour the project site and the surrounding community. This tour allows team members to converse about the site and its context, including both good and bad development patterns as well as possible design solutions.

PROCESS

In advance of the tour, the charrette manager coordinates with the project sponsor to establish a loose itinerary, including a project site tour and visits to important examples of development relevant to the project. The manager considers the various types of development that could be included in the project, such as storefront retail, multifamily housing, small and large lot housing, neighborhood commercial, and parks. The tour should include a sampling of the relevant design typologies, focusing on inventive good examples but also on examples of poor development. This can help the team understand what the community has come to expect from development and help the code writers see what their codes should prohibit.

Members of the charrette team will be looking for opportunities to study aspects of the community relevant to the project. The architects may be looking at building typologies and taking photographs, the engineers may be pacing off street widths, the landscape architects may be taking stock of the foliage and park design, and the urban designer may be pacing off the town square. This allows the team to share knowledge and build a shared understanding and vocabulary.

TIP

Dealing with the Unexpected in the First Meeting

The first public meeting can sometimes be seen by opposition groups as an opportunity to undermine the project by calling into question its validity. It is important that a skilled facilitator lead the meeting with all the tools and techniques to handle difficult meetings at his or her disposal. The facilitator must have an agreed upon agenda, the desired outcomes for the meeting, and ground rules. The ground rules are established and agreed upon at the beginning of the meeting and are invoked during the meeting to handle unexpected interruptions. ■

20-year Vision Exercise

In one popular visioning exercise, the facilitator asks participants to imagine that they have left their community for 20 years. When they come back, their community has changed. The facilitator then asks the participants what the place will look like 20 years hence, once the project has been completed. Participants are asked to envision their personal best-case scenario for the community. The facilitator leads the visioning exercise by asking, "Who lives here?", "What are they doing?", "What is the housing like?", and "How are people getting around?" ■

The Importance of Clearly Communicating Expectations

More than one opening public meeting has taken an unexpected turn because the participants did not have a clear understanding of the meeting purpose and desired outcomes. This was the case at a public meeting attended by several hundred people on the opening night of a charrette. The charrette team had been in town the previous month and had conducted a public kick-off meeting during which the participants engaged in small table exercises to create community vision ideas. At the end of that meeting, the charrette team members announced that they would go back to their offices and develop design alternatives to be presented at the beginning of the charrette. However, more than 100 people who showed up on the first night of the charrette had no knowledge of the previous month's kick-off meeting. The charrette manager was not more than 10 minutes into the presentation of the design alternatives when a riot erupted. Many people were disappointed that they were seeing design ideas presented before they had a chance to participate. The meeting had to be stopped and redesigned immediately into a workshop so that the new participants could contribute

>>

2.1.3 Primary Stakeholder Meetings

INTRODUCTION

The opening and closing public meetings are the most important events of the charrette. Before the first public meeting, the charrette manager must arrange meetings with the primary stakeholders who can make or break the project. The manager and selected team members gather knowledge that may be crucial in preparing for public meetings. In addition, it may be important to pay homage to an individual or group, such as a neighborhood association.

PROCESS

The meetings with primary stakeholders usually include other team members who either have a relationship with the stakeholders or specific knowledge of the meeting content. The meetings are held in the charrette studio or at the stakeholder's office, and they often take place while the rest of the team is touring the project site. Primary stakeholders may include elected officials, landowners, and lead community activists. It is important that these people understand the charrette process and how they can be most effectively involved. This is also an opportunity to elicit last minute information that might help the charrette manager prepare for the first public meeting, such as the latest political activity of opposition groups. If knowledge about the project's opposition can be gathered in time, the charrette manager is able to contact these people to head off a confrontation at the meeting.

2.1.4 Charrette Public Meeting #1

INTRODUCTION

The outcome of the first public meeting can have a great effect on the success of the charrette and therefore must be well planned and facilitated by the charrette manager. It is a challenge for the charrette team to explain the project to the public, present basic planning principles, and orchestrate a participatory workshop in no more than two and a half hours.

The overall goal of this first public meeting is for participants to gain a complete understanding of the project and how they can be involved. They should leave with a sense of excitement about participating. They should want to come back and feel compelled to bring their friends. Gathering stakeholder input in the form of notes and drawings is the other main goal.

Another important meeting outcome is the establishment of a standard for how people are treated. It is in this first meeting that the charrette team establishes its credibility as a professional group whose primary interest is in helping create the best solution for all parties. The manner in which the charrette team conducts itself during this meeting will, to a great extent, determine the manner in which all participants conduct themselves. If participants believe that the charrette team members are working collaboratively with the community, they will be more likely to participate and less likely to challenge the charrette process.

PROCESS

The first charrette public meeting is divided into two parts. The first involves an informational presentation, including a "food for thought" lecture, by members of the charrette team, lasting no more than 45 minutes. The second part of the meeting is an interactive, hands-on workshop involving all participants.

Room Arrangement

Seating a maximum of eight people at small tables is an ideal arrangement for the opening meeting. Each table should be equipped with flip charts and aerial photographs of the project area as well as tracing paper, markers, and sticky notes. There should be a reception table at the door with several sign-in sheets and handouts that describe the project and the process. A good way to encourage people to attend the meeting is to provide food, ideally on a dedicated table on one side of the room.

Informational Presentations

Meeting start up

If at all possible, the meeting should start with a welcome by an elected official. This sends the message that the charrette is a public event endorsed and monitored by local representatives. The presence of political leadership in the room sends the signal to participants that the charrette is taken seriously by their government and therefore has a better chance of implementation, one more reason that it is worth their while to participate. It is usually necessary to provide some coaching so that elected officials stay on topic and keep their comments short.

After the welcome, the facilitator (usually the project or charrette manager) takes the first few minutes to explain the meeting purpose, desired outcomes, agenda, and ground rules for participation. After this initial meeting set-up, which takes no more than five minutes, the charrette team is introduced.

Project description and technical background

After the set-up, a description of the project mission, goals, and process is presented. The whole project process should be covered, especially the post-charrette implementation and adoption phase. The charrette schedule is presented and opportunities for further stakeholder participation, be-

yond this first public meeting, are highlighted. Next, there may be brief presentations by charrette team members on the most important existing conditions, such as market and transportation.

Food for thought lecture

A presentation on planning principles follows the project description. The content of this lecture may vary, but the intent is to provide participants with some basic knowledge of planning principles before they engage in the hands-on workshop exercises. Using the local community as a case study to present examples of planning principles is the most effective way to communicate this information and its relevance. These examples often include elements such as corner stores, small local parks, a variety of housing types, and walkable streets and paths.

Hands-on Workshop

The purpose of the hands-on workshop is to engage as many people as possible in a discussion about their community and the project. The desired outcome of the workshop is a mapping of the current physical conditions and a prioritized list of desired vision elements for the community captured in drawings and words.

One common model for conducting a hands-on workshop is to organize it into four phases (detailed below). The first phase is the introduction of all parties at the table, the second phase is the existing conditions exercise, the third phase is the creation of a group vision for the project, and the fourth phase is a report back.

Staffing

During the hands-on workshop, a facilitator and a recorder are located at each table. Ideally, each table's facilitator and recorder are members of the charrette team. When there are not enough members of the team to staff each table,

>>

to the creation of the community vision. In retrospect, the project managers realized that this particular project was too volatile to start the charrette with design alternatives, even though the kick-off meeting validated the process. For projects with complex political situations, it is wise to err on the conservative side by beginning the charrette with a hands-on workshop rather than with a presentation of design alternatives. ∎

Table 18 **Sample Charrette Public Meeting #1 Agenda Worksheet**

Topic	Process	Person	Time (min.)
Welcome	Personal introduction, no props	Community Leader	3
Meeting start ups ■ Facilitator introduction ■ Agenda ■ Meeting purpose, desired outcomes ■ Ground rules	PowerPoint and flip chart presentation	Facilitator	7
Project, Process, People ■ Project mission, sponsors, description ■ Project process, how people can be involved ■ Introduce charrette team, related projects	PowerPoint and flip chart presentation	Charrette Manager	10
Technical background – most influential existing conditions ■ Economic, transportation, environmental	PowerPoint and flip chart presentation	Specialist(s)	15
Clarification questions	Take questions from the audience with a handheld microphone	Facilitator	10
Food for thought lecture (to prep for workshop) ■ Project context, local planning, inspire a sense of "a historic moment" ■ Teach basic good planning principles using local examples where possible	PowerPoint presentation	Charrette Manager	15
Public hands-on workshop ■ Instructions for existing conditions and visioning exercises ■ Small group work	Each table has a design leader and recorder with instructions	Facilitator, Community Members	60
Report back ■ Table representative presents top points	Each table chooses a representative who does a three-minute report on the table's top five items, facilitator keeps time	Community Members	25
Wrap up ■ Meeting assessment (positives then suggested upgrades) ■ Next steps ■ Adjourn	Two recorders with flip charts	Facilitator	5
		Total time	150

the charrette manager looks to local agency planning staff, universities, and volunteer groups for additional facilitators and recorders. In this case, the charrette manager holds a brief training session, usually about an hour before the evening meeting. The facilitators and recorders complete a crash course in table facilitation and the group exercise process. As a last resort, the charrette manager may ask a community member at the table to volunteer as a recorder.

The table facilitator's main goal is to create a safe environment that encourages people to participate. Before the community members begin their work, the charrette manager provides the instructions and framework for the exercise and the ground rules. The ground rules may include: "talk with your pen," "be considerate," and "practice listening." Part of the table facilitator's job is to make sure that everyone can participate in the discussion without any one person dominating. The facilitator is also responsible for ensuring that the work is accomplished and that the recording takes place.

The recorder's job is to capture each person's contribution as well as decisions made by the group, such as prioritizing. The recorder writes the comments on a flip chart making sure to check for accuracy with the participants. If the recorder is a volunteer community member, he or she should also participate in the exercises.

Existing conditions exercise

This exercise acknowledges the participants as experts. After all, they are the ones who know the most about their community. This is their chance to tell the team what they know in order to create the best plan possible. They identify the best places and the worst places, where the kids like to go and where residents gather. Existing conditions are completed first to allow the participants to provide information that the charrette team may not already know. It also reinforces the message that the charrette team values the exper-

tise of the community members.

One method for conducting this exercise is to have everyone write down a few ideas before the talking begins. The facilitator then goes around the table asking each person to state one point, such as, "This cafe is where everyone meets on Saturday morning before soccer games." They are encouraged to draw on the aerial map while the recorder writes their points on the flip chart. This exercise usually lasts about 30 minutes.

Visioning exercise

Creating a group vision is the goal of the visioning exercise. The table facilitator asks each person to write down a set of ideas before the discussion begins. Then, again going around the table, each person states one of his or her vision ideas, while the design leader encourages them to draw the ideas and the recorder writes them on flip charts. The goal is to record as many of the ideas as possible, especially by drawing on tracing paper over the aerial photograph. It is also important to have a written record of the group's ideas on the flip charts. At the end of the visioning exercise, the facilitator asks the table to prioritize its top three vision items to report back to the larger group.

The highlight of the meeting is the report back, when a community representative from each table gives a brief summary (maximum three minutes each) of the top vision items discussed at the table. It is critical that the representative be one of the community members, not a staff person. The results of the existing conditions exercise are not reported. This half hour of community member presentations is a very positive way to end the meeting. At this point community members take ownership of the meeting. They are presenting what they alone know about their neighborhood.

The meeting ends with a discussion of next steps. The charrette manager may end by saying "You have given the charrette team plenty to do. You told us what was important

Facilitator Training: Making the Process Work

Harrison B. Rue
Executive Director, Thomas Jefferson Planning District Commission Founding Director, Citizen Planner Institute

The Citizen Planner Institute (CPI) believes that the training of community and staff members as workshop and process facilitators is a key strategy for project success. Trained community members work to encourage broad workshop participation and become strong project supporters assisting in long-term implementation. CPI's Facilitator Training workshops are part of an extensive public involvement strategy, focused on interactive, hands-on workshops. Training for community leaders and agency staff gives the public process over to the community—although a strong moderator is needed to keep the workshops on track. Local organizers identify a diverse group—neighborhood leaders, business people, and community activists, all required to have good people skills. This group facilitates the workshops and helps publicize the events. Agency staff are trained separately to participate in the public workshops, and can help facilitate as needed.

After presentations to introduce new design, modeling technology, or policy solutions, the basic ground rules are explained and participants practice several exercises: one-on-one conversations (reporting back each other's ideas), "post-it note visions" (a quick and accurate way to identify shared values), group exer-

>>

\>\>

cises to identify issues on big paper and use a "dot vote" to prioritize, and—the key role—facilitating small group hands-on sessions, using markers on large maps.

RoadWork exercises (from my book, *Real Towns: Making Your Neighborhood Work*), completed prior to the public workshops, help participants understand their own neighborhoods, basic smart growth and new urbanist principles, and how to identify areas where change is desired. While a short handout helps facilitators remember the rules, an "open architecture" public process takes the pressure off—the moderator explains to everyone exactly how meetings will be run before every exercise. The public workshops are *always* productive. The training also helps participants apply the principles in other community exercises—while strengthening community support for the overall concepts and specific projects. ∎

about your neighborhood and now it is up to us take this information, combine it with our physical, political, and financial constraints, and develop some alternatives for your consideration at our next meeting. Please come back in a couple of nights to see if we listened to you, and please bring your neighbors." A successful first public meeting ends with participants excited to come back for the next meeting.

Conclusions for 2.1 Charrette Organization, Education, Vision

The first day sets the pace, direction, and tone for the rest of the charrette. Who the charrette team meets with and how all the meetings are conducted has a huge effect on whether the charrette can move forward with minimal resistance or whether it will face an uphill climb. Therefore, this day needs to be planned well in advance. Careful thought should be given to the meetings, their agendas, and the participants. By the end of the first day, all participants, including the politicians, landowners, project sponsor, and secondary and general stakeholders should understand with complete clarity the purpose of the charrette, the scheduling, and how they are able to participate.

The dynamic planning strategies at play in the charrette organization, education, vision sub-phase are:

1. **Work collaboratively.** By meeting with the primary and general stakeholders before beginning design, the team sends the message that the charrette is a collaborative effort.

2. **Conduct a multiple day charrette.** The team begins a creative workshop capable of facilitating transformative community change due in part to its continued presence over the week.

3. **Hold the charrette on or near the site.** Locating the charrette studio in the center of the community provides access that is supportive of active stakeholder participation.

2.2 Alternative Concepts Development

2.2.1 Concepts Team Meeting

2.2.2 Alternative Concepts Development

2.2.3 Initial Stakeholder Reviews

2.2.4 Alternative Concepts Refinement

2.2.5 Charrette Public Meeting #2 or Open House

INTRODUCTION

On the morning of the second day of the charrette, the charrette team is ready to face the challenge of creating a set of alternative concepts based on all of the research and data that has been gathered and compiled over the past several months. This includes the input from the previous night's public meeting (charrette public meeting #1). The charrette manager must coordinate a balance between maximizing the creativity of the charrette team and keeping the project on track toward a feasible outcome. This is an exciting time for the charrette team members. They will finally get the chance to start creating a plan.

The purpose of the alternative concepts development phase is to quickly arrive at a large set of plan alternative concepts that can be reviewed by the primary stakeholders for subsequent revision and then presented at the next public meeting (charrette public meeting #2). This is a very in-

Tips for Charrette Studio Management

Oliver Kuehne, Senior Town Planner
HDR|LCA+Sargent Town Planning

1. Pin-up space: If your charrette studio lacks wall space and/or you want to separate the workstations from the public areas, consider building a divider out of multiple 4'x8' sheets of 1/2" drywall. Use white duct tape to connect the sheets and set them up at an angle for stability. Drywall is cheap and you'll always find a local handyman who's happy to pick it up after the charrette. You can also lean large foamcore boards against the walls. These are lightweight but more expensive and won't work free standing. Sufficient lighting of displayed drawings is important; clamp-on lights will do the job.

2. Clean up the studio **every** morning: Take out the trash, throw out drawings you don't need anymore (keep in mind, though, sometimes old ideas offer more insights than new ones), and put the ones you want to save on a pile or pin them up. Put all the supplies back on the supply table, except for each person's personal set. Consider putting one person in charge of cleaning up the studio before everybody else arrives.

3. Post important charrette information in the studio: Charrette schedule, task and to-do lists, maps, drawings, pre-charrette analyses, and other project info. Keep everything up to date. Post internal information in the workstation area and public information near the studio entrance. ■

tense phase, during which the charrette team must work quickly and efficiently. Because there are only two days to accomplish this challenging task, the pressure is on the charrette manager to run a well-organized studio where the team's need for private working time is weighed against the need for public review.

2.2 Alternative Concepts Development Tools and Techniques
- 2.2.1 Concepts Team Meeting
- 2.2.2 Alternative Concepts Development
- 2.2.3 Initial Stakeholder Reviews
- 2.2.4 Alternative Concepts Refinement
- 2.2.5 Charrette Public Meeting #2 or Open House

2.2.1 Concepts Team Meeting

INTRODUCTION
The purpose of the concepts team meeting is to assign tasks and organize the work for the following two days. During the meeting, the charrette team debriefs on the previous night's public meeting, particularly the results of the hands-on workshop. The team then identifies the central themes from the workshop and translates these themes into a manageable number of alternative approaches, usually no more than four. After identifying three or four conceptual approaches, the team creates a number of potential plan options for each alternative.

PROCESS
Prior to the meeting, the drawings and flip charts from the previous night's hands-on workshop are posted on the studio wall. Each table facilitator reports on the results from his or her table. The charrette manager then facilitates a discussion about the workshop results with the goal of gaining agreement on three or four conceptual approaches. While

identifying these approaches, the charrette team discusses various alternative design plans for each approach. Once the approach and alternatives are identified, the charrette manager assigns individuals or small teams to study them. In order to keep the project on schedule the meeting should end by 10 or 11 a.m. so that the team can get to work on producing alternatives.

2.2.2 Alternative Concepts Development Introduction

The purpose of alternative concepts development is to create a set of alternatives based on the conceptual approaches identified in the charrette concepts team meeting. The primary stakeholders can then review these alternatives according to the objectives, strategies, and measures (1.1.1), and revisions can be made.

PROCESS
Usually, the planners, urban designers, and landscape architects lead this process. However, other specialists such as transportation planners sometimes join in the planning and design. The work done during this initial phase is generally conducted at the level of the overall plan, although each team member is encouraged to study the project by drawing elevations and sections as well as perspective rendering drawings. Investigations at different scales and from different viewpoints are always encouraged.

The charrette team must consider the ideas from the hands-on workshop during the first public meeting as well as the engineering, economics, statutory requirements, and especially the OSM (see 1.1.1), while developing the alternative concepts. The charrette manager may choose to have charrette team members work individually or in groups of two or three. An effective method for analyzing and rat-

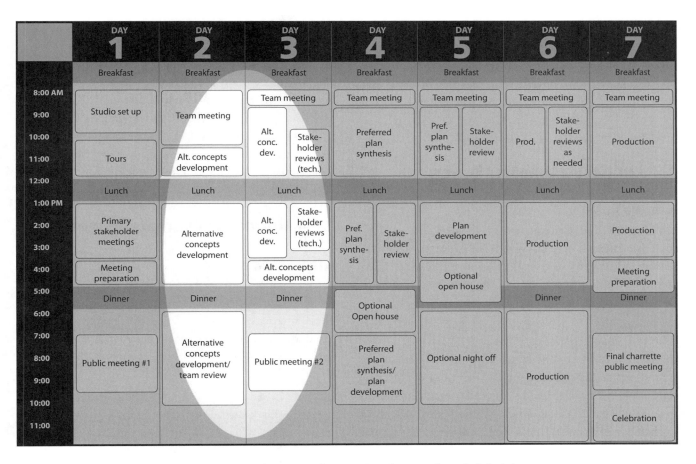

	DAY 1	DAY 2	DAY 3	DAY 4	DAY 5	DAY 6	DAY 7
	Breakfast	Breakfast	Breakfast	Breakfast	Breakfast	Breakfast	Breakfast
8:00 AM			Team meeting	Team meeting	Team meeting	Team meeting	Team meeting
9:00	Studio set up	Team meeting	Alt. conc. dev. / Stake-holder reviews (tech.)	Preferred plan synthesis	Pref. plan synthe-sis / Stake-holder review	Prod. / Stake-holder reviews as needed	Production
10:00							
11:00	Tours	Alt. concepts development					
12:00	Lunch	Lunch	Lunch	Lunch	Lunch	Lunch	Lunch
1:00 PM							
2:00	Primary stakeholder meetings	Alternative concepts development	Alt. conc. dev. / Stake-holder reviews (tech.)	Pref. plan synthe-sis / Stake-holder review	Plan development	Production	Production
3:00							
4:00	Meeting preparation		Alt. concepts development		Optional open house		Meeting preparation
5:00	Dinner	Dinner	Dinner	Optional Open house		Dinner	Dinner
6:00							
7:00	Public meeting #1	Alternative concepts development/ team review	Public meeting #2	Preferred plan synthesis/ plan development	Optional night off	Production	Final charrette public meeting
8:00							
9:00							
10:00							Celebration
11:00							

Figure 22 *2.2 Alternative Concepts Development Sample Schedule*

ing the concepts is to use a simple spreadsheet that lists the OSM elements. This spreadsheet can be used for rating the developing concepts and the emerging preferred plan throughout the charrette. This ongoing analysis and rating provides an invaluable record for the decisions made during the charrette.

This initial sketching phase usually lasts no more than a couple of hours before the charrette manager calls for a review or pin-up (see text box in this section), early in the af-

ternoon of day two. This review is critical for establishing the project direction. This is the first time that the team will review the entire range of alternatives they have been exploring. The charrette manager directs the pin-up and encourages an open debate between all team members. This analysis exposes the weaknesses and strengths of each concept. It usually lasts between an hour and 90 minutes. During this review, the weak ideas are discarded, the strong ones are highlighted, and new ideas are developed. Two plans are

TIP

Managing the Public at the Charrette Studio

Because the charrette studio is open to the public during most working hours, the charrette manager must be ready to deal with unexpected visitors. For instance, it is not uncommon for a community member or group to arrive unannounced at the studio with "their plan." Sometimes, a community member has done his or her homework and is proposing an alternative plan. It is important for the charrette manager to recognize these efforts as important contributions. It may even be appropriate to invite these people to join the effort and give them a spot at the table with the planners and designers. However, they must agree to the ground rules of the charrette: the best ideas win and no plan receives special favor, regardless of its author. In most cases, people are happy to hand off their plan to the team for its consideration. The charrette manager then directs a member of the charrette team to redraw it so that the plan can be judged for its design merits and not by the quality of the drawing technique. These proposed plans are then brought into the pin-ups and possibly into public forms. Community members who bring these plans to the charrette should be applauded for their extra efforts on behalf of their community. By proposing an alternative, they are participating in the charrette in good faith. Often, these people become the final plan's biggest promoters. ■

"One of the things that I recommend to city leaders is to get away from planning with just words. Words don't suffice, yet most comprehensive plans are more verbal than visual. Words like 'multifamily' get bad responses, terms like 'historic neighborhood' get smiles. How is that possible, since there is usually lots of multifamily housing in historic neighborhoods? You need to use pictures to get to the core issues in planning and reach consensus. Yes, this is a little subversive: Zoning's sacred cows are usually slaughtered when you use pictures instead of words."

Victor Dover, AICP
Principal, Dover, Kohl & Partners
Excerpted from the 2000 Smart Growth Conference Proceedings

often merged into one by combining each plan's strengths. Creating a refined set of alternatives that the charrette team members can take back to their tables and continue to work on is the desired outcome of this review. At this point, the concepts are ready to show to primary stakeholders for initial reviews and feedback.

2.2.3 Initial Stakeholder Reviews

INTRODUCTION
Holding meetings with primary stakeholders during the alternative concepts development phase allows the charrette team to get an early read on the feasibility of the emerging concepts. Gaining approval from the primary stakeholders is the first hurdle for the alternative concepts.

PROCESS
Initial stakeholder reviews are usually held at the end of the second day or the beginning of the third day of the charrette, as soon as the charrette team has developed and refined a set of concept alternatives. Meetings are usually held in the charrette studio. The charrette manager should not wait until he or she arrives at the site to schedule these very important meetings. Particularly because many of these stakeholders work for public agencies such as public works, fire protection, and transportation, it is necessary to schedule them in advance of the charrette. The charrette manager and members of the charrette team involved with the subject matter should attend. The rest of the team members continue to work on their concepts within earshot of the meeting. This way, the majority of the team can continue working without missing the proceedings. Occasionally, it is necessary to meet with primary stakeholders off-site. This is often the case with high-level officials who have limited free time in their schedules.

These initial stakeholder reviews provide an opportunity to show the key decision makers a wide range of concepts to which they can respond. For instance, an early meeting with a transportation agency can be very useful in identifying acceptable street networks and designs. These meetings may also serve to educate local transportation planners early on in an effort to gain their ultimate support. This is especially true when the charrette team is considering street designs that do not conform to local standards.

2.2.4 Alternative Concepts Refinement

INTRODUCTION
The purpose of alternative concepts refinement is to reduce the set of alternative concepts to a manageable number. These alternatives are then tested for feasibility and prepared for presentation at the next public meeting (charrette public meeting #2).

Figure 23 *A pin-up review by the charrette team*

PROCESS

The charrette team's focus during day three is developing the alternative concepts drawings and documents to a level appropriate for public presentation. The team should be working not only on drawing plans but also on developing elevations and sections and creating perspective renderings. These drawings should not be too polished. In fact, it is better for them to look a little rough. Hand drawn sketches do the best job of communicating to the public that it is still early and many changes are yet to come. Computer generated drawings look too finished for this stage of the charrette. Preliminary financial and transportation analyses can be started at this time as well.

Following the meetings with primary stakeholders, the charrette manager often calls for another pin-up. During this pin-up, the charrette team identifies the strengths and weaknesses of each alternative with the aim of merging good ideas, eliminating bad ones, and developing new ideas. The charrette manager may choose this time to mix things up a little by asking designers and planners to swap plans. This is a fun and challenging way to improve a plan by introducing a "new set of eyes." When using this technique, the rule is to build upon the work of others and avoid backtracking. It is important for the charrette team to refer continually to any project performance measures, such as the OSM document, when making refinement decisions.

2.2.5 Charrette Public Meeting #2 or Open House

INTRODUCTION

The second charrette public meeting is usually held on the evening of day three. This meeting involves community members in a phase of the planning process to which they may not be accustomed: a design feedback session. The purpose of the meeting is to educate all stakeholders about the alternative concepts that have emerged since the first public meeting and to facilitate a well-rounded dialogue among all of the relevant viewpoints represented. During this meeting, the charrette team seeks to gather enough information to narrow the concept alternatives into a preferred plan. It also hopes to hook the community members on the process. For many, this meeting is a revelation about how a community planning process can be conducted.

PROCESS

The second public meeting features a presentation of the concept alternatives by the charrette team, followed by a discussion of each alternative's merits, during which input from the public is actively solicited. This meeting may be held as a forum, a workshop, or an open house (see 1.5.4 for more on meeting types).

The forum, or one big meeting, is the preferred option. The advantage of the forum is that there is one conversation that is heard by everyone, during which all relevant knowledge is present and accessible. However, for groups larger than 60 it can be difficult to involve a large enough percentage of the attendees. Meetings this large may call for a workshop, breaking the forum down into smaller groups of 15 to 20 people.

For either format, the meeting begins with the charrette manager presenting a brief overview of the project and a summary of the proceedings of the first few days of the charrette. Next, the concept alternatives are presented, preferably by the members of the charrette team who authored the alternatives.

After the alternatives are presented, the manager facilitates a discussion among team members about the merits and disadvantages of the concepts, drawing the public into the discussion. The agreed upon objectives, strategies, and

Sample Alternative Concepts Development Drawings

Figure 24 *Pleasant Hill BART Station Area Charrette Alternative Concept A*

Figure 25 *Pleasant Hill BART Station Area Charrette Alternative Concept B*

Figure 26 *Pleasant Hill BART Station Area Charrette Alternative Concept C*

Pin-up Process

The charrette pin-up is a direct adaptation of a traditional teaching method at the core of architectural education. The pin-up is the moment of truth for the architectural student. At the pin-up, the blurry-eyed student presents and defends his or her design project to a "jury" after days of intense late-night work. The jury consists of faculty members and invited guests, some of whom may be famous architects. Other students in the class also participate. While the jury's critique is the focus, anyone may participate. They must, of course, be willing to subject themselves to criticism from the jury. During the pin-up, the project's strengths and weaknesses are identified and suggestions for improvement are offered. The pin-up is the proving ground for the project in which the best ideas advance, regardless of their source.

The pin-ups that occur in the charrette are modeled after these intense academic sessions. A charrette team member presents the plan alternative under consideration. The other charrette team members, sponsor staff, invited guests, and the occasional walk-in stakeholder make up the jury. The pin-up brings together a group of specialists and single interest parties to collaborate in a generalist approach in the pursuit of a holistic solution. ∎

measures (OSM) are referenced often during this meeting. These measures are used as an objective touchstone for decision making. This meeting should be a balanced educational experience for all parties. By the end of the meeting it is usually apparent which alternatives merit continued study. The charrette manager ends the meeting by summarizing the next steps that the team will take over the following few days as it works toward developing the preferred alternative. It is always important for the charrette manager to check that participants understand which alternatives will be cast aside and which ones will be merged with other options.

Holding an open house is another option for this meeting. This method is recommended only in situations when the project management team determines that the level of controversy in the project is low enough that a forum is not necessary. The open house is not actually a single group meeting but a series of small meetings between community members and charrette team members so should not be attempted this early in a highly controversial charrette (see 2.3.4 for more on the charrette open house).

Conclusions for 2.2 Charrette Alternative Concepts Development

The second and third days of the charrette are in some ways the most intense. The ability to balance creativity, efficiency, and stakeholder involvement is a true test for the charrette manager. In 48 hours, starting with a nearly clean slate, the charrette team gathers public input, develops a broad set of alternative concepts, tests them for feasibility, presents them to stakeholders, revises them, and prepares them for presentation in a major public meeting. It is important to keep in mind the point of view of the general stakeholders. To them, the second public meeting is impressive, in-

formative, and inspiring. Just two nights ago they left the charrette team with piles of ideas, and in that short time a set of alternatives has been well-described, creatively drawn, and presented. On top of that, the stakeholders' major ideas have been considered and either incorporated into the designs or excluded with explanations. After attending this meeting, even skeptics are inclined to continue to participate in the charrette.

The dynamic planning strategies at play in the charrette alternative concepts development sub-phase are:

1. **Compress work sessions.** There is a huge amount of work to complete, and a number of meetings for the charrette team to attend, in the period between the first and second public meetings. This time constraint can produce very creative results.

2. **Communicate in short feedback loops.** The second public meeting happens only 48 hours after the first. These meetings are intentionally scheduled close together to make sure that the direction of the concepts alternatives is correct.

3. **Use design to achieve a shared vision and create holistic solutions.** From the beginning, the charrette team studies concept alternatives by producing drawings that allow a large group of diverse stakeholder to understand the project and its complexity. Drawings are the primary vehicle for education during the charrette.

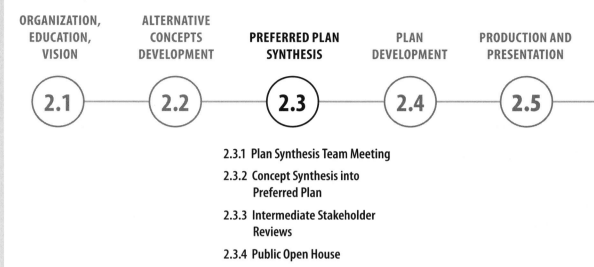

2.3 Preferred Plan Synthesis

ORGANIZATION, EDUCATION, VISION — **2.1**

ALTERNATIVE CONCEPTS DEVELOPMENT — **2.2**

PREFERRED PLAN SYNTHESIS — **2.3**

PLAN DEVELOPMENT — **2.4**

PRODUCTION AND PRESENTATION — **2.5**

2.3.1 Plan Synthesis Team Meeting

2.3.2 Concept Synthesis into Preferred Plan

2.3.3 Intermediate Stakeholder Reviews

2.3.4 Public Open House

INTRODUCTION

It is the charrette team's goal to arrive at a preferred plan after the second public meeting, around the midpoint of the charrette. This usually occurs at the end of day three and no later than day four. This schedule allows enough time for the team to develop the preferred plan and to prepare all the necessary documents for presentation at the final meeting.

It is around the midpoint of the charrette when transformative moments often occur that enable unexpected solutions to emerge. The process of synthesizing the preferred plan from seemingly conflicting concerns requires focusing on underlying common needs. Individuals are usually so fixated on their perceptions of possible solutions that the common needs are overlooked. The charrette team's duty is

The Power of Taking the Time to Listen

Bill Lennertz
Executive Director, National Charrette Institute

One afternoon during an intense charrette a couple visited the charrette studio. While the man was introducing himself, his wife began to cry. They said that they had recently built a house in a development that directly abutted the project site. When they bought the land they were told that the highest density that would ever be built across from them would be large lot single-family homes. Now the county was planning a huge multi-family affordable housing project. I told them that I understood their alarm and asked if I could visit them at their house.

Later that afternoon I met them at their home. They were very gracious and appreciative that I was concerned enough to make the effort to stop by during a clearly busy time in the charrette. We had tea as I listened to them talk about their concerns that the pristine mountain view from their patio door might soon be replaced with a view of a high density housing project. I asked them how they would feel if their view looked as though a mirror

>>

to seek solutions that go beyond basic problem solving to provide a framework for positive community transformation. Stakeholder groups are sometimes surprised when the charrette team develops new solutions that are acceptable to a diverse group of interests. The emergence of an unexpected preferred plan can cause people to change positions that were based on their limited expectations.

2.3 Preferred Plan Synthesis Tools and Techniques
- 2.3.1 Plan Synthesis Team Meeting
- 2.3.2 Concept Synthesis into Preferred Plan
- 2.3.3 Intermediate Stakeholder Reviews
- 2.3.4 Public Open House

2.3.1 Plan Synthesis Team Meeting

INTRODUCTION
The plan synthesis team meeting takes place the morning following the second public meeting. It is a defining moment in the charrette. The charrette team and sponsor staff review the results of the second public meeting and devise the work plan for the plan synthesis phase of the charrette. Clues for developing the preferred plan are uncovered during this meeting.

PROCESS
Before the plan synthesis team meeting begins, the charrette team posts the exhibits from the second public meeting on the studio walls. The charrette manager facilitates a pin-up review by the charrette team and sponsor staff that analyzes the feedback from the previous evening and charts the next steps. A clearly preferred alternative may become apparent at this time. If not, the team must agree upon the options that should be pursued and merged and whether

new ones must be created. The charrette manager then creates team assignments for the next period of work.

2.3.2 Concept Synthesis into Preferred Plan

INTRODUCTION
The purpose of concept synthesis is to continue the process of merging the alternative concepts by taking into account all information from the second public meeting as well as any agreed upon measures of success. The charrette team must stay focused and on task. The charrette manager, knowing that a solution will soon become apparent, directs the team and helps to maintain a high level of creativity.

PROCESS
While there is no one methodology for synthesizing several alternative concepts into one preferred plan, there are steps common to any process. These steps involve testing for feasibility and assessing alternatives against a common set of measures. Stakeholder meetings and studies conducted by charrette team specialists are important components of feasibility testing. These studies include economic feasibility models, transportation models, and environmental impact models.

The pin-up is the most common method of review employed during the charrette. It is discussed in detail in section 2.2. The charrette manager monitors the team's progress and makes a judgment regarding the best time to hold a pin-up. During the pin-up, a debate occurs among the charrette and sponsor team members, and possibly members of the primary stakeholder groups, over the merits of the concept schemes. One common method for synthesizing is to attempt to create one plan from the best elements

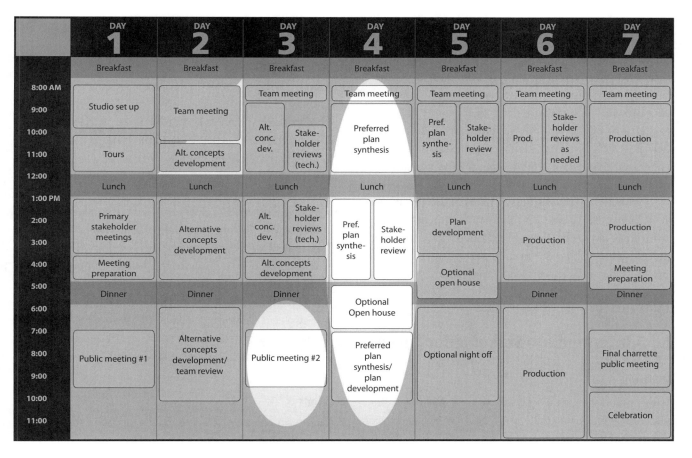

	DAY 1	DAY 2	DAY 3	DAY 4	DAY 5	DAY 6	DAY 7
	Breakfast	Breakfast	Breakfast	Breakfast	Breakfast	Breakfast	Breakfast
8:00 AM			Team meeting	Team meeting	Team meeting	Team meeting	Team meeting
9:00	Studio set up	Team meeting	Alt. conc. dev.	Preferred plan synthesis	Pref. plan synthe-sis	Stake-holder review	Prod.	Stake-holder reviews as needed	Production
10:00			Stake-holder reviews (tech.)				
11:00	Tours	Alt. concepts development					
12:00	Lunch	Lunch	Lunch	Lunch	Lunch	Lunch	Lunch
1:00 PM							
2:00	Primary stakeholder meetings	Alternative concepts development	Alt. conc. dev.	Stake-holder reviews (tech.)	Pref. plan synthe-sis	Stake-holder review	Plan development	Production	Production
3:00							
4:00	Meeting preparation		Alt. concepts development				Meeting preparation
5:00				Optional open house			
	Dinner	Dinner	Dinner	Optional Open house		Dinner	Dinner
6:00							
7:00		Alternative concepts development/ team review		Preferred plan synthesis/ plan development	Optional night off		Final charrette public meeting
8:00	Public meeting #1		Public meeting #2			Production	
9:00							
10:00							Celebration
11:00							

Figure 27 *2.3 Preferred Plan Synthesis Sample Schedule*

had been placed at the fence line so that they would see houses like theirs on comparably sized lots. They said that if something had to happen that that wouldn't be so bad. I took a digital picture through their sliding glass door. Returning to the studio, I asked our renderer to draw a picture of what I described, so that the homeowners could see exactly what it would look like from their family room. The next evening, they came to the public meeting and I showed them the drawing. They were very relieved and said that they could live with it. I asked permission to show it in the meeting. It turned out to be a big selling point for the project.

This is an example of what you can do during a multiple-day charrette. The multiple days allow you to deal with the unexpected, and it is always in the unexpected where the greatest opportunities lie. This story exhibits the inclusive and open spirit of the charrette. You never know who will walk through the door in a charrette. It is important to resist the urge to deflect these people and to listen to what is going on. Most people need only go through the standard reception/gallery process, but there are always a few who represent the opportunity for collaboration on a breakthrough solution. This serves the dual purpose of solving a problem and gaining supporters. ∎

"Managed Chaos"

The charrette is a highly creative event that can be chaotic at times. As with any creative process, a great deal of excitement builds around the creation of new ideas during the beginning phase. This is often followed by a period of chaos, when doubt may creep in that a feasible and collaborative plan is possible, as the team attempts to synthesize the alternative concepts into a preferred plan. Charrette veterans have learned to recognize and work through the phase of chaos and uncertainty without creating a crisis. They know that if the chaos is allowed to run its course and if everyone relaxes and keeps working toward the project vision, after the smoke clears, the answers will become evident. Charrette managers often warn the project sponsors about this chaotic phase. This can be a very unsettling part of the charrette for a sponsor, but it is made easier with a explanation prior to the charrette of the creative planning and design process that is likely to occur. ∎

of the alternatives. One after another, ideas are discarded or moved forward, and the best ideas begin to emerge. Because these pin-ups occur in the charrette studio, it is not uncommon to welcome visiting stakeholders to join in. In this case, stakeholders are treated as members of the greater team providing input that reflects their unique viewpoints. In the spirit of the pin-up, they must be ready to defend their positions like any member of the team. These unscheduled critiques are often among the most creative educational moments of the charrette.

As with any creative process, there can be a moment of chaos before clarity emerges. This can definitely be the case at this stage of the charrette. The seasoned charrette veteran understands that this is a normal part of the creative process. A clear possibility may not be apparent, but it is just around the corner.

2.3.3 Intermediate Stakeholder Reviews

INTRODUCTION

At this point, it may be necessary to hold additional stakeholder reviews. For example, the team may be at a decision-making point, weighing two alternatives. Before the final decision can be made, primary stakeholders must be consulted. Or, if a new idea emerges that may affect a stakeholder, he or she must be consulted before the idea can be accepted and further refined.

PROCESS

The charrette manager should ask primary stakeholders for their cell phone numbers (or other preferred number) so that they can be contacted when needed. Sometimes decisions can be made over the phone. If not, the stakeholder must either come to the studio or the charrette manager must visit the stakeholder at his or her location.

2.3.4 Public Open House

INTRODUCTION

An open house is a relatively easy way to solicit further public input. An open house is often held during the preferred plan synthesis phase. At this point in the charrette, the general stakeholders have already been through two feedback loops (charrette public meetings #1 and #2), which provided several hours of open public forum discussions about the evolution of the design. The preferred plan synthesis phase is a good time to invite people to visit the charrette studio and chat with the planners and designers about the details. This type of event works particularly well on a Saturday or Sunday afternoon. It provides an additional opportunity for members of the public to comment when they have more time. Day four is the best time for an open house in the seven-day charrette model. Open houses are not recommended during the last two days of the charrette because this time is devoted to intense design development and production.

PROCESS

Ideally, an open house is held in the charrette studio. It is a relatively simple meeting to set up: The design team posts its drawings around the studio and engages in conversations with visitors about the work up to this point. This is a casual meeting with little set-up or break down. The charrette team can work right up until the meeting and return to work as soon as it is over. It is also possible to hold informal presentations in an open house. Perhaps the transportation planner has developed street sections or a transportation analysis that he or she can share at this time. In this case, the charrette manager gauges a moment when it appears that the maximum number of people are present and then asks them to gather around the transportation planner's table to listen to a brief presentation.

Conclusions for 2.3 Charrette Preferred Plan Synthesis

The creation of the preferred plan is a defining moment in a charrette. Here, pressure is on the charrette team to create the design solutions that will satisfy the issues and needs of the project sponsor and the stakeholders. Often this involves the discovery of a solution that, up to this point, no one had considered and that will allow the project to move forward. This discovery can represent a transformative event for the project and perhaps the community. People whose opposition was based on a misconceived set of solutions may now support the project. They may even emerge from the charrette with a different viewpoint regarding their community's plan for growth.

The dynamic planning strategies at play in the charrette preferred plan synthesis sub-phase are:

1. **Work collaboratively.** All parties must work in close collaboration in order for the plan to progress quickly.

2. **Design cross-functionally.** A multidisciplinary approach is essential for the type of "out-of-the-box" solutions required by complex projects.

3. **Compress work sessions.** The pressure to produce a preferred plan by the fourth day of the charrette provides the positive intensity necessary for breakthrough solutions.

4. **Use design to achieve a shared vision and create holistic solutions.** The charrette team's primary negotiating tool is design. Drawings serve to focus everyone on the problem and assure a shared understanding of the preferred plan.

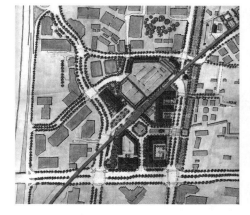

Figure 28 *Pleasant Hill BART Station Preferred Plan*

2.4 Plan Development

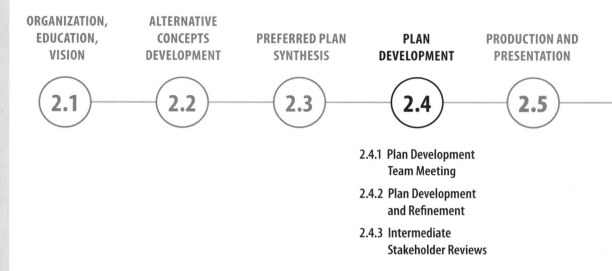

ORGANIZATION, EDUCATION, VISION **2.1**

ALTERNATIVE CONCEPTS DEVELOPMENT **2.2**

PREFERRED PLAN SYNTHESIS **2.3**

PLAN DEVELOPMENT **2.4**

PRODUCTION AND PRESENTATION **2.5**

2.4.1 Plan Development Team Meeting

2.4.2 Plan Development and Refinement

2.4.3 Intermediate Stakeholder Reviews

INTRODUCTION

Intensive, collaborative planning processes that last less than three days typically allow enough time to produce an agreed-upon plan but seldom allow enough time to conduct feasibility studies. All too often an abbreviated charrette results in a plan that must either undergo major revisions or never comes to fruition. A failed effort like this sows the seeds of distrust that can lead to community-led obstruction or apathy.

In dynamic planning, detailed testing of the preferred plan during the charrette phase provides immediate feedback to the stakeholders regarding feasibility. This immediate feedback provides the information necessary to adjust the plan during its development, thereby reducing time spent pursuing fruitless alternatives. During the plan development phase, the charrette team members study environmental impacts and economic feasibility and develop

Twelve Typical Charrette Website Elements

Peter J. Musty
Urban Designer, CharretteCenter Town Design

A website is a great resource before, during, and after the charrette. If it is well designed and useful, it will add weight, legitimacy, and trust to the process.

1. **Latest Plans:** Profile of the latest plans in storyboard fashion. Formatted like an article for easy reading. Usually on the homepage.

2. **Image Gallery:** Thumbnail catalogue of every image recorded at the charrette. Valuable for publishing efforts later in the process. Public comments may be added to each image as an interactive element.

3. **E-mail Links:** Prominent contact link on the homepage.

4. **"What Is a Charrette?":** Definition of the charrette process.

5. **Daily Schedules:** Public participation schedule and more detailed team schedule.

6. **Studio Location and Directions**: Directions and maps for download.

7. **Charrette Team Profiles:** Charrette team members' qualifications.

>>

implementation documents such as zoning plans and codes. A draft of the overall implementation action plan is also created. In addition, the team investigates elements of the plan such as schools, public squares, parks and trails, street design, and building heights that are important to primary stakeholder groups. The elements that contribute to or have a major impact on the community must be clearly illustrated. The implementation documents and detailed studies created in the plan development phase help to gain stakeholder support by showing how the plan will benefit them and how it will be built.

2.4 Plan Development Tools and Techniques
- 2.4.1 Plan Development Team Meeting
- 2.4.2 Plan Development and Refinement
- 2.4.3 Intermediate Stakeholder Reviews

2.4.1 Plan Development Team Meeting

INTRODUCTION
During the plan development team meeting, the charrette team and project sponsor determine the tasks and assignments for the plan development sub-phase of the charrette. They identify the adjustments required for the completion of the preferred plan as well as the studies necessary to address the critical interests of the primary stakeholders and to assure overall project feasibility.

PROCESS
The meeting begins with the charrette team posting the latest drawings and documents on the studio wall for review. The charrette manager refers to the objectives, strategies, and measures (1.1.1) and the charrette products list (1.1.2) when identifying which parts of the plan to study in detail, keeping in mind what will be required for the fi-

nal presentation. The stakeholder analyses (1.1.3 and 1.2.3) provide direction when choosing the studies that will address critical stakeholder interests. For instance, if one of the "wins" for a primary stakeholder is the preservation of a grove of trees, then it might be necessary to produce a detailed plan of the area showing how the trees are accommodated. With the commencement of plan development, some charrette team members may be switching from working on the overall plan to the detailed studies. The charrette manager drafts a schedule to assist in managing the large number of documents now under production.

2.4.2 Plan Development and Refinement

INTRODUCTION
During plan development and refinement, the charrette manager strives to fully utilize the individual talents of the team members by assigning tasks that employ each person's background and strengths. This part of the charrette leverages the diverse capabilities of charrette team members as they change assignments. It is not unusual for someone to begin the charrette working at the scale of an entire neighborhood or even a region and end up working on site plans of example building types.

PROCESS
The charrette manager monitors the progress of each team member while keeping an eye on the production schedule. Each charrette team member now shifts to focusing on his or her own studies rather than on the plan as a whole. The economist is running financial pro formas, the transportation planner is creating street sections, the architects are creating form-based codes, for example (see table 13 in 1.5.2). During this period, the charrette studio becomes somewhat less available to visitors. Once the charrette progress-

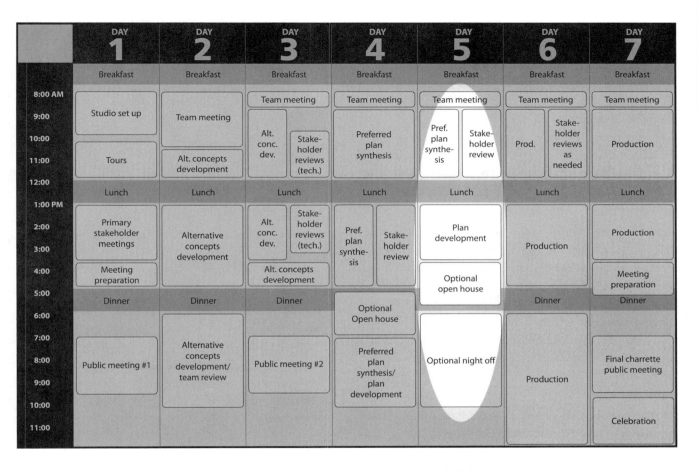

The following table is shown in the figure:

	DAY 1	DAY 2	DAY 3	DAY 4	DAY 5	DAY 6	DAY 7
	Breakfast	Breakfast	Breakfast	Breakfast	Breakfast	Breakfast	Breakfast
8:00 AM			Team meeting	Team meeting	Team meeting	Team meeting	Team meeting
9:00	Studio set up	Team meeting	Alt. conc. dev.	Preferred plan synthesis	Pref. plan synthesis	Prod.	Stakeholder reviews as needed	Production
10:00							
11:00	Tours	Alt. concepts development	Stakeholder reviews (tech.)		Stakeholder review		
12:00	Lunch	Lunch	Lunch	Lunch	Lunch	Lunch	Lunch
1:00 PM							
2:00	Primary stakeholder meetings	Alternative concepts development	Alt. conc. dev.	Stakeholder reviews (tech.)	Pref. plan synthesis	Stakeholder review	Plan development	Production	Production
3:00							
4:00	Meeting preparation		Alt. concepts development		Optional open house		Meeting preparation
5:00	Dinner	Dinner	Dinner	Optional Open house		Dinner	Dinner
6:00							
7:00	Public meeting #1	Alternative concepts development/ team review	Public meeting #2	Preferred plan synthesis/ plan development	Optional night off	Production	Final charrette public meeting
8:00							
9:00							
10:00							
11:00							Celebration

Figure 29 *2.4 Plan Development Sample Schedule*

>>

8. **Design Principles:** Values and principles used throughout the project.

9. **Research and Project Site Information:** Questions can be answered in the studio simply by referring people to this section of the website.

10. **Links and Special Resources:** List web links to relevant projects, organizations, and resources.

11. **Press Page:** Links to local press coverage of the charrette and related issues.

12. **Discussion and Review Board or Survey:** Obtaining feedback directly through the web page can supplement the public participation events—but should **never** replace them. ∎

Plan Development Detail Studies from the Pleasant Hill BART Station Charrette

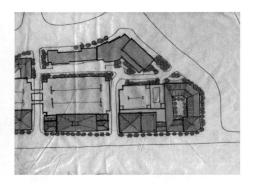

Figure 30 *Block A Detail Study*

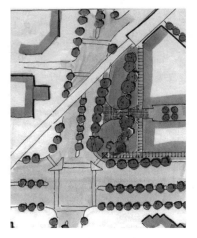

Figure 31 *Oak Grove Park Study*

es through the initial period of intense collaborative work and enters the plan development phase, the need for input is reduced. Community members are no less welcome; they are just confined to the gallery, allowing the charrette team members in the studio to focus on the final production tasks at hand.

2.4.3 Intermediate Stakeholder Reviews

INTRODUCTION

Because of the creative nature of the charrette, new ideas continue to emerge even as the team focuses on detailed studies and presentation documents for the final charrette public meeting. Significant new contributions to the preferred plan may require further meetings with the affected parties. These meetings will assure that the final presentation holds no unwelcome surprises for primary stakeholders that could undermine their support.

PROCESS

Intermediate stakeholder reviews are facilitated by an agreement with primary stakeholders to be "on call" to the charrette manager. Sometimes the matter can be solved over the phone, other times the stakeholder may have to come to the studio for a meeting. If neither option is possible, it may be necessary for the charrette manager to take the drawings to the stakeholder. It is never too late to run an idea by a primary stakeholder in order to avoid misunderstandings that may result in costly rework. In situations when large-scale disagreements remain between stakeholders about basic assumptions, such as whether or not development should occur, both options should be explored in depth and weighted against the objectives, strategies, and measures. It is important that all concepts, even the no-build option, be presented in light of their impacts and the short- and long-term trade-offs.

Conclusions for 2.4 Charrette Plan Development

The charrette plan development sub-phase of the charrette focuses on the project's feasibility and potential impacts. Without this work, a preferred plan will not be based in reality. Planning processes that create untested "visions" may never come to fruition. These exercises waste the valuable time and resources of the participants and create apathy toward the sponsoring organization. This sub-phase is essential to the holistic approach of dynamic planning and therefore should not be undervalued or cut short.

The dynamic planning strategies at play in the charrette plan development sub-phase are:

1. **Produce a feasible plan.** For a preferred plan to represent a feasible project, it must be rigorously tested for feasibility (e.g. economic impacts) and stakeholder support.

2. **Study the details and the whole.** Studies at various scales that cross-reference information from different specialties can identify potential fatal flaws in the preferred plan.

ORGANIZATION, EDUCATION, VISION

ALTERNATIVE CONCEPTS DEVELOPMENT

PREFERRED PLAN SYNTHESIS

PLAN DEVELOPMENT

PRODUCTION AND PRESENTATION

2.1 — 2.2 — 2.3 — 2.4 — **2.5**

2.5 Production and Presentation

INTRODUCTION

During the last day and a half of the charrette, the charrette team prepares for the final charrette public meeting. The presentation of the preferred plan is carefully orchestrated and designed to be an educational and inspirational event for the community. This meeting is often highlighted by a dramatic public affirmation of the preferred plan. A successful final charrette public meeting can provide the momentum for the long-term support needed for a project to survive the inevitable obstacles on its path to implementation.

The amount of attention given to the production and presentation sub-phase is a distinguishing feature of dynamic planning. The charrette team makes an intense effort during this sub-phase to produce drawings and documents of the highest professional quality. Special care is taken to produce beautiful, informative drawings and carefully prepared data to deliver a comprehensive presentation of the preferred plan and implementation strategies. The final presentation is, at its best, an impressive and entertaining event, one that makes the community proud of its collaborative effort during the previous week.

The schedule is designed to allow the charrette team to create, test, and develop the preferred plan early enough to allow sufficient time to properly prepare the final presentation. A note of caution is therefore in order: Sponsors will often attempt to cut corners by reducing the length of the production and presentation sub-phase. The opportunity to gain strong community support can be lost by abbreviating the time it takes to prepare a complete and professional presentation.

2.5 Production and Presentation Tools and Techniques
- 2.5.1 Production Team Meeting
- 2.5.2 Final Stakeholder Reviews
- 2.5.3 Production
- 2.5.4 Final Charrette Public Meeting

2.5.1 Production Team Meeting

INTRODUCTION
The charrette manager identifies and distributes the tasks, responsibilities, and schedule for the final production effort during this charrette team meeting.

PROCESS
Charrette team members post their existing drawings and documents on the studio wall for review. The charrette manager works with the team to determine which drawings and documents still need to be created and which ones

require further work. The charrette manager creates a production schedule for drawings and documents, complete with drawing descriptions, production method, assignments, and due times. Each member of the charrette team receives a copy of the production schedule before setting forth to produce his or her work products.

2.5.2 Final Stakeholder Reviews

INTRODUCTION
During the final hours of the charrette, it may be necessary to check in once again with some of the primary stakeholders. The production phase is an intense, fast-paced time and while it may seem counter-intuitive to take the time for a stakeholder meeting, this effort can go a long way toward building project support. Insights from meetings with primary stakeholders can occasionally inspire an eleventh hour adjustment to the final meeting presentation that will increase the probability of its acceptance.

PROCESS
Final stakeholder reviews occur on an as-needed basis. When necessary, the charrette manager contacts the primary stakeholders and asks them to come to the studio. Typical primary stakeholders that merit consultation at this time are elected officials, community leaders, and public agency managers. The charrette manager may choose to hold a last-minute preview of the upcoming public meeting presentation for these primary stakeholders. The charrette manager may also arrange a preview for elected officials well ahead of time in order to accommodate their schedules. This preview should occur no later than the morning before the final charrette public meeting to allow enough time to make any last-minute adjustments.

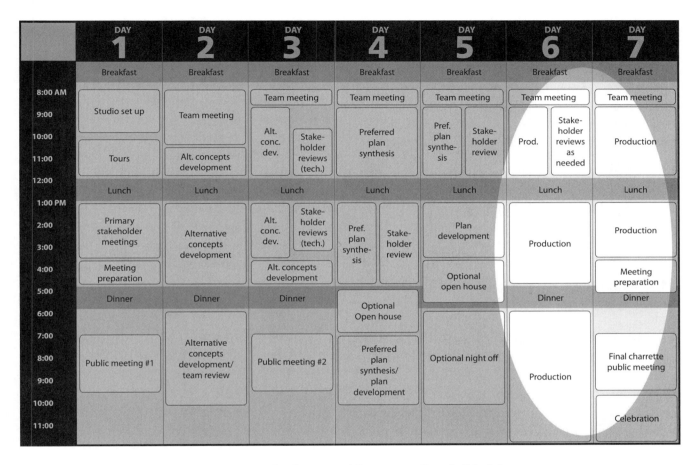

	DAY 1	DAY 2	DAY 3	DAY 4	DAY 5	DAY 6	DAY 7
	Breakfast	Breakfast	Breakfast	Breakfast	Breakfast	Breakfast	Breakfast
8:00 AM			Team meeting	Team meeting	Team meeting	Team meeting	Team meeting
9:00	Studio set up	Team meeting	Alt. conc. dev. / Stakeholder reviews (tech.)	Preferred plan synthesis	Pref. plan synthesis / Stakeholder review	Prod. / Stakeholder reviews as needed	Production
10:00							
11:00	Tours	Alt. concepts development					
12:00	Lunch	Lunch	Lunch	Lunch	Lunch	Lunch	Lunch
1:00 PM	Primary stakeholder meetings	Alternative concepts development	Alt. conc. dev. / Stakeholder reviews (tech.)	Pref. plan synthe-sis / Stakeholder review	Plan development	Production	Production
2:00							
3:00							
4:00	Meeting preparation		Alt. concepts development		Optional open house		Meeting preparation
5:00	Dinner	Dinner	Dinner	Optional Open house	Dinner	Dinner	Dinner
6:00	Public meeting #1	Alternative concepts development/ team review	Public meeting #2	Preferred plan synthesis/ plan development	Optional night off	Production	Final charrette public meeting
7:00							
8:00							
9:00							
10:00							
11:00							Celebration

Figure 32 *2.5 Production and Presentation Sample Schedule*

Charrette Production

Andrew Georgiadis
Town Planner, Dover Kohl & Partners Town Planning

During the charrette, designers produce a range of images, including the illustrative master plan, plan diagrams, rendered perspectives, photographs, and graphs. Some of them are entirely digital, such as AutoCAD or Photoshop files which are converted into PowerPoint slides, while others are handcrafted pieces.

All images must be transformed into digital files for the purpose of publication and presentation. Therefore, there should be several scanning stations in the studio. Each designer scans drawings as they are completed. Dover Kohl currently uses 8.5" x 11" HP scanners.

The illustrative master plan must be given priority over all other exhibits. Our typical master plan measures 36" x 48" but may be longer if it is a corridor study. The plan must be scanned no later than the morning of the presentation, meaning that it must be completed the evening before the presentation. When a large-format scanner is available, we send the master plan off-site to be scanned. If one is not available, we scan the plan in pieces and join them with Photoshop. We prefer large-format scanning, not only because this process consumes less time, but also because the final image will be seamless. Because we prefer not to color the original black-and-white version of the plan, the linework must

2.5.3 Production

INTRODUCTION

During the last day and a half, the charrette segues from the creative phase of developing the plan into the mechanical production phase. By now, the charrette team and the stakeholders have worked many long hours to arrive at a preferred plan that has been studied and tested for feasibility. What remains is the task of simply and clearly illustrating and documenting the plan. The production phase tests the management and organizational skills of the charrette manager, who must plan and organize the work ahead of time in order to ease the pressure and stress associated with tight deadlines.

During production, the charrette studio is in full swing, embodying the energy and spirit of the 19th century École des Beaux Arts architecture school, for which this contemporary process is named. Music is playing, espresso is brewing, and the charrette team is working at full tilt. Like an orchestra that finally has a chance to perform after hours of painstaking rehearsals, the charrette team creates an ensemble of images and data that together describe an inspiring and informative path to community transformation.

PROCESS

Most charrette practitioners utilize digital presentation software such as PowerPoint. The use of this technology saves time during the last day of the charrette (especially compared with 35-mm film technology that required several hours for processing). An efficient charrette studio is equipped with a computer station capable of digitizing drawings and transferring them into the software. The type of equipment used varies from firm to firm, but the typical set-up includes several laptop computers, a digital camera, one or more printers, and one or two scanners connected by a wireless hub. Drawings that are too large for an aver-

age size scanner can either be digitally photographed or sent out to a print shop that has a large-bed scanner.

The charrette manager prepares for the final PowerPoint presentation well in advance. Once an outline for the presentation is created, the software template can be prepared for the images. Images are then inserted into the presentation document as they become available. The charrette manager refers to the production list while monitoring the progress of the charrette team. Deadlines for the production of drawings and documents are staggered in order to avoid a holdup at the scanners and printers. Time for review and refinement should be built into the schedule.

The presentation of the preferred plan is usually composed of sections related to the different plan elements. These sections may include: land use, transportation, market and economics, urban design and architecture, codes and policy, and management strategies. It is common for each team member to work on his or her part of the presentation simultaneously (on separate laptops). This creates an additional organizational complexity for the charrette manager who must coordinate and combine the individual pieces into a unified presentation. The vast amount of information prepared by each specialist during the charrette makes it challenging to create a concise and complete presentation lasting no more than 90 minutes. The charrette manager must therefore be ready to help team members reduce their sections for the sake of a manageable presentation. Ideally, time should be set aside for a presentation rehearsal at least two hours before the meeting. This is in addition to the special presentation held earlier for primary stakeholders.

Table 19 **Final Charrette Public Presentation**
The final public presentation is a concise yet comprehensive review of the project and the plan. It typically takes up to 90 minutes to cover this material. Because of its length, the presentation must be carefully designed to be engaging. While the technical elements (usually delivered by each specialist) should be made as interesting as possible, they should also be interspersed with the visually attractive design/plan components.
SAMPLE FINAL CHARRETTE PRESENTATION ELEMENTS
Project Overview
■ Project mission, sponsors, charrette team
■ Charrette role in the approvals process
Charrette Review
■ Day-by-day review
■ Evolution of preferred plan
• Explanation of decision-making process
• Objectives, strategies, and measures for decisions on plan evolution
Preferred Plan
■ Master plan
■ Sub-area studies
■ Transportation
■ Market/economics
■ Codes
Implementation Action Plan
■ Implementation plan
■ Next steps

2.5.4 Final Charrette Public Meeting

INTRODUCTION

The final charrette public meeting has the potential to create a wave of public support that can carry a project through the inevitable obstacles to its implementation. It is the high point of the charrette, the culmination of many days of hard work by the charrette team and stakeholders. The level of expectation and energy at the final charrette public meeting is very high. The seasoned charrette manager capitalizes on this moment by orchestrating an event that will have a lasting impact on the project. The meeting should be educational and inspirational, concluding with a call for support of the final plan. The desired outcome of the public meeting is for people to leave so excited at the prospect of the project moving forward that they are willing to assist in its implementation.

PROCESS

A final charrette public meeting can last up to two and a half hours. It is broken into three segments: (1) project process and preferred plan presentation, (2) public input in the form of an open forum discussion and open house, and (3) a reception.

The project process and preferred plan presentation usually lasts no more than 90 minutes and is commonly divided into three parts. Part one is a summary of the project and the charrette process in the context of the larger approvals process. This provides an update for first-time attendees. The summary includes the proceedings from each day of the charrette as well as a description of the evolution of the plan. The second part is a comprehensive presentation of the preferred plan. This is usually accomplished with short presentations by the charrette team member specialists on such topics as transportation, economics, and codes. The third part covers the implementation plan and next steps (see Table 19).

be complete the morning before the day of the final presentation to allow for copies to be made for the coloring phase. We use a combination of markers and colored pencils to render the plan. We photograph the exhibits produced during the charrette only as a last resort.

After the scanning of the illustrative master plan and other drawings has occurred, the images must be formatted, renamed, and resampled for the PowerPoint presentation. By this stage, a folder has been established as a repository for these PowerPoint-ready files so that the principal or charrette manager who is presenting may easily insert images into the digital slide show.

While the PowerPoint show is being created, a team member plots large versions of the most important images, such as the illustrative master plan and renderings. When we have access to a plotter (such as when we work in a local engineer's or architect's office) we do the plotting. Usually, though, we must send the file to a printing company for plotting. The master plan is plotted out at its own scale (for example, 36" x 48"). Perspectives are plotted out at 24" x 36". These plots must then be mounted on boards and are unveiled at the end of the PowerPoint presentation, just as the lights are turned on. ■

The Importance of Including the Media

It is crucial to have the press involved throughout the charrette and especially at the final charrette public meeting. It is common to schedule a preview of the final presentation for the press before the public meeting, answer questions, and provide copies of the drawings for publication in the next day's newspaper. Some newspapers are so interested in covering the issues surrounding community growth that they will publish separate supplements on the project and the charrette process. ∎

The presentation is followed by an open forum discussion. The meeting facilitator takes comments with the assistance of at least two people roving the audience with wireless microphones. The forum is a pivotal moment for the charrette; the manner in which it is facilitated can lead either to success or failure. When opening the forum, the charrette manager should never simply ask people what they think about the preferred plan. Too often this type of open-ended question acts as an invitation for a negative commentator to direct the discussion. Once this happens, the meeting can take a negative turn, with other critics adding their voices to the discussion. People who were inclined to speak positively about the plan may lose their nerve, especially if they are not comfortable speaking in public. Suddenly, the meeting can take a nosedive from which it is hard to recover. In order to maintain a positive discussion, the meeting leader or facilitator first asks people what they like about the preferred plan. The facilitator then asks for suggestions for improvements. At this point, people may voice their disagreement—or even opposition—but must not be allowed to finish their critiques without providing a suggestion for improvement. This facilitation method allows for an open and critical discussion in pursuit of the best final plan.

After the forum, the facilitator concludes the formal meeting with a description of the next steps. It is essential that participants understand that their involvement does not end here. It should be made clear that the charrette products are in draft form and in need of review, testing, and revision. The revision process will occur over the four to six weeks following the meeting, after which a follow-up public meeting will be held. The public should be encouraged to continue to stay involved during the review and revision period. E-mails updating people on the project's progress should be sent out regularly, and frequent updates should be made to the project website. It should also be made clear that the next public meeting will provide another opportunity to review the revised plan and offer further input.

Before adjourning the meeting, the charrette manager may take the opportunity to call for an affirmation of the plan. If it is obvious that the atmosphere of the room is overwhelmingly positive, then he or she may venture to ask, "Did we get it right? Are we on the right track?" At this point the audience usually erupts into a round of applause. It is very important that elected officials and the press are present to witness this expression of public support for the plan. An informal open house usually follows the meeting. Participants are invited to circulate the room, discuss the charrette drawings and documents on display with the charrette team members, and complete exit questionnaires.

A post-meeting celebration is a wonderful way to end the charrette on a positive note. Whether it is a full-blown party or a simple reception, this event provides time for the sponsor, charrette team members, and stakeholders to discuss the project in a more relaxed atmosphere. Some project sponsors use the post-meeting celebration as a marketing event by inviting potential investors, developers, Realtors, tenants, and the press.

See the Pleasant Hill BART case study in Section Four for example final charrette products.

Conclusions for 2.5 Charrette Production and Presentation

The final charrette public meeting is a highly anticipated and energetic event. This meeting has the potential to garner support and momentum to carry the project through both anticipated and unforeseen obstacles for years to come. The experienced charrette manager is well aware of this potential and prepares for it from the early planning stages of the charrette. The charrette manager creates the production lists and presentation templates in anticipation of the intense production and presentation period. Veteran charrette team members hold an advantage in this sub-phase, but a skilled group of professionals new to the process, led by a well-organized charrette manager, can be very effective. The final charrette public meeting presentation should be considered a pivotal part of a larger strategy for project implementation. Therefore, the time and resources necessary for a successful final event should be allocated.

The dynamic planning strategies at play in the charrette production and presentation sub-phase are:

1. **Produce a feasible plan**. Compared with the number of documents prepared by the team over the course of the charrette, a relatively small number are chosen for the final presentation. Those that are chosen must build the case for project feasibility.

2. **Compress work sessions.** The deadline of the final charrette public meeting, and the limited amount of time available to prepare for it, catalyzes the team's efficiency and creativity.

Phase Three:
Plan Implementation

INTRODUCTION

During the plan implementation phase of dynamic planning, the project management team works to assure the continued and expanded support of the project as it is guided through adoption and development. This work includes the continued involvement of stakeholders as the charrette team tests, refines, and finalizes the charrette products. The plan implementation phase can be the most volatile part of any project. Even following a successful charrette, the project is far from over, and it is critical to maintain momentum through its completion.

Sometimes, in the interest of controlling the budget, the project sponsor will choose to minimize the involvement of the charrette team during the implementation phase. Often in such cases, team members are called back to the project only when things begin to go wrong. When this happens the charrette team may find itself in the difficult position of repairing damage caused by poor post-charrette stakeholder communications.

The passage of time can be one of the biggest enemies of project implementation. It is preferable that the implementation phase be as short as possible to reduce the risks associated with changes in political and regulatory leadership. Dynamic planning can dramatically shorten the overall project process but uncontrollable factors, such as market changes, can sometimes cause the plan implementation phase to last years. There are multiple challenges to project implementation when the process takes months or years. These challenges may include maintaining the interest and support of charrette stakeholders over a long period of time and educating new stakeholders about the agreements that were forged during the charrette.

It is important to use all means available to get agreements completed during the charrette, when everyone is there. If you fail to get an agreement during the charrette, then you will be back to the usual methods of endless meetings. Remember that the charrette is a special opportunity to conclude negotiations. (See the Plan for Central Hercules case study in Section Four for an example on the importance of concluding negotiations during the charrette.)

These potential realities make the work prepared during the plan implementation phase all the more important. The project status communications, product refinement, and final meetings have the potential to create the political and regulatory foundations needed for a project to weather an extended approvals and construction period. The charrette is a training session for local community members, staff, and officials who will be in charge of implementing the plan. A successful charrette forges a shared set of agreements on a vision and how to achieve it. Often when there is a change in the leadership of a primary stakeholder group, other parties take up the responsibility to see that the project is completed according to the charrette vision.

A famous example of this occurred with the Kentlands development in Gaithersburg, Maryland. In this project, the bank took charge of the project during the implementation phase. The neighbors and city officials made it clear to the bank that in order for the project to be approved it would have to adhere to the vision of the charrette. The result is a very successful, built, smart growth project.

Plan Implementation Sub-Phases
- 3.1 Project Status Communications
- 3.2 Product Refinement
- 3.3 Presentation and Product Finalization

3.1 Project Status Communications

INTRODUCTION

The first few weeks following a charrette represent a window of opportunity in which to guarantee positive momentum for the project. If weeks pass without communication between the project management team and the stakeholders, then any one person or group has the opportunity to control the discussion. A lack of attention during this short time frame has led to small groups of well-organized community members initiating a referendum opposing the project.

Communications and meetings following the charrette should focus on maintaining the support of the primary stakeholders. One of the most effective ways to keep the project on track after the charrette is to broadcast a vari-

STORY FROM THE FIELD

Charrette Implementation

James Kennedy
Redevelopment Director, Contra Costa County
Community Redevelopment Department

Charrettes have proven to be a very effective tool for obtaining positive and sustainable outcomes for complex land use settings. But the work does not end with the conclusion of the charrette. The experiences of Contra Costa County, California, in implementing the results of the Pleasant Hill BART Station Transit Village charrette are revealing.

The implementation of the charrette outcome required three levels of action, all of which needed to occur to retain the public trust gained during the charrette. First, the charrette outcome had to be translated into a form in which Contra Costa County could approve land use entitlements. Critical elements to accomplish this included: the preparation as part of the charrette of a coding document and the retention of a "town architect" to act as an intermediary between participants, the development team, and the county.

A second action was the incorporation of the charrette result into the property land use

>>

ety of communications regarding the project's status. It is also important to simultaneously establish a dialogue between the project management team and the primary stakeholders.

During the charrette, the charrette manager has the lead responsibility for most of the activities. After the charrette, during the plan implementation phase, the majority of the responsibility shifts back to the project manager. The project manager must be on the lookout for any changes in the primary stakeholder group. When new people important to the project present themselves they must be contacted immediately and educated about the project and the charrette proceedings.

3.1 Project Status Communications Tools and Techniques
- 3.1.1 Project Management Team Debriefing
- 3.1.2 Public Communications

3.1.1 Project Management Team Debriefing

INTRODUCTION
The purpose of the project management team debriefing is to compare notes on the results of the charrette while the charrette is still fresh in people's minds. The project manager holds a series of meetings with those who are most closely involved in the project, including the project management team, the project sponsor, and any project steering committees. During these meetings, the project management team must agree upon a communications strategy and plan for the implementation phase. The team must also identify any areas of the final charrette plan that require review and possible revision. These meetings are one way to assure that the team and primary stakeholders remain supportive of the project.

PROCESS
Project management team debriefings should ideally begin the day after the charrette. During this first meeting, the charrette manager leads the group through a review of the charrette and the final public meeting outcomes. Topics for discussion include the role of the press and post-charrette community politics. It is also useful to revisit the stakeholder analysis to identify any key people or groups who require special communications in order to ensure that they support the project. Another goal is to identify areas of the charrette plan that may require potential revisions. At the end of the meeting, assignments are distributed to the charrette team for document review and revision. Finally, a communications plan should be drafted identifying major channels for communications and the meetings required with primary stakeholders.

Over the following several months, the project manager holds meetings with the project management team, the project sponsor, and project steering committees. In this way, people are kept up to date on the project status, revisions are reviewed and checked with primary stakeholders, and any necessary adjustments are made to the communications plan.

3.1.2 Public Communications

INTRODUCTION
Because most people have access to instant information via the Internet, it is imperative that the project manager and sponsor take the initiative to publicize the outcomes of the charrette as soon as possible. The project sponsor staff should be the first to communicate the project status. They should establish their position as the primary source of information regarding the outcome of the charrette. Failure to do so provides the opportunity for others to step in and

create their own versions of the proceedings. A comprehensive public communications plan includes strategies for written informational pieces about the charrette as well as meetings with primary stakeholders.

PROCESS

The public communications plan is guided by the most current stakeholder analysis and the post-charrette communications strategy. The most immediate means for communication is the project website, which should be immediately updated to include the proceedings and final products of the charrette. Other communication methods include articles in local newspapers and informational flyers produced by the project management team. Sometimes the local newspaper has a significant enough interest to create a Sunday supplement covering the complete charrette process.

Members of the project management team should also meet with primary stakeholders during this period. These include one-on-one meetings with elected officials and the leaders of neighborhood associations and public agencies. It may also be necessary to make presentations about the charrette outcomes at community and church meetings. The project management team should do whatever it takes to reassure the community during the potentially volatile implementation phase.

Conclusions for 3.1 Project Status Communications

The charrette is a powerful community event that can release a wave of momentum. Those who are the first to catch this wave often determine the post-charrette political direction. In this age of instant communication it is relatively easy for an individual or group to quickly gain the position

as "the" information source regarding the charrette. It is becoming more and more common for a small group of organized community members to emerge after the charrette and take control of the debate through the use of the Internet. Therefore, the project management team must seize control of the message by communicating the correct version of the charrette proceedings in as many ways as possible. Public relations experts say, "If you don't set the table, someone else will set it for you." This adage certainly applies to post-charrette communications.

The dynamic planning strategies at play in the project status communications sub-phase are:

1. **Work collaboratively.** Collaboration doesn't stop at the end of the charrette. The final position of the stakeholders on the project can depend as much as on how they are treated after the charrette as while it is happening.

2. **Communicate in short feedback loops.** Immediate communication after the charrette keeps the feedback loop process intact.

>>

entitlements. This was accomplished by using the county's Planned Unit District (PUD) zoning, which essentially allowed the county to incorporate into the land use ordinances the entire charrette results, including the Codes, Development Standards, and Landscape Standards. Without a flexible zoning tool, the results of the charrette simply could not have been implemented.

The third action was the presence of an entity to carry much of the financial burden associated with the charrette development program. The Contra Costa County Redevelopment Agency's ability to finance critical public facilities, place making amenities, and infrastructure was a vital element in achieving the desired outcome.

At its conclusion the land use entitlement process for the Pleasant Hill BART Transit Village ended with unanimous approval and no public opposition. From the perspectives of both the developer and the county the investment in the charrette allowed the parties to achieve the one elusive commodity that had been missing from all prior efforts for the site: permitting certainty. ∎

3.2 Product Refinement

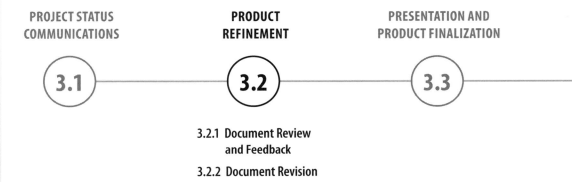

INTRODUCTION

One of the primary goals of dynamic planning is to accelerate the project implementation phase by minimizing rework. It is not uncommon for very few revisions to the preferred plan to be necessary during the engineering and construction process. This can translate into substantial cost savings in the implementation phase, particularly when compared with conventional planning processes.

During the product refinement sub-phase, the charrette team performs a final round of testing and refinement of the preferred plan. This is completed as soon as possible after the charrette, while the information is still fresh in the team members' minds. This exercise not only assures plan feasibility but also promotes the continued involvement of the primary stakeholders in the testing process. This will help to maintain the critical support of primary stakeholders through project implementation.

Strategic Actions and Implementation

Elizabeth Plater-Zyberk
Founding Principal, Duany Plater-Zyberk & Company

A list of strategic actions for implementation can be a helpful part of the charrette report. In community building there are three categories of strategic actions: design, policy, and management. These three categories are interrelated and can be addressed concurrently during the charrette. It is important to distinguish which type of solution is required for each issue that arises. Crime, for example, is a problem that can be addressed by policing techniques, a management action; however, design can facilitate the management of a safe environment with building facades having "eyes on the street."

Implementation can be further encouraged by identifying the actor (who) for each action (what) and the time frame (when). For example:

Design Actions
Design actions relate to the physical environment, such as "provide landscaped traffic calming circle for the intersection of Galiano and Salzedo Streets." Recommending that specific design and construction projects that are feasible in the short term be undertaken immediately after the charrette reinforces the plan with an early example of its intent.

>>

3.2 Product Refinement Tools and Techniques
- 3.2.1 Document Review and Feedback
- 3.2.2 Document Revision

3.2.1 Document Review and Feedback

INTRODUCTION
The primary purpose of document review and feedback is to solicit input from the charrette team and the primary stakeholders regarding the feasibility of the preferred plan. The documents referred to here are the charrette products: the drawings, analysis, reports, and policies that make up the preferred plan. Therefore, the primary stakeholders, public agencies, elected officials, and neighborhood leaders, as well as the charrette and sponsor team members, should all be involved in the review and feedback cycle.

PROCESS
During the document review and feedback period, each charrette team member reviews and analyzes the areas of the plan for which he or she is responsible. The transportation planner may model the performance of the street network. The finance and marketing experts may run pro formas that measure market and financial feasibility. The civil engineer may review the grading and drainage plan. During this time, the charrette manager is communicating with representatives of regulatory agencies to assure that the preferred plan meets their requirements and that they are supportive of the plan. Community feedback is solicited through the project website, during community meetings, and in one-on-one meetings with community leaders. If the charrette team anticipates the need for major revisions to the preferred plan it may be necessary to confirm the primary stakeholders' support of the revisions before the final project public meeting.

Some members of the charrette team focus on the implementation plan at this time. The basic elements of the implementation plan will have been outlined in the charrette as part of the feasibility testing. During this revision phase, those elements are expanded and refined through discussions with those who will take positions of responsibility during the implementation phase. The implementation plan can be organized into three areas: design, policy, and management issues (see text box in 3.1 introduction). During this period, the charrette manager communicates with people who have major roles in the implementation plan to ensure that they understand and agree to their responsibilities.

3.2.2 Document Revision

INTRODUCTION
The review and feedback period ideally takes no more than one month to complete. By then all pertinent information required to make the necessary revisions to the preferred plan should be available to the charrette team. Any potential weaknesses, as well as opportunities for improvement, have been identified and the team must now decide which changes to the plan will be made.

PROCESS
During the document revision period, the charrette manager convenes a meeting of the project management team for the purposes of reviewing the recommendations of the project team members and deciding on the final revisions to the preferred plan. During this process, the team must continue to refer to the objectives, strategies, and measures (1.1.1) agreements to assure the primary stakeholders that the revisions adhere to the previous agreements. After this meeting, the charrette team finalizes its revisions in preparation

for the final review with primary and general stakeholders. At this stage it is important that revised drawings and documents do not look completely finished. Stakeholders must be shown that, even at this late stage of the process, the plan is a work in progress and that their input can still make a difference to the outcome.

Conclusions for 3.2 Product Refinement

Product refinement is an essential step for assuring that the preferred plan is feasible both physically and politically. Failure to attend to the stakeholder communications and plan testing required in this phase can cause delays or even termination of the project. The time and money spent during this sub-phase provide insurance for project implementation. It is a small sum to pay when compared with the resources required to start a project from scratch.

The dynamic planning strategies at play in the product refinement sub-phase are:

1. **Design cross-functionally**. The charrette team continues to work together to test and refine the preferred plan.

2. **Confirm progress through measuring outcomes.** The OSM is utilized by the team throughout document review and feedback as a tool for testing the plan.

3. **Produce a feasible plan.** The primary goal of the refinement work is to assure that the plan is feasible according to all agreed upon measures.

>>

Policy Actions
Policy actions are the regulations that control development to ensure public benefit by private development. These include comprehensive plans, zoning codes, and form-based codes. They provide the regulatory basis for the plan's implementation, promoting physical predictability during building and rebuilding, an important encouragement for investors and property developers. Example: "Revise the zoning code to allow open air shopping and dining."

Management Actions
Management actions precede design and policy in importance. Maintaining a safe, clean, and functioning environment can be integrated with supportive design and policy. For example, to ensure the success of a main street renewal, creation of a business district to manage parking and trash removal and to run promotions and festivals complements the effect of appropriately designed retail frontages and streetscape. ∎

3.3 Presentation and Product Finalization

PROJECT STATUS COMMUNICATIONS

3.1

PRODUCT REFINEMENT

3.2

PRESENTATION AND PRODUCT FINALIZATION

3.3

3.3.1 Final Project Public Meetings

3.3.2 Project Closeout

INTRODUCTION

The dynamic planning process concludes with a final set of public meetings and production of the project report. It is the opportunity to complete the final feedback loop with the general stakeholders and to solidify their support. Upon completion of these final meetings, the charrette team can complete the final set of drawings and project documents with confidence.

TIP

The Final Charrette Report

David Brain

Professor, New College of Florida

The final charrette report can be a very effective tool for civic education when translated into a widely disseminated publication. It can also provide the support community members and leaders need to carry the shared understanding and collaborative spirit of the charrette into the implementation of a vision.

It is important to keep a final report tight and focused. An introductory section should articulate the overall purpose and orientation of the plan and should also reemphasize the way the plan grew out of a participatory process. Essentially, the report should be grounded directly in the discussions that occurred during the charrette.

It is a good idea to assign someone to observe and take detailed notes of discussions throughout charrette public meetings. These notes are invaluable when writing an accurate final report, reflecting the richness of charrette discussions and documenting the process of formulating proposals responsive to the diverse points of view that often emerge.

In the context of a master planning process, final reports generally present two major categories of proposals. First are the general controls that constitute the implementation framework: e.g., the regulating

>>

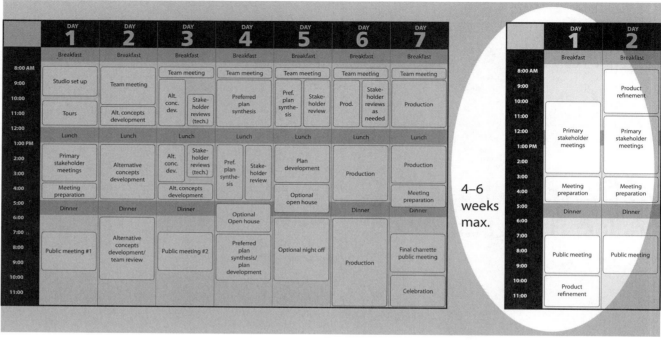

Review
& revise

Final
review

Figure 33 *3.3 Presentation and Product Finalization Sample Schedule*

3.3 Presentation and Product Finalization Tools and Techniques
- 3.3.1 Final Project Public Meetings
- 3.3.2 Project Closeout

3.3.1 Final Project Public Meetings

INTRODUCTION

The final project public meetings are a great opportunity to defuse any post-charrette project opposition and to shore up community support. The meetings should be designed in part to provide a safety net for people who are new to the project. The concerns of these people are best accommodated as they are in the charrette, through a feedback loop consisting of proposal, feedback, and response.

PROCESS

The final project public meetings ideally occur four to six weeks after the charrette. If they are held any later than this, there is the potential for a change in leadership that can have a destabilizing effect on the project. This event can be a stand-alone evening meeting or a pair of evening meetings occurring one or two days apart. The two-meeting model is especially effective for projects that remain volatile after the charrette or for projects with significant post-charrette revisions. This provides an important forum for those who were either absent from the charrette or for those who maintain serious reservations about the state of the project. In this format, a select group of charrette team members returns to the community for two days. The first day is spent meeting with primary stakeholders. The recommended plan revisions are presented that evening in a public meeting during which the team solicits another round of community input. The team works the next day

to incorporate the public input into a final set of recommended revisions. This final revised plan is presented the next night at another public meeting. This process provides the advantage of a final feedback loop with the primary and general stakeholders. This is an effective method for dealing with people who, for one reason or another, were not at the charrette. These people may enter the meetings much the same way as one would enter the first meeting of the charrette, with questions and on guard. In the two-meeting process, their concerns can be addressed and responded to in a short period of time. This format has proved very effective for solidifying community support. It also gives the project management team the confidence to finalize the documents knowing that the plan is feasible and will be supported by the majority of stakeholders.

Table 20 **Sample Final Project Public Meeting Agenda (7:00–9:30 p.m., first night)**	
7:00	Meeting start ups
7:15	Project goals/process refresher
7:30	Clarification questions
7:45	Recommended revisions to charrette plan
8:15	Discussion forum
8:50	Next steps
9:00	Open house

>>

plan and its associated policies, architectural and urban codes, general standards covering relevant components of the plan. Second are specific catalyzing projects that simultaneously demonstrate key principles and constitute strategic interventions that can be implemented relatively quickly. Such projects build faith in the plan, as well as momentum in the implementation process.

A three-part format can be very effective when presenting each specific proposal within the overall framework of the plan. These three sections are observation, discussion, and recommendation. The initial observation states the facts of the case as discovered during the charrette. The discussion section explains the issues at stake, documents differing points of view as they arose in the charrette process, and explains the rationale for the proposed solution. The recommendation describes the specific actions to be taken in response, and is thereby clearly connected to a charrette-based rationale. The final charrette report should enable people who were not at the charrette to understand not only the specifics of each proposal, but the underlying rationale as it emerged from the process. ■

TIP

The Three-legged Stool: Charrettes, Urban Design, and Form-based Codes

Peter Katz
President, Form-Based Codes Institute

As wonderful as the charrette process is, it does not do its work alone. Within the context of new urbanism and smart growth development, the charrette is just one leg of a three-legged stool. The other two legs are *compelling urban design* and *form-based development regulations*.

When community members first see a dramatic new vision of their community, they are often taken aback. But as they start to consider new possibilities, they take a "transformative leap." They wonder if they could really have a public square and a new branch library like the one shown in the rendering. Despite fears of increased density and related impacts, community members *will* accept growth if it is packaged in a compelling urban design that includes features they want in their community.

The next stage in the charrette may involve a certain amount of skepticism on the part of community members. They question whether the beautiful images and project features they are seeing ever could ever be realized.

3.3.2 Project Closeout

INTRODUCTION

A dynamic planning project concludes with the creation of a set of documents that concisely describes the project, the process, and the plan. These documents should cover the entire dynamic planning process, highlighting stakeholder involvement and decision making. An important purpose of these documents is to stand as a public record to assist any forthcoming adoption processes or formal plan applications. The documents must also be capable of educating those who did not participate in the process previously. For some, the closeout signals the end of their involvement with the project and for others it represents the beginning of their implementation responsibilities.

PROCESS

The project manager is responsible for the assembly of the final project report that commonly includes a regulating or zoning plan, the form-based codes, the project process report, and the all-important implementation action plan. It is a comprehensive report that documents the project and, as some project sponsors have said, makes it "bulletproof" to any legal challenges. One way to assist in the assembly of this report is to staff the charrette team with a recorder who is assigned to document the proceedings of the charrette for inclusion in the final report. After assembling a draft version of the report, but before producing the final version, the charrette manager circulates the draft among the primary stakeholders and the charrette team members for review.

Conclusions for 3.3 Presentation and Product Finalization

The presentation and product finalization sub-phase provides the opportunity for the project management team to make the final technical and political adjustments necessary to send the project into the public approvals process with positive momentum. If the team has been diligent in attending to the details of the dynamic planning process, particularly by maintaining the feedback loops with the stakeholders, then project closeout should hold no surprises and should proceed with ease. Projects that adhere to this model have a history of experiencing very little opposition throughout the public hearings process.

The dynamic planning strategies at play in the presentation and product finalization sub-phase are:

1. **Produce a feasible plan.** The final project documents are the main project implementation tools.

2. **Use design to achieve a shared vision and create holistic solutions.** The success of the final presentations is strongly dependent on descriptive and inspirational design drawings.

Table 21 **Example Final Report Table of Contents from an Area Master Plan Project**

1. Introduction	**5. Plan**
■ Mission and vision	■ Charrette log — the evolution of the plan
■ Project process	■ Preferred plan documents
■ Summary of the preferred plan	● Preferred illustrative plan
2. Background	● Illustrations and perspectives
■ Project chronology	● Economic analysis
■ Regional context	● Transportation system
■ Comprehensive plan	● Transit plan
3. Physical and financial context	● Parking analysis
■ Site description	● Regulating plan
■ Market analysis	● Form-based codes
■ Transit opportunities	**6. Appendices**
■ Transportation existing conditions	■ Financial model assumptions and structure
4. Public Process	■ Traffic counts and other relevant traffic background
■ Public involvement process	■ Public proceedings log
■ Summary of stakeholder issues	■ Design concept iterations
■ Objectives, strategies, and measures	■ Public comments made during events
■ The charrette	

>>

Form-based codes, which represent actual development ordinances, help to address such concerns. The codes work best when they are developed in draft form during the charrette. Presenting the proposed ordinance alongside the finished renderings brings increased confidence that what is drawn might actually be built. Furthermore, by riding the wave of enthusiasm that accompanies the charrette process, the form-based codes can become law much more quickly, thus minimizing the inevitable watering-down process that can severely compromise a worthy development plan. ■

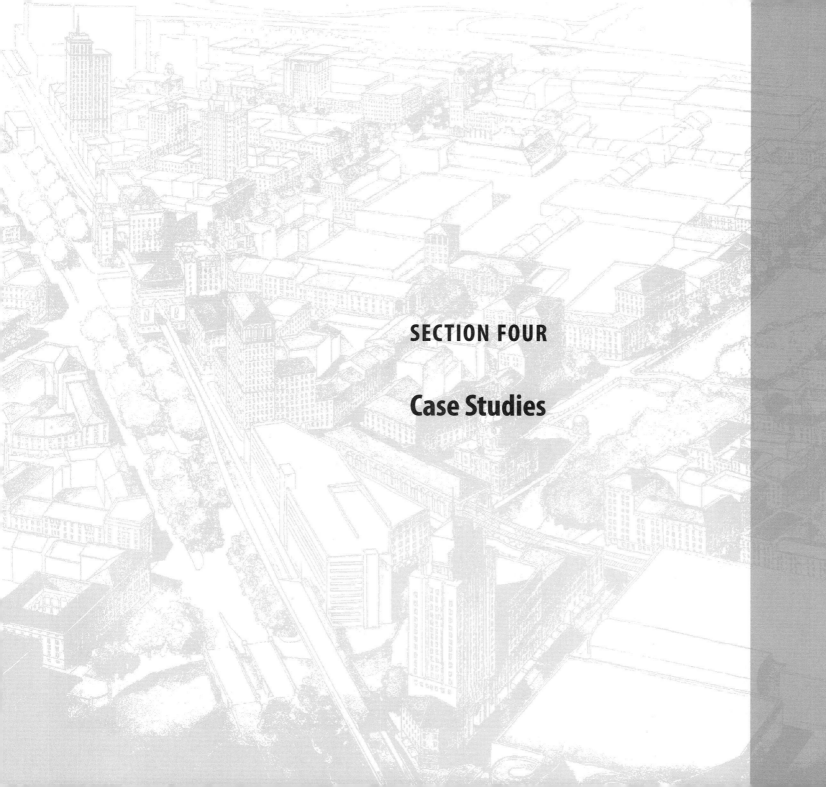

SECTION FOUR

Case Studies

4

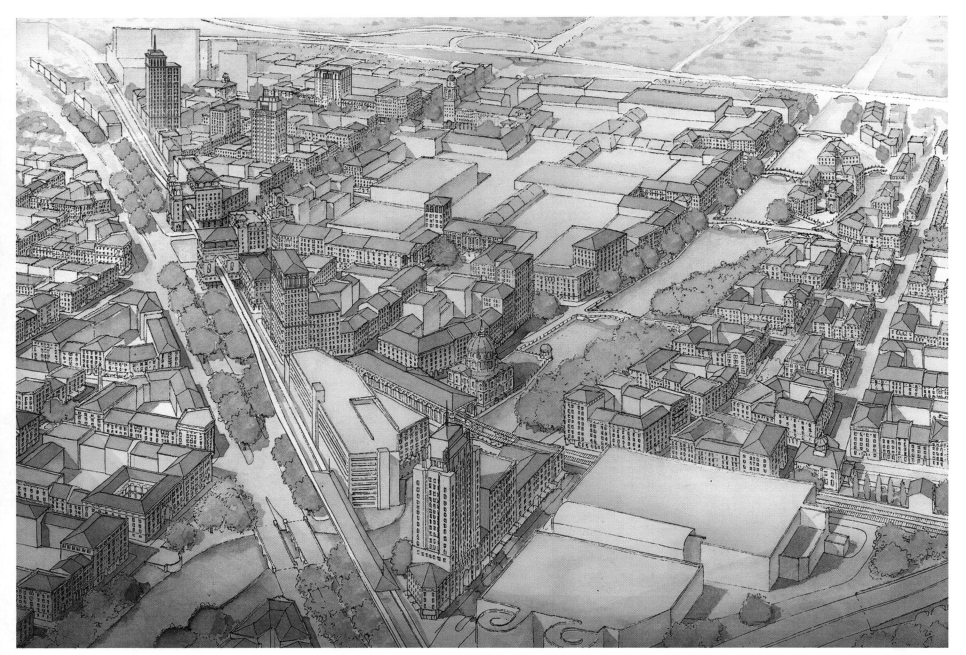

Figure 34 *Downtown Kendall, Florida. Aerial view showing existing shopping mall surrounded by street-oriented retail with housing above.*

Downtown Kendall, Florida

INTRODUCTION

In a dramatic success story of transformation, Downtown Kendall, in Miami-Dade County, Florida, is evolving from a suburban-style commercial center to an urban, mixed-use downtown. In an environment of skepticism among community members, county government, neighboring municipalities, developers and business owners, the combination of the dynamic planning process and the principles of new urbanism resulted in a creative vision that will forever alter Downtown Kendall. During the charrette, it was discovered that both residents and private developers valued pedestrian connectivity and high-quality public spaces, and this agreement resulted in a new urban plan with streets, arcades, squares, and greens. The charrette as a public forum allowed these parties to recognize their shared values and begin to implement them.

HISTORY OF THE SITE

Until recently, the site existed as a 338-acre commercial crossroads in suburban Miami-Dade County. With limited-access highways on two sides, and in spite of its commuter rail stations, the area was auto-oriented with empty buildings and huge parking lots surrounding the 1.4 million sq. ft. Dadeland Mall. Talk of transforming this area into a pedestrian-friendly, mixed-use new urbanist development—"Downtown Kendall"—was laughable; there was no "downtown." Prior to the 1960s, the area was farmland. With the 1960s came the mall, highways, and car dealerships. During the 1980s the transit system was established, and several office towers and a high-rise hotel were built.

WHAT LED TO THE CHARRETTE?

This history, the location, and the infrastructure led to the area's designation in the county's Comprehensive Development Master Plan as a "future urban center." The area includes two major heavy rail stations used by commuters (Dadeland South and Dadeland North). Dadeland South is the end of the line, a transfer point to the South Miami-Dade Dade Busway, with multiple bus lines converging at these stations.

Residents were fed up with development patterns, and they were making things difficult for developers by opposing permits. Paul Vrooman, Chamber South's then-marketing director, began to wonder about the region's growth. He remembers asking himself, "Where are the gathering places if there are only malls? Where will people watch the Fourth of July fireworks and listen to jazz concerts?" Chamber South, the South Miami-Dade/South Miami/Kendall chamber of commerce, was impressed by the changes that had occurred in downtown South Miami as a result of a master plan designed by town planners Dover Kohl & Partners. Chamber South asked Dover Kohl for its help transforming Downtown Kendall into an urban center.

Private business and property owners in the area were motivated to participate by the fact that permitting new development had become more difficult. Nearby residents, frustrated by sprawl, agreed that a new start on planning was needed for the area. Dover Kohl recommended that the project be co-funded by the county and private property owners within the project area. The agreement of the property owners to share the cost was a transformative event

Mission

"The vision of the Downtown Kendall project is to create a thriving center of activity in Kendall with a consistent and appealing urban identity. This community will include a strong shopping presence as well as residential projects, hotel and convention facilities, community activity features and green space in a pedestrian-friendly environment. There should be a comprehensive community-based plan for this which calls for an intense use of space that serves as a model of urban infill development."

— Mission statement adopted by the Kendall Council of Chamber South (local chamber of commerce)

during the pre-charrette process.

Chamber South proposed that Dover Kohl partner with Duany Plater-Zyberk & Company (DPZ). Firm principals were excited to work together, as they had in the past, and in a region where their offices are located. Victor Dover writes, "We thought it deserved attention from as many of the leading urbanists as possible."

PROCESS DESCRIPTION

In addition to designers and town planners at Dover Kohl & Partners and DPZ, many other individuals and organizations played major parts before and during the charrette. Chamber South was the convener, led by its president, Donna Masson. Miami-Dade County was the largest funder, the regulator that was to adopt the results of the charrette. There was a multi-stakeholder committee composed of more than 20 assembled by Chamber South. It included local business leaders, property owners (led by chair Richard Norton), and neighbors from nearby neighborhoods (led by activist Albert Harum-Alvarez). Rick Hall, a new urbanist traffic engineer, was brought in to consult. South Florida Water Management, the county transit authority, and attorneys representing property owners and developers were also involved throughout the charrette.

Although there had been stakeholder group meetings prior to Dover Kohl's involvement with the project, meetings were opened to the public after the firm was brought in. Also, to prepare the community for the charrette, public lectures and rallies, hosted by the chamber and county, were held. Speakers included Peter Katz, new urbanist author and consultant; Elizabeth Plater-Zyberk, dean of the University of Miami School of Architecture and founding principal of DPZ; and Kristen Paulsen Pickus, planner and smart growth educator. The lectures covered such topics as edge cities, retail, and how "great cities can do great things." They were used to inform and inspire with nu-

merous examples of other communities around the country that were developing with similar goals.

The charrette took place over seven days in June of 1998 at the Dadeland Marriott. Before, during, and after the charrette, the *Miami Herald* tracked the story closely.

A Transformative Charrette Moment

Around the time when the charrette team and Chamber South were preparing for the charrette, a developer arrived with an application to build a tower complex, the Dadeland Galaxy, on the site of a former Cadillac dealership. The proposed building rose 390 feet, but the height limit was only 300. The developer asked for a variance for the Dadeland Galaxy project that was stridently opposed by business owners and neighbors. The proposed building was cited during public meetings as another example of "out of control" development. The variance was approved by the county, which prompted a neighboring municipality to file a lawsuit objecting to the process. The neighboring Village of Pinecrest brought forward a complaint that the county had not followed the proper public procedure in approving Dadeland Galaxy. Village residents claimed that their objections were not given due process. The whole situation contributed to an environment of distrust, especially between county leaders and local residents. This impasse provided an opportunity for the charrette to focus and solve a core issue.

The solution, generated during the charrette, was a new approach to building height in which limitations were measured in stories, not feet. However, the number of stories could no longer be varied. The developer who had originally requested the variance to build a 390-foot-tall building abandoned that plan and is currently building a six- and seven-story development. The method of measuring height in feet led developers to maximize square footage by minimizing ceiling height, an option that results in less attractive and cramped spaces. Measuring building height by stories

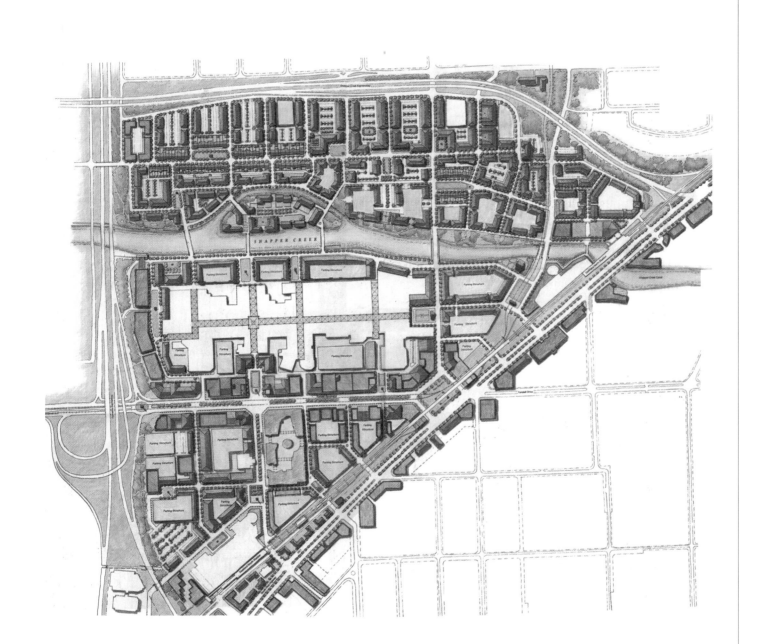

Figure 35 *Downtown Kendall long term illustrative plan. Existing mall is in the center.*

eliminates the advantage of low ceiling heights. Developers could build higher by raising the ceiling height and, in turn, improve the living spaces. The resulting flexibility in floor to floor dimensions contributes to variety in the skyline while maintaining a cap on overall floor area. Additionally, fewer tenants in the new buildings results in less traffic.

CHARRETTE RESULTS

The intent of the charrette plan was, in Victor Dover's words, to replace Kendall's "chaotic development" with "coherent town building." The charrette resulted in unanimous approval of the final plan by the Miami-Dade Planning Commission. Subsequently, the same team produced the Downtown Kendall Urban Center District Code, which was approved unanimously by the Miami-Dade County Commission, and is today guiding the build-out of Downtown Kendall.

Kendall's existing superblock pattern was transformed in the plan created during the charrette, resulting in smaller blocks and more streets. However, the county street standards were not capable of delivering the quality of streets and sidewalks required in the pedestrian-oriented development model. In this model, developers would be required to spend considerable resources to propose and negotiate alternate street designs for every project submittal. With this in mind, the county planning department hired transportation engineer Rick Hall to design a street template that made the developers' jobs easier and increased the feasibility of better street design. The street template would eliminate the developers' costly and time-consuming process.

IMPLEMENTATION DESCRIPTION

Although the owners and managers of Dadeland Mall (Simon Properties and Lend-Lease Corporation) participated in the charrette, soon after the ordinance was adopted they filed a property-rights claim. They did not buy into the street-oriented model and wanted to be able to maintain their standard mall development, fearing that the ordinance would hinder "business as usual." They wanted to be excepted from the ordinance. By returning to the basic principles of the charrette plan, refining language regarding grandfathering of pre-existing rights, and subtly modifying the official maps to incorporate new information from the mall owners, a compromise was found. In response to the claim brought by the developers, urban designer Jonathan Barnett and urban economist Chris Leinberger were brought in to consult on creating a workable compromise. Barnett suggested small changes to the master plan while Leinberger made a powerful economic argument in favor of street-oriented development. A solid base of public support helped ease the changes, which strengthened the original plan.

During the first 18 months following the plan's approval, more than 3,000 dwelling units, commercial space, and hotels proceeded through the permitting process. The new development met with rapid market acceptance. Currently, approximately six city blocks, named "Downtown Dadeland," including residential and commercial uses, have been developed. Another eight city blocks comprising an urban quarter named "The Colonnade" are under construction, including a 25-story high rise that is mainly residential.

LESSONS LEARNED

Establishing the right relationship between public and private sponsors was an important foundation for this project, in particular, its initiation and guidance by the nonprofit Chamber South and a diverse and inclusive guiding committee. The process of design investigation using short feedback loops enabled the charrette team to develop a win/win solution to the building height controversy.

Figure 36 *Downtown Kendall under construction. Pedestrian-scale streetfront with residential towers behind.*

Figures 37 and 38 *Transformation of street into boulevard with street-oriented retail*

Figure 39 *View of Bedford Avenue live-work units*

Bedford Avenue, Nashville, Tennessee

INTRODUCTION

Bedford Avenue in Nashville, Tennessee, is an example of how a residential avenue evolved into a commercial street. Decades of struggle over the future of the street pitted developers against residents and residents against residents. Land values and market pressures were causing developers to seek commercial rezoning while most of the residents were concerned about losing their residential quality of life. Strong political leadership combined with a charrette process brought an end to the deadlock by creating an overlay zone with design goals and objectives, a concept plan for development, and a form-based code that would allow commercial development to coexist with the existing residential neighborhood.

HISTORY OF THE SITE

For 40 years, people along Bedford Avenue in Nashville were caught in a tug-of-war. Because it is a highly desirable area of the county, with markets for both residential and commercial, people had been fighting to zone the area either completely residential or completely retail. Bedford is a single street between a single-family neighborhood called Woodmont Estates (Cross Creek is a street in this neighborhood that backs up to properties on Bedford Avenue) and the Green Hills Mall (a regional shopping mall). The Green Hills area is southwest of downtown and the inner city neighborhoods. While it has been around for quite a while, it is mostly suburban. The Green Hills area envelops Bedford Avenue as well as Woodmont estates and Cross Creek. According to Mary Jon Hicks, a neighborhood ac-

tivist, Bedford homeowners were beginning to lease out their houses as rental spaces and these were becoming dilapidated. Some Bedford owners of the rental houses wanted to sell their property for commercial use so that they could make top dollar and rid themselves of the rundown houses. However, the houses were zoned residential. Still others wanted nothing to do with the business district and wanted a barricade between it and their homes.

WHAT LED TO THE CHARRETTE?

Metro councilman Jim Shulman understood the neighborhood's opposition to rezoning and development—the residents (quickly turning into NIMBYs) did not want new commercial development abutting their properties. The policy plan for the area, a document that the planning staff uses to make recommendations to the Metro council, called for Bedford to be a transition between the Woodmont Estates neighborhood and the Green Hills Mall area. Over the past 40 years, individual property owners as well as developers with proposals for the entire street had been trying to rezone it commercial. In 2002, district council member Jim Shulman requested that the planning department work on a compromise. The planning department's design studio saw the need for a process that would allow a workable compromise and proposed a charrette. Shulman became the project's champion, welcoming attendees at all of the public meetings with the design studio leading the charrette. His presence as an elected official reassured the attendees that their concerns would be taken seriously.

As the process moved forward, Mary Jon Hicks acted as

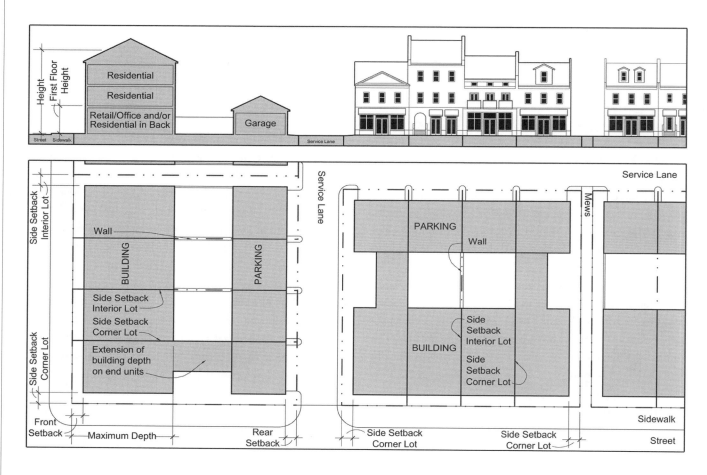

Figure 40 *Form-based code graphic for live-work units*

a mediator and information conduit and worked with the planners to reach a compromise with the residents of Cross Creek. Shulman and Hicks decided to use the charrette to develop a plan that reflected the community's desires instead of waiting for a developer to come to them with an acceptable plan.

Before the charrette began, a notice was mailed out to every property owner within 300 feet of the proposed development inviting them to the public meetings. At this point, there were no proposals on the table. One major pre-charrette meeting was held two weeks before the start of the

charrette. The ground rules (no grandstanding, no personal attacks, no one could erase anyone else's comments during work with maps) for the charrette and subsequent public meetings were laid down. Approximately 50 people attended. Metro planning staff described the purpose of the charrette and what the charrette process would be like. Then, attendees broke into small groups to confirm the study area. It was solely an informational meeting to prepare the public for the commencement of the charrette.

A critical part of the charrette occurred when the city hired an independent market analyst, acceptable to both the residents and the potential developers. The background economic analysis illustrated to the neighborhood that the current low-density residential use was not viable and that there was a need and a strong market for more intense development. These results were presented during the pre-charrette meeting.

PROCESS DESCRIPTION

The three-day charrette was held in February of 2003 in the Junior League headquarters in Green Hills, about a block from the development site. On the first day, input from the public was gathered through a visioning session where attendees broke into small groups, looked at aerial maps of the study area, and answered questions regarding what they liked about the area, disliked about the area, and what they preferred for the future growth of the area. On the second day, all vision maps were consolidated into a single plan examining all of the relevant issues. Design on three different design concepts started that afternoon; one was completely residential, one was completely retail, and the last plan combined both. That evening, staff presented the consolidated issues and the three concept plans to the public. Following the presentation and subsequent discussion, the community decided on the preferred direction, which was a combination of two concepts being studied and developed. The final presentation was accepted on the evening of the third day.

The charrette ended with an agreed-upon design plan for the area, and an urban design zoning overlay was proposed to implement the plan. Overall, the charrette enabled the community to establish a direction for the neighborhood and identify a way to implement it.

Because this project addressed a discrete question concerning street rezoning, the charrette organizers were able to complete this charrette in three days. Although it was a thorny situation, in the end it had a relatively simple dy-

namic. The process was also helped along by capable political leadership, both at city hall and at the neighborhood level, with a shared desire to solve the problem.

IMPLEMENTATION DESCRIPTION

The charrette produced a land use compromise: One side of the street would be residential and office and the other side would be mixed-use. However, both sides would be visually compatible with one another as prescribed in the form-based code of the overlay.

After this successful charrette, there remained a disagreement regarding the manner in which the infrastructure would be built. Metro had to find a way to build the development incrementally as there was no master developer for the entire area. The agreed-upon plan required that the entire street be upgraded because of the proposed change in character from suburban residential to urban mixed-use. This became a huge issue for all involved, yet the overlay was adopted with this requirement. Eventually, a primary developer emerged and submitted a proposal to develop and upgrade two-thirds of the street. Once this was proposed, a phased upgrade of the street for future development became possible. Completion of the first phase of the development was set for 2007.

LESSONS LEARNED

When people have been entrenched in their positions over a period of years it is sometimes necessary to bring in a third-party mediator to facilitate a dialogue and present new options. Previous meetings among residents ended in yelling matches. With the planning department acting as a third-party mediator and identifying the critical missing analysis, in this case an independent economic analyst, the historic distrust and posturing was removed during the charrette and all sides were able to communicate more freely and with great results.

Figure 41 *Bedford Avenue illustrative masterplan showing compatibility of westside residential and eastside commercial*

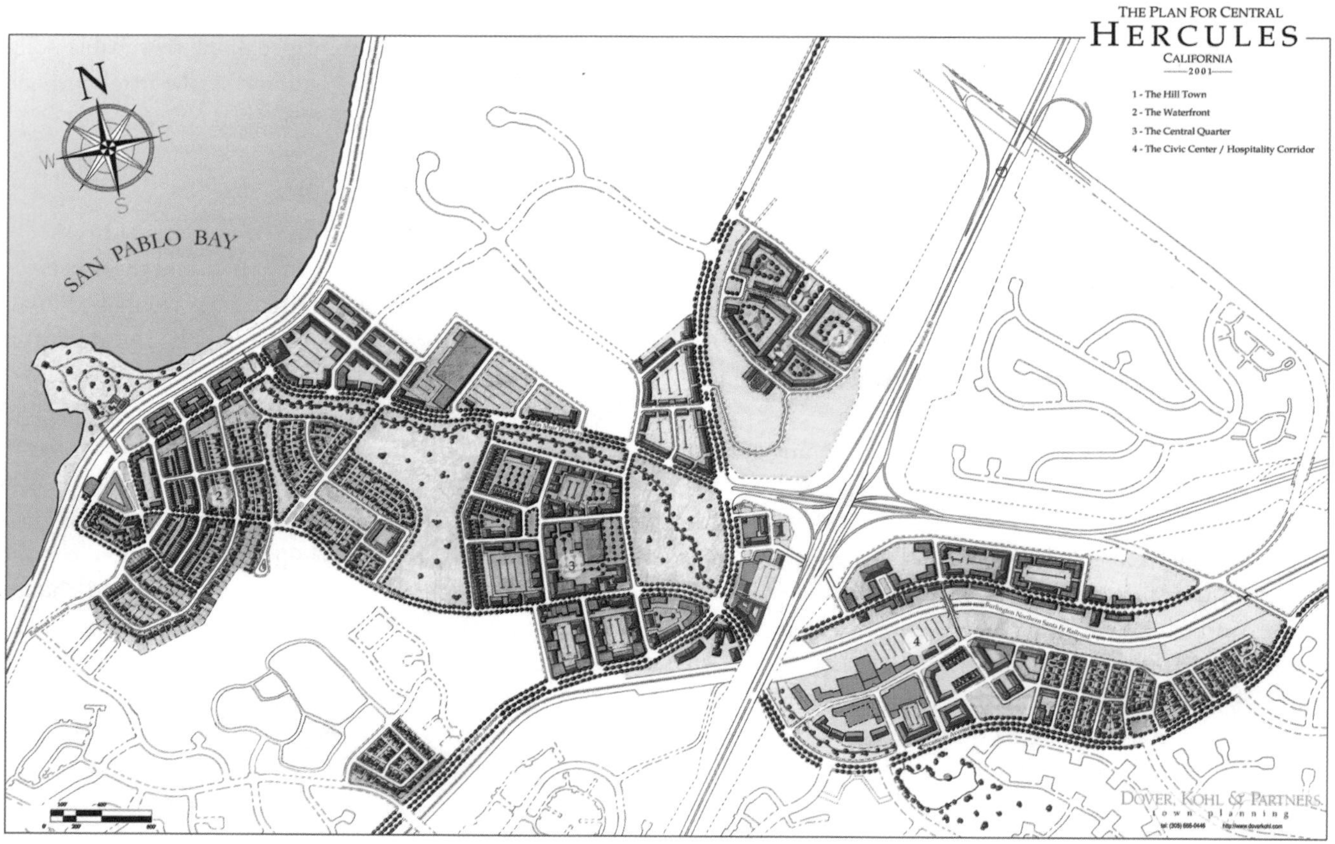

THE PLAN FOR CENTRAL
HERCULES
CALIFORNIA
—2001—

1 - The Hill Town
2 - The Waterfront
3 - The Central Quarter
4 - The Civic Center / Hospitality Corridor

Figure 42 *Hercules
Illustrative Master Plan*

Figure 43 *View along Snapper Creek*

The Plan for Central Hercules, Hercules, California

INTRODUCTION

In the 1990s, the small city of Hercules in the San Francisco Bay Area was beginning to feel development challenges to its previous identity as a quiet bedroom community of newly constructed homes. Land values were increasing and plans for commercial and residential development were again being discussed after several years of recession. A group of citizens, most of whom were involved with the Hercules Planning Commission, saw this growth pressure as an opportunity to create a traditional town center instead of the usual suburban sprawl.

New development in the Bay Area is frequently met with local opposition. But because community members in Hercules were invited to craft plans in advance of developer proposals, a different dynamic was established. The charrette created the vision and momentum for change that politicians could not ignore. It created an irresistible picture of a town center along with a plan and the first form-based code in California. It created a civic contract between a group of elected officials (and their successors) and the people who participated in the charrette to build a vision of the downtown.

HISTORY OF THE SITE

During the 1970s, large parcels of the Hercules Powder Company factory site, formerly an explosives manufacturing facility, were sold to homebuilders for residential development. Originally established in 1881, the Hercules Powder site was a nine-square-mile incorporated town, comprising a company-owned workers' hamlet surrounded by factory buildings, railroads, storage bunkers, and plenty of open space (to buffer accidental explosions). After homebuilders constructed and sold about 6,500 mostly single-family detached houses on the hills in the late 1980s, the center of the new city remained an undeveloped piece of land, strewn with remnants of the dynamite plant. Hydrology, roadway, and geologic conditions suppressed values and, therefore, development plans. This 426-acre brownfield in the middle of single-family homes remained undeveloped until the late 1990s. Around this Central Hercules area, community members in the comfortable bedroom community of Hercules remained curious and wary about the final shape of development for their town.

WHAT LED TO THE CHARRETTE?

By the late 1990s, there were several controversial development proposals for the Central Hercules area powder company site. In addition, the city's financial condition indicated a strong need for commercial, particularly retail, development. The Hercules Planning Commission and City Council, with funding from the Hercules Redevelopment Agency, landowners, and developers, initiated the project by hiring Dover Kohl & Partners, an urban design firm specializing in charrettes.

PROCESS DESCRIPTION

In the months leading up to the charrette, the Hercules Planning Commission and Redevelopment Agency organized a steering committee, planned the actual charrette event, located and obtained resources, and worked with city staff on logistics. Additionally, a series of regular meetings with the city council, planning commission, and the steering committee were held to ensure that anyone interested in the process had the opportunity to contribute ideas on the organization of the event, which set the expectations and limits of the charrette and its outcomes.

One month before the charrette was slated to begin, a public "town hall" meeting was held. It was publicized during the preceding weeks through handouts, posters (in businesses and on A-frame signs in traffic islands), announcements made during televised city council and planning commission meetings, and in newspaper articles. At the standing-room-only town hall meeting, Victor Dover of Dover Kohl delivered an inspirational lecture on urban design.

The 10-day charrette began on June 19, 2000, in an inactive Wells Fargo bank branch. Public presentations were held in the nearby Hercules Swim Center Gymnasium. In addition to Dover Kohl, Fehr & Peers Traffic Consultants aided with transportation matters, Zimmerman/Volk Associates consulted on housing, Robert Gibbs worked on retail, and DK Associates, a civil engineering firm, consulted as well.

The plan produced during the charrette was intended to provide a greater level of assurance to developers, landowners, and neighbors that the center of Hercules would be constructed in a manner aligned with the public's desires, namely: increased walkability, an appropriate amount of wildland preservation (some wetlands are present on the site), and a greater mix of uses. Additionally, the plan specified a higher quality of architectural design and a greater ability to attract retail businesses to the center of Hercules.

The charrette received regional coverage in the local press. Neutral to positive stories were published almost daily. This helped to keep the public abreast of the unfolding activities, including those who were unable to make it to the public meetings. The final products of the charrette included a regulating plan, narrative report, and a form-based code. Hercules became the first California city to adopt such a code.

IMPLEMENTATION DESCRIPTION

One of the Hercules developers with a key parcel of waterfront land was committed to new urbanism. His original plan for the area improved over the course of the charrette and it was the first to be built, soon after the charrette. The waterfront development showed the reality of the decisions made during the charrette and proved that they were feasible. The new development transformed the industrial waterfront into a walkable, mixed-use neighborhood. Planning Commissioner Richard Mitchell notes that the usual opposition to development proposals was absent on the waterfront area applications.

LESSONS LEARNED

During the charrette, the fire chief of the independent fire service agency reviewed and indicated approval of the proposed palette of street sections. However, the chief retired shortly after the code was written and adopted by the city. His successor disavowed several of the street sections in the palette. This unfinished business at the conclusion of the charrette set the stage for subsequent difficult conflict between the city and the fire agency. Lesson: Get it in writing! Use all means to get these agreements completed during the charrette, when everyone is there. If you fail to get an agreement during the charrette, you will be back to the usual methods of endless meetings. Remember that the charrette is a special opportunity to conclude negotiations like these.

7. Neighborhood Lane

The Neighborhood Lane is designed with traffic calming in mind. This street section is used primarily in residential areas or secondary streets. On-street parking is located on both sides.

A. Building Placement:

Build-to-line location: 0 to10 ft. from
(Typical)   R.O.W. line

Space Between
Buildings: 0 ft. if attached
                       6-15 ft. if detached

B. Building Volume:

Bldg. Width: 16 ft. minimum
                 160 ft. maximum

Bldg. Depth: 125 ft. maximum

Bldg. Height: 2 stories minimum
                 4 stories maximum
                 55 ft. Maximum

C. Notes:

1. Appurtenances may extend beyond the height limit.
2. Parallel parking permitted on both sides of the street.
3. The alignment of floor-to-floor heights of abutting buildings is encouraged to allow for shared use of elevators.

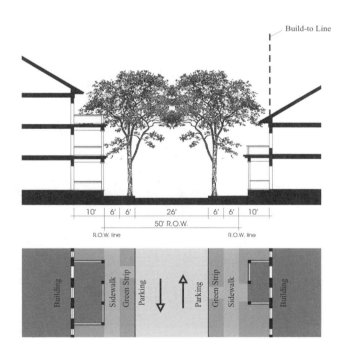

Regulating Code for the
Central Hercules Plan

Figure 44 *Page from form-based code*

Role of the Press

A reporter for *The Green Hills News* attended every public meeting and spoke to the public and planners afterwards. This supplied a constant stream of publicity. After the charrette was completed, the project received more attention from the citywide press, including *The Tennessean*.

Figure 45 *Pleasant Hill BART. A view from the station drawn by the developer's architect as part of the development package five years after the charrette.*

Pleasant Hill BART Station, Walnut Creek, California

INTRODUCTION

Contra Costa County leadership had been talking about creating a transit-oriented village around the Pleasant Hill BART station, in Walnut Creek, California, for 25 years. Several attempts were made, but it was not until the right partners were in place that a plan was settled upon. These partners included the landowner, Bay Area Rapid Transit System (BART); the developer, Millennium Partners; and the public planning authority, Contra Costa County Redevelopment Agency.

Donna Gerber, then a county supervisor, was looking for a solution that the neighborhood association would embrace and that would also work for Millennium and BART. She saw that new urbanism and the charrette process could possibly be an answer to this stalled situation.

HISTORY OF THE SITE

Walnut Creek in Contra Costa County, California, received its name from the walnut groves that covered the beautiful valley west of Mount Diablo. Prior to the building of I-680, the area was predominantly bungalow and ranch homes nestled among the orchards. Residents were either associated with the walnut industry or had relocated from the urban San Francisco Bay Area. The arrival of the highway interchange, adjacent to the local Pleasant Hill BART station, began to transform what was once a quiet agricultural valley into a regional transportation hub.

In the early 1980s, a specific plan for the 140-acre BART station area was adopted by Contra Costa County calling for a higher density, mixed-use transit-oriented communi-

ty. Since 1986, more than 2,400 housing units, two hotels, offices with more than 4,000 employees, and more than $40 million in major public infrastructure improvements had been built within walking distance of the Pleasant Hill BART station. The accumulation of this development activity increased strain on the once convenient lifestyle of the single-family ranch home neighborhoods surrounding the station area. The increase in traffic congestion created the greatest impacts on residents.

During the 1980s, developer-driven programs were proposed for the Pleasant Hill BART station area. These failed attempts were primarily commercial developments with heavy office or entertainment retail uses. At that time, Contra Costa County and BART required that a developer pay to build a parking garage to house the 1,477 surface commuter parking spaces that the development would replace, in addition to the parking required for the new development itself. This burden had the effect of limiting the financially feasible options to large-scale commercial uses. The regional market orientation of these projects raised the objections of both neighbors and surrounding cities. Neighbors were concerned about the traffic impacts, and the cities were concerned about competition with their own commercial developments. Community members were given limited opportunities to participate in the development proposals, and when they were engaged there were too few options on the table. It looked to the community participants as though the heavy commercial and entertainment uses were a foregone conclusion and that their input had no potential impact on the proposal outcomes.

	THURSDAY, FEB. 22	FRIDAY, FEB. 23	SATURDAY, FEB. 24	SUNDAY, FEB. 25	MONDAY, FEB. 26	TUESDAY, FEB. 27	WEDNESDAY, FEB. 28
	Breakfast	Breakfast	Breakfast	Breakfast	Breakfast	Breakfast	Breakfast
8:00 AM		Team meeting	Team meeting	Team meeting	Team meeting	Team meeting	
9:00	Studio set up	Alt. conc. dev. / Stake-holder meeting	Neighbors meeting	Preferred plan synthesis	BART technical meeting and staff review	Final production	Technical advisory committee / team meeting
10:00							
11:00	Technical advisory committee mtg.	BART technical meeting	Alternative concepts dev.		Design development		
12:00	Lunch	Lunch	Lunch	Lunch	Lunch	Lunch	Lunch
1:00 PM	Afternoon tour of site and local New Urbanism examples with team, TAC, and citizens	Pedestrian & bicycle access meeting	Alt. conc. dev. / Stake-holder review	Preferred plan synthesis / design development	Production	Presentation preparartion	
2:00							
3:00		Retail meeting					
4:00		Staff review meeting	Public workshop and pin-up review				
5:00	Dinner	Dinner		Dinner	Dinner	Dinner	Dinner
6:00							
7:00	Public kickoff meeting	Alternative concepts development	Preferred plan synthesis	Design development	Public meeting on transportation	Final public meeting	
8:00							
9:00		Team review	Team review		Production		
10:00							

Figure 46 *Pleasant Hill BART Station Charrette Schedule*

By the late 1980s many residents of the surrounding neighborhoods believed that any additional development other than locally serving service and residential uses would push the traffic problem over the edge. This made for a difficult political environment for developing the 18 acres of parking immediately adjacent to the station. When the Contra Costa County Redevelopment Agency undertook planning for this redevelopment, it met public resistance on all fronts. It wasn't until the agency initiated a process that invited local employees, residents, and business owners to help plan the area surrounding the station that any progress was made.

WHAT LED TO THE CHARRETTE?

Following a failed attempt to plan a regional entertainment complex on the property in 1999, Donna Gerber invited author Peter Katz to deliver a series of lectures on new urbanism. Gerber was interested in the potential of a new urbanist approach to provide needed services, quality housing, and community amenities while minimizing traffic growth. When the community responded positively to the lectures, Gerber and County Redevelopment director, Jim Kennedy proposed a charrette.

PROCESS DESCRIPTION

To plan the Pleasant Hill BART project and conduct the charrette process, a consultant team was selected by a steering committee. The steering committee represented the Contra Costa County Redevelopment Agency, BART, the designated developer, and the neighborhood. Members of the neighborhood association were part of the selection committee, which was a unique component of the process. Five years later, community members were still overseeing the project as part of the Pleasant Hill BART Municipal Advisory Council.

The steering committee chose the planning firm Lennertz Coyle & Associates to lead a team of consultants, including transit planners Nelson\Nygaard, transportation engineers Fehr & Peers, market economists Strategic Economics and CSG Advisors, retail consultant and architect Seth Harry, architects Opticos Design, computer imaging consultant Steve Price of Urban Advantage, and public outreach specialist Communities by Design. After the charrette, Geoffrey Ferrell Associates wrote the form-based codes and McLarand Vasquez Emsiek & Partners became the project architect.

The consultant team held an initial public meeting that sought to take one more step toward reestablishing the trust between the community members and the project sponsors: Contra Costa County, BART, and the developer. This public kick-off meeting was held six weeks before the start of the charrette to inform the public about the project and the charrette process and to solicit their ideas for the neighborhood. During the meeting, community members worked in small groups to discuss how the project related to the area and what a vision for the developed site might look like. The consultants then took this input and combined it with the other critical information such as market demand, financing requirements, and site constraints to develop alternative concepts for the site.

One month later, the consultant team of architects, planners, engineers, and economists held a six-day charrette that resulted in a comprehensive plan for the site. Public meetings were held for anyone who wished to attend, and stakeholder meetings were scheduled with neighbors, a technical advisory committee, bicycle and pedestrian advocacy groups, and BART representatives, to name a few. The charrette team worked with all of the input from these meetings and developed alternative concepts. These concepts were brought back to the stakeholders and general public numerous times throughout the week at public meetings and open houses and were revised according to additional input. The charrette team took the refined plans and synthesized them into one comprehensive plan representing the best of all ideas. Steve Potter, a participant in the charrette, noted that, "The charrette process invited my neighbors and me to share our opinions and suggestions in designing a positive addition to our community . . . [T]he charrette process has developed a plan that no one group of people could — it has drawn the best from those who participated."

The Pleasant Hill BART Municipal Advisory Council consists of seven people who either live or work in the area. Members of the Municipal Advisory Council are appointed by the Contra Costa County Board of Supervisors and their role is to advise the board on any development projects within the planning area.

A Transformative Charrette Moment: Ad Hoc Charrette Transportation Meeting

Traffic was the primary point of contention for the neighborhood residents. Over the years, people watched as traffic on Treat Boulevard became worse and worse. The most vocal neighbors held the firm conviction that development on the scale discussed so far in the charrette would make traffic a great deal worse. They also did not trust the traffic studies because they were based on the county's two-year-old traffic

Figure 47 *View of station square with high rise offices in background*

counts. During the charrette, it quickly became apparent to the charrette team that these issues would have to be put to rest. During the second day of the charrette, a couple of neighbors emphasized the problem with the validity of the traffic counts. The charrette manager and county planners decided to order new counts to begin the next day. This announcement to the neighbors (during a public meeting) was a profound moment in which an important issue that had previously been ignored by the county was validated and addressed quickly.

That same day, community members continued to object to the alternative designs that were presented. Participants insisted, "You just don't understand. No matter how well you design it, the traffic will only get worse." The charrette team recognized that the project could not move forward without a definitive answer to this objection. The charrette team scheduled an ad hoc transportation meeting

for the next evening of the charrette. Sixty people attended this meeting, during which the consulting engineers were successful in changing people's understanding of this pivotal issue. First, the engineers illustrated the dynamics of growth in the county. They showed that because of supply and demand, the development proposed for the site would be built somewhere else within the county and, if it was built elsewhere, it would make the overall traffic problem in the county a lot worse. In other words, because of its proximity to the major transportation access points, the station area was the best place for this development. The final proof was in the analysis that showed, to everyone's surprise, that the alternatives under consideration in the charrette would add only 5 percent more traffic to Treat Boulevard.

Figure 48 *Photo of existing conditions along Treat Boulevard*

Figure 49 *Computer-generated drawing of retail along Treat Boulevard*

CHARRETTE RESULTS

Over the course of the six-day process, form-based zoning and architectural codes; market and financial feasibility analyses; street and transit circulation plans; a pedestrian paths and parks plan; a transit plan for buses, taxis, and kiss and ride; regulating plan; and illustrative renderings depicting the future state were all created and refined. In the end, the charrette resulted in a comprehensive and detailed plan that met the basic requirements of all parties, ending the deadlock.

IMPLEMENTATION DESCRIPTION

In 2002, Contra Costa County Supervisors unanimously approved the plan with no attendee speaking in opposition and incorporated the charrette plan into the area specific plan. The county created a position for a town architect who was hired to ensure that incoming development applications adhered to the form-based codes created during the charrette.

It is notable that in the years since the charrette, the results have survived the continued scrutiny of community members, ongoing partnership negotiations between the public and private entities involved, and the passing of the project to a new design firm. Projects are often compromised during the volatile implementation phase, but the plan created during the BART charrette broke ground in 2006 with its original vision in place.

LESSONS LEARNED

Extremely contentious situations require at least a six-day charrette. This allows for time to deal with the unexpected. For instance, the ad hoc transportation meeting was made possible because there was sufficient time to pull it together. The results of this charrette would not have been possible in a shorter time frame.

Strong political leadership is invaluable. This project spotlights the benefits of the leadership of an elected official who is able to facilitate the creation of a vision and keep the project on track.

An accurate base plan is extremely important. The team did not have an accurate base map to work from at the charrette. It was only 24 months later that the engineering team discovered this fact. The result, although it did not drastically alter the charrette plan, did cause considerable rework that could have been avoided if the correct base plan had been available during the charrette.

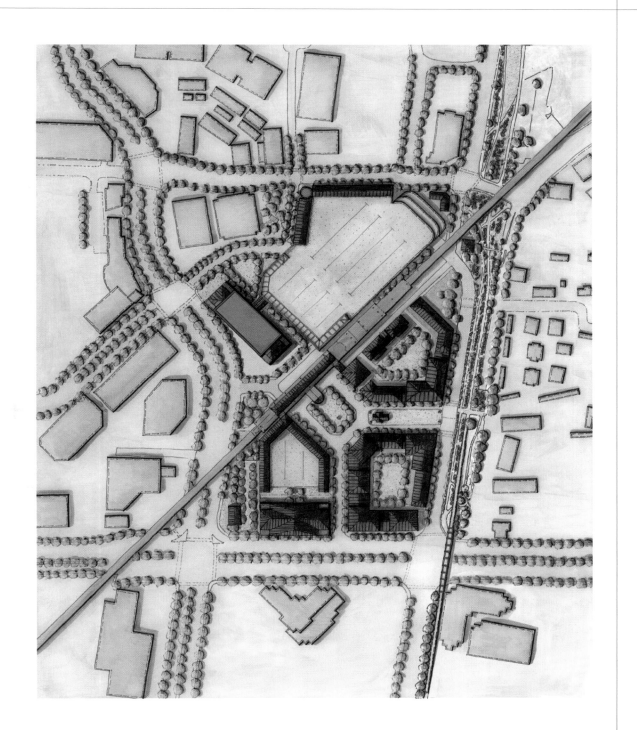

Figure 50 *Final charrette plan*

Final Charrette Products, Pleasant Hill BART Project

Figure 51 *Aerial view from southeast*

Figure 53 *View of station square with townhouses and public park in the foreground*

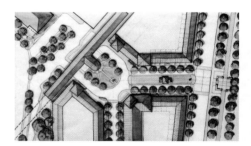

Figure 54 *Detailed study of station*

Figure 52 *View of station square with Mt. Diablo in background*

Figure 55 *Retail surrounding station square*

Figure 56 *Main street retail with housing above*

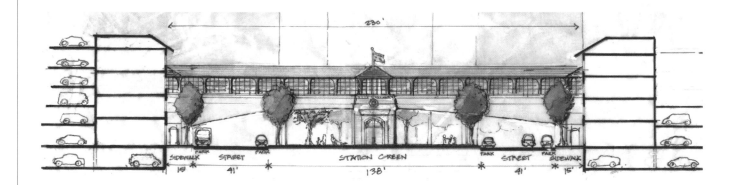

Figure 57 *Sectional study of station square showing parking strategy*

Figure 58 *Residential green showing townhouses with Mt. Diablo in background*

Figure 59 *Elevation of renovated BART station*

Figure 60 *View of townhouses from regional trail*

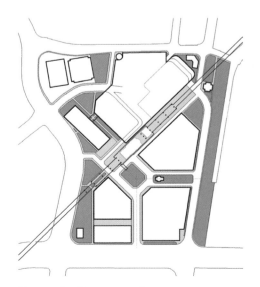

Figure 61 *Open space diagram*

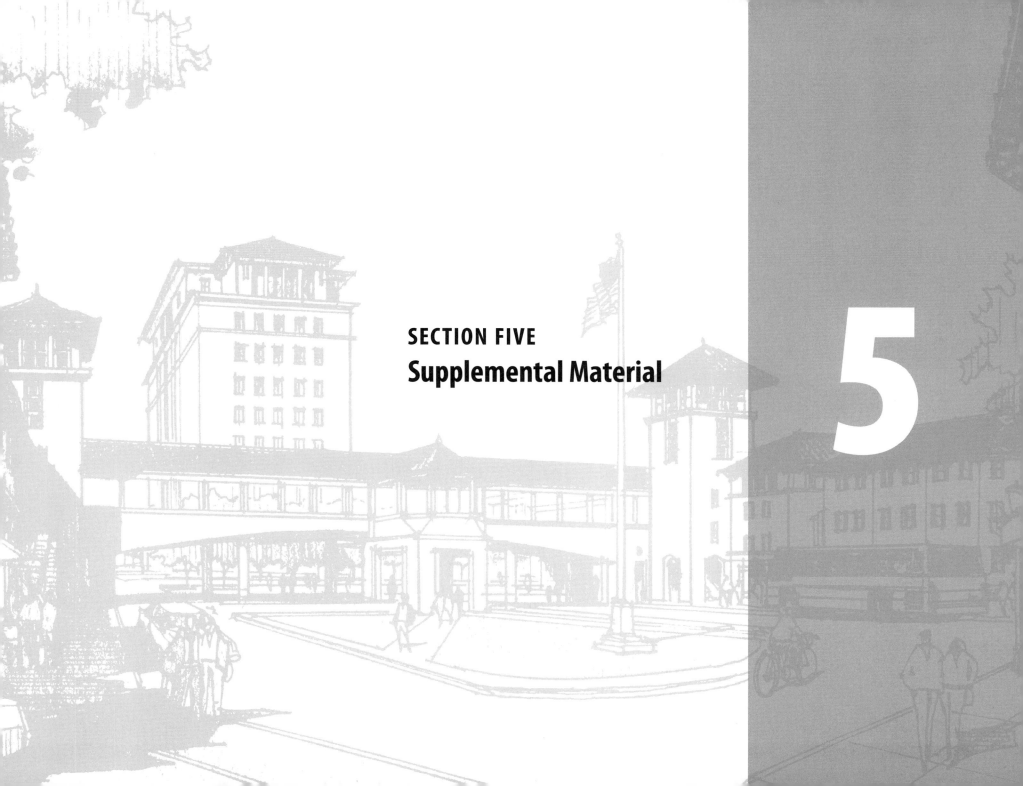

SECTION FIVE
Supplemental Material

5

Frequently Asked Questions

Can a governmental planning agency run a charrette?

A third party is often required to neutralize a contentious political environment. The third party facilitator is a person recognized by all participants as someone genuinely committed to protecting the people and the process during a charrette. The third party role is invaluable for creating an atmosphere of trust for all participants. At minimum, the charrette requires someone who can effectively play the third party role when necessary. In many cases, local planning agency staff members have too much history in a community. Although it is a bit of a high-wire act, it is possible for a conscientious charrette leader to both assume a third party role and provide content.

Why does a charrette have to last multiple days?

One of the unique traits of a charrette is the series of feedback loops. Three loops are the minimum required to facilitate a change in participants' perceptions and positions. Within these three major feedback loops, designs are created based upon a public vision, and presented within hours for further review, critique, and refinement. Four consecutive days are required to accommodate three feedback loops, scheduled at least a day apart. These feedback cycles foster a holistic understanding of complex problems by all participants and form the basis of a plan that reflects all vital viewpoints. It results in true buy-in by everyone involved, who are thereby inspired to support the plan, allowing it to overcome the inevitable challenges on its path to implementation.

When is a charrette not the right choice?

A project or community is not "charrette ready" if the primary stakeholders are unwilling to participate in good faith throughout the process. For instance, if the major decision makers will not participate in the charrette there may be reason to put things on hold until they will. Even if people cannot physically attend the charrette, if they are willing participants in the process then the charrette team can find some way to include them, such as meeting at their office. Another indicator of charrette readiness is the availability of the data required to make informed decisions at the charrette. For instance, if there is a lack of information about the housing market, it may be worthwhile to postpone the charrette until a market study can be completed.

What is the difference between a visioning workshop and a charrette?

Charrettes are often confused with visioning sessions. The purpose of vision development is to establish a description of a future state based on shared community values that acts as a guide for the project decision-making process. The visioning process can include one or a number of efforts including educational lectures, workshops, neighborhood walks, and preference surveys. According to practitioner Gianni Longo, visioning sessions are driven by community members and comprehensive. They take into account the "long horizon," and they work best for master plans. They produce goals, principles, policies, and initiatives. A visioning session, or series of sessions, gets a community ready for a charrette. Most of the time, visioning sessions are held well in advance of the charrette but sometimes a charrette begins with one, depending on the individual community's needs. Visioning sessions are valuable during the process of charrette preparation. Holding a visioning workshop is a great way for a community to come to an agreement on its basic values and the vision of those values as implemented. It is important to have a set of shared values, principles, and vision statements before the charrette begins. Therefore, we include visioning workshops in the "Research, Education and Charrette Preparation" section of our curriculum.

What are the most common causes of failed charrettes?

Not scheduling enough time for the charrette

Often, first-time charrette sponsors resist holding a charrette that lasts more than three days. When a sponsor has not been through a complete dynamic planning process, it is difficult for her to understand the benefits of holding a four- to seven-day charrette. Sponsors are often concerned about the resources necessary (both money and time) to complete a lengthy process. However, there are risks associated with charrettes that are too short. Inevitably, unexpected political or engineering challenges that require extra analysis or meetings will arise during the charrette. If the charrette is too short to accommodate these analyses and meetings, the contentious issues may not be settled. An abbreviated process will not allow enough time for the charrette team to solve the problem and produce the final documents in an informative and attractive format for the final presentation. It is a disservice to the project sponsor and all involved not to be able to fully test the preferred plan and create the documents necessary to explain it.

Late to the game stakeholders

There are numerous examples of projects in which a small but well-organized group of opponents successfully undermined the charrette outcome. However, when potential blockers are identified and engaged early on, they often end up as promoters. Success depends on the charrette team's level of understanding of the opponents' interests and its ability to establish a mutually beneficial relationship. It is also important to have an involvement plan in place for those people arriving to the charrette late or after it has concluded. It is particularly important to be able to show latecomers the decision-making process used and records of the feedback loops.

Incomplete base data

The charrette is a major undertaking requiring significant resources for its preparation and execution. Once the charrette begins, it is crucial that the necessary resources and base data are readily available for the charrette team to take the project to the level of detail required to assure feasibility. There should never be a time when a team member says something like, "If we only knew exactly where the heritage trees were located then we could precisely plan the location of the main boulevard."

Shortchanging the implementation phase

Sometimes, in the interest of controlling the budget, the project sponsor will choose to minimize the involvement of the charrette team during the implementation phase. Often, team members are called back to the project only when things begin to go wrong. When this happens, the charrette team may find itself in the difficult position of repairing damage caused by poor post-charrette stakeholder communications.

Charrette Scheduling Variations

VARIATIONS ON THE MULTIPLE-DAY CHARRETTE

The structure of the charrette schedule varies with the level of physical and political complexity of a project. Projects that have challenging site conditions or complex design constraints may call for specialized staffing and extra days. Weeklong charrettes provide highly contentious projects with extra time for conflict resolution. There are many variations of the multiple day charrette model. Most models begin and end the charrette on a weekday and include a weekend open house. Other models begin the charrette with a public workshop on the weekend. Following are a few examples from veteran charrette firms.

Time	Wednesday November 2	Thursday November 3	Friday November 4	Saturday November 5	Sunday November 6	Monday November 7
8:00 AM 9:00 10:00 11:00	• Set up site- all day • Final details and script run-thru w/staff	• (8am) Kick-off Meeting w/ entire team and key participants. • Site tour	• (8-10 am) **1st PIN-UP REVIEW** of alternatives by design team, key participants and interested citizens.	• (9-11 am) **2nd PIN-UP REVIEW** by entire design team, key participants, and interested citizens.	• Begin presentation drawings and finalize proformas. • Final check off by key players as required	• Complete presentation documentation
12:30-1:30		Lunch	Lunch	Lunch	Lunch	Lunch
2:00 3:00 4:00 5:00	• Team arrives • Team meeting	• Design team begins on various plan options	• Design team works on focus projects and overall district design • **OPEN HOUSE**	• Team adjusts designs, & continues design development • Complete design development.	• Continue presentation production	• Production work ends • Wrap-up meeting with staff • Clean-up and pack
6:30-7:30		Dinner	Dinner	Dinner	Dinner	Dinner
8:00 9:00	• (7:30 pm) **PUBLIC KICK-OFF MEETING**	• Design team completes alternatives	• Design team develops focus projects.	• Evening off!	• Continue presentation production	• (7:30 pm) **PUBLIC PRESENTATION OF CHARRETTE RESULTS** • Partytime!

1. Opening public meeting on Wednesday night

2. Mid-course open house

3. Final charrette public meeting on Monday night

Figure 62 *Sample 6-Day Charrette Schedule: Mercer Island Town Center, Lennertz Coyle & Associates*

Name of Charrette		THURSDAY	FRIDAY	SATURDAY	SUNDAY	MONDAY	TUESDAY	WEDNESDAY	THURSDAY	FRIDAY
		DAY 1	DAY 2	DAY 3	DAY 4	DAY 5	DAY 6	DAY 7	DAY 8	DAY 9
DRAFT Charrette Schedule	August 25 - 31									
	8:30 AM	Team DKP Depart MIA	Breakfast	Breakfast	Breakfast	Breakfast	Breakfast	Breakfast	Breakfast	Breakfast
Name of Lead Firm Project Principal	9:00	**①**	DKP setup studio	**②**	DESIGN	DESIGN	DESIGN			
Project Principal	10:00		TECHNICAL MEETING #1	Hands on design workshop	TECHNICAL MEETING #4	TECHNICAL MEETING #6	TECHNICAL MEETING #8	DESIGN	DESIGN	Return
Project Director	11:00		**③**		**③**	**③**				
Design Team	12:00 PM		Lunch		Lunch	Lunch	Lunch	Lunch	Lunch	
	1:00		DESIGN	Lunch						
Visualizations Name of Consulting Firm	2:00		TECHNICAL MEETING #2	Facilitator de-briefing	TECHNICAL MEETING #5	TECHNICAL MEETING #7				
Transportation Consultants	3:00	Teour site and surroundings					DESIGN	DESIGN	PRODUCTION AND FINAL PRESENTATION PREPARATION	
Name of Consulting Firm	4:00		TECHNICAL MEETING #3		DESIGN	DESIGN				
Market Consultants Name of Consulting Firm	5:00									
	6:00		Team review		Informal pin-up	Informal pin-up	**⑤** Public open house	Informal pin-up		
Development Team	7:00	Team meeting & dinner		Dinner	Dinner	Dinner	Dinner	Dinner	Final presentation	
Name of Consulting Firm or Client	8:00		Kick off presentation and public open house						**⑦**	
	9:00									
	10:00		**④**		DESIGN	DESIGN	DESIGN AND PRODUCTION	DESIGN AND PRODUCTION	Studio clean-up	
	11:00									
	MIDNIGHT						**⑥**			

Legend:
- project team meetings
- technical meetings
- community meetings

1. Thursday set-up and organization
2. Saturday morning public hands-on workshop w/optional picnic
3. Technical meetings with project sponsors, agency staff, etc., as needed
4. Charrette begins with a Friday open house and "food for thought" lecture
5. Tuesday afternoon open house mid-course reviews
6. Production begins after the open house
7. Thursday night final charrette public presentation

Figure 63 *Sample 7-Day Charrette Schedule with Weekend Start Option, Dover Kohl & Partners Town Planning*

Owl's Head Charrette Schedule
January 19–27

DPZ Team
Project Principal
Project Manager
Project Coordinator

Design Team

Design Consultants

Lodging:

Studio:

	MONDAY DAY 1	TUESDAY DAY 2	WEDNESDAY DAY 3	THURSDAY DAY 4	FRIDAY DAY 5	SATURDAY DAY 6	SUNDAY DAY 7	MONDAY DAY 8
8:00 AM	Breakfast	Breakfast	Breakfast	Breakfast	Breakfast	Breakfast	Breakfast	Breakfast
9:00	①		Team session	Team session		Team session	Morning off ??	DESIGN & PRODUCTION
10:00		Team session			Team session			
11:00			MEETING #2 Town Center/Cultural/Retail	MEETING #4 Transportation/City/County/State				
12:00 PM	Team arrives and travels to Freeport	INTERNAL MEETING Grit & Grace presentation and lunch	Lunch in	Lunch in	Lunch in	Lunch in	Lunch out	Lunch in
1:00	Lunch in	DESIGN	DESIGN		DESIGN			
2:00		MEETING #1 Elected officials/Planning/Public works/Infrastructure			MEETING #6 Residential Architects/Builders/Contractors		DESIGN & PRODUCTION	DESIGN & PRODUCTION
3:00	Project overview and site tour		MEETING #3 Recreation/Amenities	DESIGN		DESIGN		
4:00	Tour DeFuniak Springs	②						
5:00	Studio set up							
6:00			④					
7:00	Team dinner	③ OPENING PRESENTATION On site		MEETING #5 Pin-up and Review Neighbors & Public	Night off	Dinner out	Dinner in	⑤ FINAL PRESENTATION On site
8:00			Dinner out	Dinner out				
9:00		Dinner out						
10:00	Hotel check-in						DESIGN & PRODUCTION	Celebration dinner ⑥
11:00								
MIDNIGHT								Team departs Tuesday PM

1. Monday set-up and organization
2. Tuesday afternoon stakeholder meetings
3. Tuesday open public meeting
4. Thursday evening public pin-up mid-course review
5. Monday night final charrette public presentation
6. Wrap-up celebration

Figure 64 *Sample 7-Day Charrette Schedule: Owl's Head, Duany Plater-Zyberk & Company*

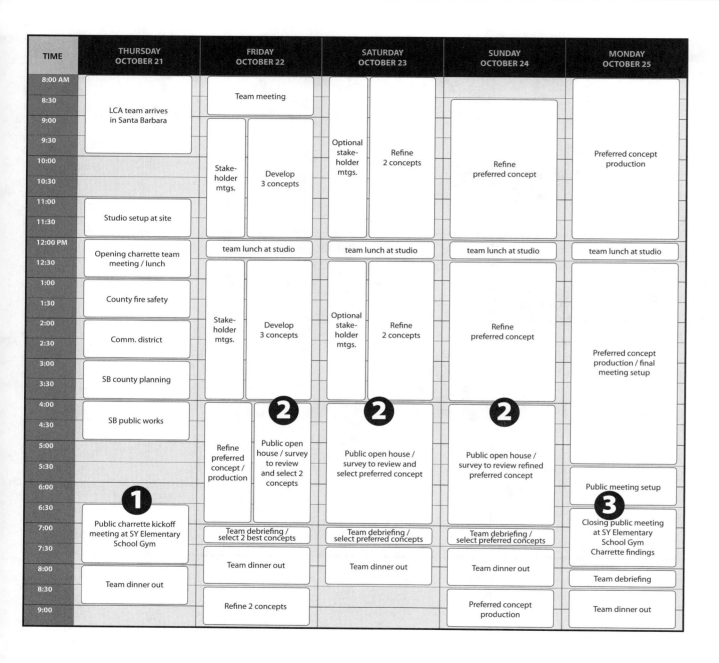

TIME	THURSDAY OCTOBER 21	FRIDAY OCTOBER 22		SATURDAY OCTOBER 23		SUNDAY OCTOBER 24	MONDAY OCTOBER 25
8:00 AM		Team meeting					
8:30	LCA team arrives in Santa Barbara					Refine preferred concept	Preferred concept production
9:00				Optional stake-holder mtgs.	Refine 2 concepts		
9:30		Stake-holder mtgs.	Develop 3 concepts				
10:00							
10:30							
11:00	Studio setup at site						
11:30							
12:00 PM	Opening charrette team meeting / lunch	team lunch at studio		team lunch at studio		team lunch at studio	team lunch at studio
12:30							
1:00	County fire safety						
1:30		Stake-holder mtgs.	Develop 3 concepts	Optional stake-holder mtgs.	Refine 2 concepts	Refine preferred concept	Preferred concept production / final meeting setup
2:00	Comm. district						
2:30							
3:00	SB county planning						
3:30							
4:00	SB public works		②	②		②	
4:30							
5:00		Refine preferred concept / production	Public open house / survey to review and select 2 concepts	Public open house / survey to review and select preferred concept		Public open house / survey to review refined preferred concept	
5:30							
6:00							Public meeting setup
6:30	①						③
7:00	Public charrette kickoff meeting at SY Elementary School Gym	Team debriefing / select 2 best concepts		Team debriefing / select preferred concepts		Team debriefing / select preferred concepts	Closing public meeting at SY Elementary School Gym Charrette findings
7:30							
8:00		Team dinner out		Team dinner out		Team dinner out	Team debriefing
8:30	Team dinner out						
9:00		Refine 2 concepts				Preferred concept production	Team dinner out

1. Opening meeting on Thursday night
2. Daily open house reviews/surveys
3. Final charrette public meeting on Monday night

Figure 65 *Sample 4 ½-Day Charrette Schedule: Meadowvale, HDR/LCA+Sargent Town Planning*

ALTERNATIVES TO THE MULTIPLE-DAY CHARRETTE

There are several alternatives to the continuous multiple-day charrette. These alternatives nonetheless reflect the dynamic planning values of collaboration, transparency, and shared learning. Like the multiple-day model, the alternatives feature feedback loops at key decision points. The main difference is in the time lapse between feedback loops. In the seven-day charrette model, the time between feedback loops is no more than a couple of days. The feedback loops in these alternative models are sometimes up to a month apart. The model used by Urban Design Associates was chosen as an example of a successful alternative to the multiple-day charrette.

THE URBAN DESIGN ASSOCIATES COLLABORATIVE COMMUNITY DESIGN WORKSHOP PROCESS

Urban Design Associates (UDA) has been conducting collaborative community design workshops for more than 40 years (see Section Two). Their process is based on values and principles similar to those of dynamic planning. It is a proven alternative to the five- to seven-day charrette model. The UDA process features three distinct phases, each marked with an event that achieves consensus.

In Phase One, information is gathered and analyzed and there is intensive public interaction to identify strengths, weaknesses, and aspirations. The product of this phase is a memorandum and a set of principles that provides a solid platform for the rest of the process. It enables all parties to agree on the criteria for design.

In Phase Two, alternative designs are developed in response to the issues and goals identified in Phase One. The central event is a three-day charrette in which alternatives are prepared in three-dimensional designs much as in the longer charrette model. At the end of the charrette there is a public presentation in which structured exercises are conducted to enable participants to evaluate the alternatives. This material is then compiled and distributed to the lead-ership group as the basis for Phase Three.

Phase Three begins the morning after the charrette with a meeting with the steering committee to review results and set the direction for determining the preferred alternative. This involves further testing for economic feasibility and for impacts on the environment and traffic. The final plan is then prepared and presented in a final public meeting. In the course of the meeting, there is another round of structured exercises to solicit objective evaluations from participants. This is most useful in determining the phasing and implementation strategies for a plan, since those items with the most consensus are generally the most attractive to implementers whether they be politicians, bureaucrats, or developers.

Phase One: Understanding—Figuring Out What Is Going On

Purpose: Develop consensus on project strengths, weaknesses, goals, and program

Process: Trip preparation includes collecting data and base maps, scheduling meetings with appropriate groups, and clarifying the leadership groups goals for the process.

Trip One (one to three days):

A team of three to six persons conducts reconnaissance of both hard and soft data. Hard data include statistical information, base maps, photo reconnaissance, reviewing legislation, collecting program information, and working with economists, traffic planners, and other specialists to understand the economic, political, and physical conditions.

The soft data include the perceptions of all those involved in the process: the worries and aspirations of community members, the ambitions of developers and community groups, and the concerns of civic leaders. Techniques include a series of structured exercises, including the use of colored dots on maps to identify strengths, weaknesses, and areas that require action. These are used in individual interviews, focus group discussions, and large pubic meetings.

Synthesis and Consensus:

Both hard and soft data are analyzed to understand the physical planning causes and effects that have led to perceptions of problems and possibilities. A summary of strengths, weaknesses, and goals as well as the graphic analyses are distributed along with a draft statement of key issues to be addressed by the planning process.

Phase Two: Exploring

Purpose: Test design alternatives to form the basis of selecting a final course of action

Process:

One-day, in-house charrette

- The results are reviewed by the design team and the client leadership. A draft consensus statement and set of principles are prepared.

- The team prepares preliminary sketches of potential design directions and alternatives.

On-site charrette (three to four days)

DAY ONE:

- The results of the analyses, draft principles, and potential directions for the plan are shared with the focus groups and the affected constituencies.

DAY TWO:

- Project team members develop and refine design alternatives in the same space in which the focus group discussions take place. The principles and designs are modified to respond to issues as they arise in the discussions. The designs are developed using interactive, three-dimensional media as well as plan and elevation drawings.

DAY THREE:

- Client, constituent representatives, and interested visitors review preliminary designs and plans with the project team at the studio in a mid-day meeting.

- In the evening at a public meeting, the alternative designs are presented. Small group discussions then review the designs and use the same techniques used in the first step. They are asked to identify the best and worst aspects of each design, use colored dots on the plans or perspectives, and make suggestions for improvement. These are summarized by a spokesperson from each group at the end of the meeting.

DAY FOUR of the charrette (document the charrette and file the materials):

- In a meeting with the client leadership, the results of the charrette are reviewed and a consensus is reached on the direction for the final plan.

Interim report:

- Summary of information gathered in Phases One and Two as well as results of the on-site charrette.

- Client review.

Phase Three: Deciding What to Do

Purpose: Refine and confirm the final decision on the preferred alternative

Process: The consulting team studies and tests the alternatives. The designs are refined and a draft report is presented.

On-site working session and presentation:

A two-day working session that includes a public meeting at which the proposed plan is presented and subjected to small group evaluation and review using the same techniques as previous sessions. The results help identify those elements of the plan for which there is broad support. This establishes priorities for action.

Refine report:

The collection of interim reports is refined and published as an illustrated document to be used in the formal approval process. This may require additional presentations before the jurisdictional bodies of the community.

Next steps:

The planning document and its individual images are used in the implementation process, either as the basis for marketing or as the first step in developing codes, design guidelines, or pattern books to ensure effective implementation.

Further Reading

PUBLICATIONS

Collaborative Planning Methodologies

Ames, Steven C., ed. *Guide to Community Visioning*. Chicago: APA Planners Press, 2001.

Cogan, Elaine. *Successful Public Meetings: A Practical Guide*. Chicago: APA Planners Press, 2000.

Doyle, Michael, and David Straus. *How to Make Meetings Work*. New York: Berkley Publishing Group, 1993.

Fisher, Roger. *Getting to Yes: Negotiating Agreement Without Giving In*. New York: Penguin Books, 1991.

Kaner, Sam. *Facilitator's Guide to Participatory Decision-Making*. Gabriola Island: New Society Publishers, 1996.

Morse, Suzanne W. *Smart Communities: How Citizens and Local Leaders Can Use Strategic Thinking to Build a Brighter Future*. San Francisco: Jossey-Bass, 2004.

Nelessen, Anton C. *Visions for a New American Dream*. Chicago: APA Planners Press, 1994.

Race, Bruce, and Carolyn Torma. *Youth Planning Charrettes: A Manual for Planners & Teachers*. Chicago: APA Planners Press, 1998.

Rue, Harrison Bright. *Real Towns: Making Your Neighborhoods Work*. Citizen Planner Institute, 2000.

Straus, David. *How to Make Collaboration Work: Powerful Ways to Build Consensus, Solve Problems, and Make Decisions*. San Francisco: Berrett-Koehler, 2002.

Smart Growth, Urban Planning and Design

Alexander, Christopher, et al. *A Pattern Language: Towns, Buildings, Construction*. New York: Oxford University Press, 1977.

Barnett, Jonathan. *The Fractured Metropolis: Improving the New City, Restoring the Old City, Reshaping the Region*. New York: Harper Collins, 2001.

Benfield, F. Kaid, et al. *Solving Sprawl: Models of Smart Growth from Communities Across America*. Washington, D.C.: Island Press, 2001.

Bohl, Charles. *Place Making*. Washington, D.C.: Urban Land Institute, 2002.

Burden, Dan. *Streets and Sidewalks, People and Cars: The Citizens' Guide to Traffic Calming*. Local Government Commission Center for Livable Communities, 2000.

Calthorpe, Peter. *The Next American Metropolis: Ecology, Community and the American Dream*. New York: Princeton Architectural Press, 1993.

Congress for the New Urbanism. *Codifying New Urbanism*. Chicago: APA Planning Advisory Service Report 526, 2004.

Dittmar, Hank, and Gloria Ohland. *New Transit Town: Best Practices in Transit-Oriented Development*. Washington, D.C.: Island Press, 2004.

Duany, Andres, and Elizabeth Plater-Zyberk. *Towns and Town-Making Principles*. New York: Rizzoli, 1992.

Duany, Andres, et al. *Suburban Nation*. New York: North Point Press, 2000.

Goldberg, David. *Choosing Our Community's Future: A Guide to Getting the Most Out of New Development*. Washington, D.C.: Smart Growth America, 2005.

Hall, Kenneth, and Gerald Porterfield. *Community by Design: New Urbanism for Suburbs and Small Communities*. New York: McGraw-Hill, 2001.

Jacobs, Jane. *The Death and Life of Great American Cities*. New York: Random House, 1961.

Katz, Peter. *The New Urbanism: Toward an Architecture of Community*. New York: McGraw-Hill, 1994.

Kelbaugh, Douglas. *Common Place: Toward Neighborhood and Regional Design*. Seattle: University of Washington Press, 1997.

Kunstler, James Howard. *The Geography of Nowhere: The Rise and Decline of America's Man-Made Landscape*. New York: Simon & Schuster, 1993.

Leccese, Michael, and Kathleen McCormick, eds. *Charter of the New Urbanism*. New York: McGraw-Hill, 2000.

Longo, Gianni. *A Guide to Great American Public Places*. New York: Urban Initiatives, 1997.

Steuteville, Robert, and Philip Langdon. *New Urbanism: Comprehensive Report & Best Practices Guide*. Ithaca, N.Y.: New Urban Publications, 2003.

Urban Design Associates. *The Urban Design Handbook: Techniques and Working Methods*. New York: W.W. Norton & Company, 2001.

Whyte, William H. *City: Rediscovering the Center*. New York: Doubleday, 1989

WEBSITES

Charrette/Public Involvement Resources

Center for Neighborhood Technology: www.cnt.org

CharretteCenter, Inc.: www.charrettecenter.com

National Charrette Institute: www.charretteinstitute.org

Neighborhood Charrette Handbook: www.louisville.edu/org/sun/planning/char.html

PlaceMatters.com: www.placematters.com

The Town Paper: www.tndtownpaper.com

U.S. EPA Public Involvement Resources: www.epa.gov/publicinvolvement

Sustainable Growth

American Institute of Architects, Center for Communities by Design: www.aia.org/liv_default

American Planning Association: www.planning.org

Congress for the New Urbanism: http://cnu.org

Local Government Commission: http://lgc.org

National Association of Realtors, Smart Growth Program: www.realtor.org/smartgrowth

New Urban News: http://newurbannews.com

Project for Public Spaces: www.pps.org

Reconnecting America: www.reconnectingamerica.org

Seaside Institute: www.theseasideinstitute.org

Smart Growth America: http://smartgrowthamerica.org

Surface Transportation Policy Project: www.transact.org

U.S. Green Building Council: www.usgbc.org

Walkable Communities, Inc.: www.walkable.org

Glossary

Alternative concepts: A number of different plan options pursued by the charrette team during the early days of the charrette after charrette public meeting #1. Alternative concepts are presented in charrette public meeting #2, after which they are synthesized into the preferred plan.

BART: Bay Area Rapid Transit System, the public transportation system in the San Francisco Bay Area.

Base data: The technical, political, and social information necessary for the creation of a detailed plan. Base data consist largely of existing conditions. They are collected prior to the charrette and often include information on the project site, transportation, market, economics, politics, environment, planning, history, and project program.

Charrette/NCI charrette: The NCI charrette is a collaborative design and planning workshop that occurs over four to seven consecutive days. It is held on-site and involves all affected stakeholders in a series of feedback loops, resulting in a feasible plan. The charrette is the second phase of the three phase dynamic planning process.

Charrette manager: The person who coordinates and manages the charrette. She can be public planning staff or a private consultant, but it is key that she is highly trained in the facilitation of a variety of in-house and public meetings. The charrette manager is responsible for more logistical elements of the charrette such as drawing production, transportation, catering, and organizing the charrette team. The charrette manager may also be the overall project manager. See also: **Project manager**.

Charrette products: Drawings and documents produced by the charrette team during the charrette to assure project feasibility. Products are initially identified in task 1.1.2, product mission and products. These may include a master plan, transportation plan, zoning codes, architectural guidelines, economic and market feasibility studies, and renderings.

Charrette ready: The point when all of the base data are in place and all stakeholders are prepared to participate in a charrette.

Charrette studio: A facility located on or near the project site where the charrette team works and holds stakeholder meetings during the charrette. It is generally open to the public throughout the charrette.

Charrette team: The core group of planners, designers, engineers, economists, and others that creates the charrette products in collaboration with the stakeholders. Team members are usually professional consultants funded by the project sponsor. The team may be supplemented by local agency planning staff members.

Cross-functional: Involving specialists from various disciplines to work collaboratively to create holistic solutions.

Dynamic planning: A three-phase, holistic, collaborative planning process during which a multiple-day charrette is held as the central transformative event. Phase one is research, education and charrette preparation. Phase two is the charrette. Phase three is plan implementation.

Feasible plan: A plan capable of being implemented. A feasible plan successfully addresses all project constraints, such as environmental, political, financial, and engineering issues.

Feedback loop: A feedback loop occurs when a design is proposed, reviewed, changed, and re-presented for further review.

Hands-on workshop: A workshop in which small groups of stakeholders and charrette team members work together on well-orchestrated, hands-on exercises for such purposes as creating a vision, community values, neighborhood asset maps, etc.

Healthy communities: Communities that improve the social, economic, and physical well being of their people, places, and natural environments.

Holistic/holism: Emphasizing the importance of the whole and the interdependence of its parts. The theory that the parts of any whole cannot exist and cannot be understood except in their relation to the whole; holism holds that the whole is greater than the sum of its parts.

LEED: Leadership in Energy and Environmental Design, a Green Building Rating System®, is a voluntary, consensus-based national standard for developing high-performance, sustainable buildings. It was developed and is sponsored by the U.S. Green Building Council.

New urbanism: New urbanism is an urban design movement that began in the late 1980s and early 1990s. New urbanists aim to reform all aspects of real estate development and community planning. The Congress for the New Urbanism established the principles of new urbanism in the Charter of the New Urbanism in 1996.

NIMBY: "Not in my backyard." Commonly used to describe people who are opposed to development proposals in their communities.

Open house: Members of the community circulate through the charrette studio or other public meeting space to review and give feedback on the design and planning work in progress. Generally information is organized into exhibits or stations that are staffed by members of the charrette team.

Pin-up: An informal plan review process in which members of the charrette team present and debate their work with their peers and stakeholders.

Preferred plan: The plan that emerges midway through the charrette from a set of alternative concepts and best solves the design problem. It is often a synthesis of two or more alternative concepts.

Project management team: The individuals who are involved with the management of the dynamic planning project from start to finish. In most projects, this team includes: the project sponsor, the sponsors' staff, and members of the lead consulting firm running the charrette. It may also include a political leader or other consultants, depending on the situation.

Project manager: The project manager is responsible for leading the entire dynamic planning process. During the charrette, the project manager maintains the primary relationships with the sponsor and the stakeholders and is responsible for leading the decision-making process and the public meetings. He can be public planning staff or a private consultant, but it is key that he is highly trained in the facilitation of a variety of in-house and public meetings. He may also act as the charrette manager or may work in concert with a charrette manager. See also: **Charrette manager.**

Project sponsor: Person or organization that funds the dynamic planning process. For example, a sponsor could be a private developer, a public agency, or a non-governmental agency.

Public kick-off meeting: A public meeting held four to six weeks before the start of the charrette to let people know about the project purpose and process, and their options for involvement. It provides an opportunity to elicit information and vision elements from the public before any design/planning work begins.

Smart growth: Community development that involves citizens in the development process, provides housing options for people of all incomes and ages, protects farmland and open space, revitalizes neighborhoods, and offers a variety of convenient transportation options. (Paraphrased from *Choosing Our Community's Future: A Guide to Getting the Most Out of New Development* by David Goldberg, published by Smart Growth America.)

Sponsor: Person or organization that funds the dynamic planning process. For example, a sponsor could be a private developer, a public agency, or a non-governmental agency. See also: **Project sponsor**.

Stakeholder: Anyone who will be reasonably affected by the project outcome. This includes project promoters, blockers, and those responsible for making decisions.

Stakeholder categories:
Primary: Primary stakeholders are those with a strong influence over the project. These individuals hold political, jurisdictional, or economic positions (elected or appointed) or they own land nearby. The primary stakeholders must be involved at all key decision-making points.

Secondary: Secondary stakeholders are those with a keen economic or political interest in the project such as community art groups, schools, and churches. It is common to hold interviews with the secondary stakeholders before the charrette.

General: General stakeholders, most commonly community members, are at the very least involved in the public meetings.

TOD (Transit-oriented development): Also known as Transit-oriented Design, TOD is compact, walkable, and centered around transit stations. In general, TODs include a mix of uses, such as housing, shopping, employment, and recreational facilities within a design that puts a high priority on serving transit and pedestrians.

Bibliography

BOOKS

Batchelor, Peter, and David Lewis, eds. *Urban Design in Action: The History, Theory and Development of the American Institute of Architects' Regional/ Urban Design Assistance Teams*. Raleigh: North Carolina State University Press, 1986.

Caudill, William Wayne. *Architecture by Team*. New York: Van Nostrand Reinhold, 1971.

Floyd, Chad. "Giving Form in Prime Time." In *Scope of Social Architecture*, edited by Richard Hatch. New York: Van Nostrand Reinhold, 1983.

————"Making Television Useful." In *The Enthusiasms of Centerbrook*, edited by John Morris Dixon. Australia: Images Publishing, 2001.

Kelbaugh, Douglas. *Common Place: Toward Neighborhood and Regional Design*. Seattle: University of Washington Press, 1997.

King, Jonathan, and Philip Langdon, eds. *The CRS Team and the Business of Architecture*. College Station: Texas A&M University Press, 2002.

Riddick, W.L. *Charrette Processes: A Tool in Urban Planning*. York, Pa.: George Shumway Publisher, 1971.

Urban Design Associates. *The Urban Design Handbook: Techniques and Working Methods*. New York: W.W. Norton & Company, 2001.

Van der Ryn, Sim, and Peter Calthorpe, eds. *Sustainable Communities: A New Design Synthesis for Cities, Suburbs, and Towns*. San Francisco: Sierra Club Books, 1986.

Watson, Donald. *Environmental Design Charrette Workbook*. AIA Committee on the Environment, 1996.

PERIODICALS

Costello, Anthony J. "Community-Based Charrettes." *Urban Design Quarterly* 49 (1994):18-19.

————"MUDS: A Focus for Urban Design Education in 'Middletown, USA.'" *Urban Design Studies* 1 (1995).

————"MUDS has a long history of filling downtown," *The Star Press*, December 1, 2002.

————"Muncie Charrette '82 Spurs Downtown." *Art Insight* 4 (1982):12.

Crosbie, Michael J, "Television as a Tool of Urban Design," *Architecture*, November 1984.

Floyd, Chad. "Riverdesign. Dayton, Ohio." *Process Architecture* 3 (1977).

Hammond, Christopher, "Greensboro's Team Effort," *Planning*, January 1996, 13-15.

Lewis, David, and Raymond L. Gindroz. "Toward a Design Process that Re-enfranchises Citizens and Consumers." *AIA Journal* 62 (1974):28-31.

Pena, William, Kevin Kelly, and Steven Parshall. "Squatters Revisited." *Tennessee Architect*, 3 (1980):17-20.

Rosenman, Marvin E. "Charrette." *Indiana Architect*, Jan 1970, 9-14.

OTHER

"A Guide to the Regional/Urban Design Assistance Team Program: R/UDAT Planning Your Community's Future," Pamphlet/flyer of the American Institute of Architects, 2004.

Caudill, William Wayne. Oral interview. By Larry Meyer for an Oral Business History Project, University of Texas, 1971. Sponsored by The Moody Foundation. Source: CRS Archives, CRS Center, Texas A&M University, College Station, Texas.

Costello, Anthony J. "Found Allies: 'Middletown, USA' Forges Partnerships that Benefit Town & Gown," 1998 ACSA East Central Regional Conference Proceedings, University of Kentucky, October 1998: 47-52.

"R/UDAT Program FAQs," Pamphlet/flyer of the American Institute of Architects, 2005.

Urban Land Institute website on Advisory Service Panels: www.uli.org/Content/NavigationMenu/ProgramsServices/AdvisoryServices/Advisory_Services.htm

Index

ABOUT NCI

The History of NCI

In 1987 on the high Texas plains outside of Austin, a group of architects and planners spent six days in a historic stone farmhouse with a developer, local officials, and community members to complete a master plan and codes for a new 500-acre community named Friday Mountain. This charrette, led by Andres Duany and Elizabeth Plater-Zyberk along with project manager Bill Lennertz, would shape the future practice of Duany Plater-Zyberk & Company (DPZ) and sow the seeds for what would eventually become the National Charrette Institute (NCI). In the six years following Friday Mountain, Bill Lennertz, working as director of the DPZ Boston office, managed many charrettes. The weeklong charrette would become the model process for DPZ's town planning work. Bill's final task before leaving the firm in 1991 was to create a charrette management handbook for future DPZ charrette managers.

In 1992, Bill joined architect Steve Coyle to form the architecture and town planning firm of Lennertz Coyle & Associates (LCA) Architects and Town Planners in Portland, Oregon. Based on Bill's six years of experiencing first-hand the power of the charrette process to facilitate community transformation, LCA chose it as the primary delivery process for their new urbanist practice.

In 1993, Bill delivered his first of many lectures about the charrette process at the annual Local Government Commission conference in San Francisco. Nine years later he conducted his first two-day charrette training at the Seaside Institute in Florida. The enthusiastic response for this training indicated the need for a rigorous charrette curriculum. In the spring of 2001, Bill, Steve, and LCA's former business manager, Aarin Lutzenhiser, created the nonprofit National Charrette Institute to research and teach charrette best practices.

In 2003, Bill and Aarin became full-time NCI staff. The first order of business for NCI was to create a charrette curriculum based on the best practices of leading firms. Bill Lennertz, Steve Coyle, and Aarin Lutzenhiser authored the original dynamic planning curriculum. This curriculum has matured into the NCI certification trainings that have been taught widely across the United States and abroad. These certification programs are the basis for this book.

NCI's Mission

The National Charrette Institute (NCI) is a nonprofit educational institution. We help people build community capacity for collaboration to create healthy community plans. We teach professionals and community leaders the art and science of Dynamic Planning, a holistic, collaborative planning process that harnesses the talents and energies of all interested parties to create and support a feasible plan. We advance the fields of community planning and public involvement through research, publications, and facilitation.

National Charrette Institute Staff

Bill Lennertz, *Executive Director*
Aarin Lutzenhiser, *Director of Operations*
Breesa Culver, *Publications Manager*

NCI Board of Directors

David Brain, New College of Florida
Steve Coyle, HDR|LCA+Sargent
Victor Dover, AICP, Dover, Kohl & Partners
Donna Gerber, California Nurses Association
Dan Slone, McGuire Woods
Joseph Molinaro, AICP, National Association of Realtors
Elizabeth Plater-Zyberk, Duany Plater-Zyberk & Company (board member emerita)
Laurie Volk, Zimmerman/Volk Associates